OPERATION COUNTRYMAN

DICK KIRBY
has also written

Rough Justice
Memoirs of a Flying Squad Officer

The Real Sweeney

You're Nicked!

Villains

The Guv'nors
Ten of Scotland Yard's Greatest Detectives

The Sweeney
The First Sixty Years of Scotland Yard's Crimebusting
Flying Squad 1919–1978

Scotland Yard's Ghost Squad
The Secret Weapon against Post-War Crime

The Brave Blue Line
100 Years of Metropolitan Police Gallantry

Death on the Beat
Police Officers Killed in the Line of Duty

The Scourge of Soho
The Controversial Career of SAS Hero
Detective Sergeant Harry Challenor MM

Whitechapel's Sherlock Holmes
The Casebook of Fred Wensley OBE, KPM,
Victorian Crimebuster

The Wrong Man
The Shooting of Steven Waldorf and
the Hunt for David Martin

Laid Bare
The Nude Murders and
the Hunt for 'Jack the Stripper'

London's Gangs at War

Praise for Dick Kirby's Books

Rough Justice 'The continuing increase in violent crime will make many readers yearn for yesteryear and officers of Dick Kirby's calibre.'
Police Magazine

The Real Sweeney 'His reflections on the political aspect of law enforcement will ring true for cops everywhere.'
American Police Beat

Villains 'This is magic. The artfulness of these anti-heroes has you pining for the bad old days.'
Daily Sport

You're Nicked! 'A great read with fascinating stories and amusing anecdotes from a man who experienced it all.'
Suffolk Norfolk Life Magazine

The Guv'nors 'They were heroes at times when heroes were desperately needed.'
American Police Beat

The Sweeney 'Thoroughly researched and enjoyable history, crammed with vivid descriptions of long-forgotten police operations . . . races along like an Invicta at full throttle.'
Daily Express

Scotland Yard's Ghost Squad 'Dick Kirby . . . knows how to bring his coppers to life on each page.'
Joseph Wambaugh, Author Of The Choirboys

The Brave Blue Line 'Simply the best book about police gallantry ever written.'
History By The Yard

Death on the Beat 'I am delighted Dick Kirby has written this book.'
Michael Winner

The Scourge of Soho 'Dick Kirby has chosen his fascinating subject well.'
Law Society Gazette

Whitechapel's Sherlock Holmes 'Dick Kirby has done an excellent job.'
The Ripperologist Magazine

The Wrong Man 'Dick Kirby gives us the gritty reality of this subject. I did not put this book down, reading it in one day, deep into the night.'
Paul Millen, Author Of Crime Scene Investigator

Laid Bare 'Kirby writes with authority and clarity . . . it's highly recommended.'
Real Crime Magazine

London's Gangs at War 'This is a riveting book and Dick has done his usual amazing research.'
London Police Pensioner

This book is dedicated to
former Detective Chief Superintendent John Simmonds,
who in the face of great adversity displayed unlimited moral courage.

And to Ann:
If love were what the rose is,
And I were like the leaf,
Our lives would grow together
In sad or singing weather.

A.C. Swinburne

OPERATION COUNTRYMAN

COUNTRYMAN

THE FLAWED ENQUIRY INTO LONDON POLICE CORRUPTION

DICK KIRBY

PEN & SWORD
TRUE CRIME

First published in Great Britain in 2018 by
Pen & Sword True Crime
an imprint of
Pen & Sword Books Ltd
47 Church Street
Barnsley
South Yorkshire
S70 2AS

ISBN 978 1 52671 254 7

A CIP catalogue record for this book is available from the
British Library.

Printed and bound by CPI Group (UK) Ltd, Croydon, CR0 4YY

Pen & Sword Books Ltd incorporates the Imprints of Pen & Sword
Archaeology, Atlas, Aviation, Battleground, Discovery, Family
History, History, Maritime, Military, Naval, Politics, Railways,
Select, Transport, True Crime, Fiction, Frontline Books, Leo
Cooper, Praetorian Press, Seaforth Publishing,
Wharncliffe and White Owl.

For a complete list of Pen & Sword titles please contact
PEN & SWORD BOOKS LIMITED
47 Church Street, Barnsley, South Yorkshire, S70 2AS, England
E-mail: enquiries@pen-and-sword.co.uk
Website: www.pen-and-sword.co.uk

Contents

About the Author

Dick Kirby was born in 1943 in the East End of London and joined the Metropolitan Police in 1967. Half of his 26 years' service as a detective was spent with the Yard's Serious Crime Squad and the Flying Squad.

Married, with four children and five grandchildren, Kirby lives in a Suffolk village with his wife. He reviews books, films and music, is a consultant for a television series and writes memoirs, biographies and true crime books – this is his fifteenth.

Kirby can be visited on his website: www.dickkirby.com

Acknowledgements

First, I have to thank John Simmonds, to whom this book is dedicated, for his enormous help. Without him it would not have seen light of day. Next, to my friend David Woodland for his very kind and thoughtful foreword, also to Brigadier Henry Wilson of Pen & Sword Books for his unfailing assistance and enthusiasm and to George Chamier for his lynx-eyed editing.

Next, my thanks to the following, who provided much needed behind-the-scenes assistance: Dave Allen from the Bow Street police station website; Julie Bedford, Sussex Police; Bob Fenton QGM, the Honorary Secretary of the Ex-CID Officers' Association; Alan Moss of *History by the Yard*; Susi Rogol, editor of the *London Police Pensioners' Magazine*; Phillip Barnes-Warden, Metropolitan Police; Chris Pearson, guest editor of *The City of London Police Pensioners' Newsletter*; Ian Dyson QPM, Commissioner of the City of London Police, and Sarah Coker, Head of Staff Office; Claire O'Malley from the Chamberlain's Department, City of London Corporation; Becky Ford, PA to the Chief Constable of Dorset Police; Norman Robertson, Branch Secretary, Dorset Branch; Martin McKay, BTPHG webmaster; Philip Bye and Andrew Lusted from The Keep, East Sussex; Fiona Irving and Richard Gould, Equiniti Pensions.

When I first declared my intention to delve into allegations regarding the murky world of police corruption, often coupled with Freemasonry in various shades of grey, several (no doubt) well-meaning people told me, pityingly, 'No one's going to talk to you, you know.' And initially, I began to think they might be right.

I requested help from a number of people; some ignored my pleas, others – for reasons best known to themselves – flatly refused. Some people did come forward but wanted to give their information anonymously. Another initially told me, 'I couldn't possibly tell you what went on, even now' – and then, later on, he did, and told me things which were quite hair-raising. Someone else said, 'I'm not talking to you over the phone' but then he did as well and told me things so matter-of-factly that when I checked them out independently and discovered they were true, I found them all the more astonishing. There were one or two, with varying degrees of menace in their voices, who told me, 'Be careful', plus another who reminded me, 'The streets are dangerous.'

One of the sources to which I appealed for assistance was the City Police Pensioners' website. Within 12 hours of my request being posted, it was viewed on 285 occasions; the vast majority of viewers were ex-CID officers – and not one of them contacted me.

But there were others who were bursting at the seams to have their stories told. 'Thank God!' one told me. 'I've been wanting to tell somebody about this for years!'

So my thanks to them and to the following, who appear in alphabetical order: Terry Babbidge QPM; John Barber; Robert Bartlett; the late Ernie Bond OBE, QPM; Mike Bucknole FNAVA, BA Hons, PgC; Peter Burgess; Mick Carter; Michael Chance; Eddy Cherry; Tony Cook; Brian Crouch; Fred Cutts LL.B; Neil Dickens QPM; David 'Ginger' Dixon; John Dougall; Christopher Draycott; Mick Dunn; Tony Forward; Liam Gillespie; Bill Hatfull; Les Knight; Anthony Lampard QPM; David Little; Alan Longhurst; Tony Lundy; Bryan Martin; James Martin; Philip Meeson; Peter Miller; Jim Mitchell; John 'Jock' Murray; John Newman; John O'Connor; Kevin Pengelly; Roderick 'Jock' Penney; Bill Peters; Frank Pillinger; Ezra Pritchard; Derek Ramsay; Paul Rextrew; Anthony Robertson; Bob Robinson; David Rowland; Charlie Scott; Jon Shatford; Keith Taylor; Geoff Todd; Max Vernon; Gwyn Waters: Ian Will; Chris Wilson; 'Harvey Yates'.

My thanks for the use of photographs go to John O'Connor, Bob Robinson, Robert Bartlett, Alan Moss and John Simmonds. Other images come from the author's collection, and whilst every effort has been made to trace copyright holders and publishers, the author and Pen & Sword apologize for any inadvertent omissions.

As always, I have blundered blinkered through cyberspace, but fortunately my daughter, Suzanne Cowper, and her husband Steve have emerged from their rural retreat to provide much-needed advice and assistance.

In addition, I have profited from the love and support I have received from my sons, Mark and Robert Kirby, my daughter, Barbara Jerreat, and her husband Rich, plus my grandchildren: Emma Cowper B.Mus, Jessica Cowper B. Mus, Harry Cowper, and Samuel and Annie Grace Jerreat.

Most of all, to my dear wife Ann – we've weathered many storms.

Dick Kirby
Suffolk, 2017

Foreword

This is a story that needs to be told and nobody is more qualified to tell it than Dick Kirby. Dick is known by many readers of true crime stories, having been a particularly effective thief-taker who served most of his career in Scotland Yard's Flying Squad and Serious Crime Squad. In an era when a series of events brought the whole detective force into disrepute and culminated in the downfall of traditional policing methods, Dick Kirby stood head and shoulders above many of his contemporaries and was acknowledged throughout the service for his personal integrity and detective ability.

Since his retirement he has written many books which pulled no punches and told it in a straightforward way without fear or favour. Nothing can be more difficult than exposing crime, especially when the perpetrators were the very persons charged with keeping the Queen's Peace but who through sheer greed betrayed their trust and used their office as a means to thieve and plunder.

Only experienced detectives like Kirby can appreciate the difficulties that can and did arise working alongside corrupt colleagues bent upon sabotaging investigations into crime, let alone those hiding behind their shield, setting up and even participating in villainy such as armed robberies. It follows the purge of a handful of crooked cops by the Metropolitan Police Commissioner Sir Robert Mark, who used a scattergun approach to destroy one of the finest crime-fighting units in the country. He used the simple expedient of interchanging uniform officers totally ill-equipped to counter professional gangsters with seasoned detectives, now placed into the uniform branch upon more routine and mundane policing matters. Mark destroyed the CID by calling it 'the most routinely corrupt organization in London', and it was only after destroying their credibility that he later conceded the CID was 'professionally and technically highly competent' and contained 'a considerable number of thoroughly honest, dedicated and skilled detectives at every level'.

Here then is the point where Kirby takes over the narrative and in his own inimitable style outlines the historic nature of corruption within the Met, before turning his attention to far-reaching criminality within the City of London Police. Kirby describes the effect this had in destroying the career of a fine detective with whom I once served, who transferred to the City of London Police and was handed the poison chalice of purging the cancer that was eating its way into the very bones of that force. That man was John Simmonds, and I can endorse the troubles that John sustained in his endeavours to bring corrupt senior police officers to justice before, sick of the cover-ups, lies and deceit, this eventually led to his retirement and yet again the loss of an honest, dedicated cop.

To the layman, what follows may be difficult to follow and comprehend, but please persevere and you will start to appreciate the difficulties encountered during the debacle known as Operation Countryman, carried out by largely inept and inexperienced country policemen who were totally incapable of handling either crooked cops or experienced thieves and robbers.

Former Detective Inspector David I. Woodland,
author of *Crime and Corruption at the Yard*

Author's Note

When the news broke of allegations of corruption in both the City of London and the Metropolitan Police Forces, and it was said that Len Burt was going to head the enquiry, many people thought that the man referred to was Commander Leonard James Burt CVO, CBE, the brilliant Metropolitan Police spycatcher, murder investigator and wartime MI5 operative, who had been commended on thirty-nine occasions and, in addition to his British decorations, had been appointed to the *Légion d'honneur*, awarded the Order of Orange Nassau and the Order of the Dannebrog. Well, they were wrong. At the time of the enquiry, Burt, who had served in the Metropolitan Police for forty-six years, had settled down to a well-deserved retirement and was eighty-six years of age. Nor was it his namesake, Detective Inspector Burt DSC, who had similarly served in Special Branch and retired on 25 March 1960. No. The Len Burt I'm referring to was forty-six years old and the Assistant Chief Constable of Dorset Constabulary, where he had spent all of his twenty-four years of service. The confusion between the two men may have arisen because the younger Burt was often credited with the success of breaking up 'The Portland Spy Ring' in 1961. However, he played only a minor role in the investigation, and the arrest of the Soviet agents which led to their convictions was due to Detective Superintendent George Gordon Smith QPM of the Metropolitan Police – dubbed 'the best spycatcher Great Britain has ever known'.

*

On the one and only occasion that I met Len Burt it was not as a result of anything to do with what later became known as 'Operation Countryman'. In fact, I probably wouldn't have recalled the meeting at all, except for what happened later in that ill-fated enquiry. It was early in 1976 when a small contingent of senior officers from the Yard's Serious Crime Squad, which also included lesser lights – namely me and the redoubtable Detective Sergeant 'Ilda 'Arris – went to Dorset Police headquarters, where we met with senior officers from that constabulary. This was because a protected witness in a blackmail case was living in Dorset; 'Ilda and

I were the liaising officers. This meeting was to establish who we
were, who the witness was and, in our absence, for the local officers
to keep a discreet eye on the witness and to take appropriate action
in the event that large, broken-faced thugs from London should
suddenly materialize.[1]

Everything was quickly sorted out and we cemented our relationship with a few drinks. During the evening I took the opportunity to regale the audience with an amusing story; it concerned a
case where I had been attacked in the street by a pair of East End
thugs, who had aggravated matters by threatening me with broken
milk bottles. This, I hasten to add, was not the humorous aspect
of the story; that occurred when I conducted the prosecution at
the Magistrates' Court. Having got them convicted, I described
the antecedents of this charmless duo, and whilst I appeared to
outline their history in a way that was scrupulously fair, the inflex-
ions I put into my voice, my hesitant pauses, eyebrow-raisings and
head-shakings gave an entirely different interpretation to the Bench
and ensured that both of them were returned to Borstal. It may not
appear to be very funny seeing this in print, but it was, if I may
say so, a well-told tale, and the punch-line raised roars of laughter
from the audience – the Metropolitan officers, that is. Burt and the
other Dorset officers simply smiled in a polite kind of way, and it
was only later that I realized they hadn't grasped the humour or the
reality of the situation. You see, prosecuting straightforward cases
like this was something that had been carried out by Metropolitan
Police officers (starting with the rank of constable) since time
immemorial. But Dorset (and many other constabularies) hadn't;
they used either an inspector to outline the facts or a local solicitor
to prosecute.

Therefore the impression I formed of Len Burt was that he was
pleasant enough but – probably through no fault of his own – a bit
naïve and rather parochial in his outlook, and I forgot all about the
incident.

I recalled it a couple of years later, when those sentiments – and
others of a more unkind nature – were shared by a considerable
bunch of other police officers.

Introduction

This book is about conscientious and brave policemen, it's about policemen who were wronged, it's about incompetence on an industrial scale and it's about policemen who were staggeringly crooked. Some were convicted; others never even stood trial. Most of all, this book is about allegations of police corruption.

There always has been corruption in the police; there always will be. When men and women are put in a position of authority, there are always those who will breach the trust which has been placed in them. And when the shit hits the fan – as it inevitably does – the public are appalled and they conveniently forget the very fine work which is carried out by the vast majority of honest police officers. All are tarred with the same brush.

So what is corruption? Put in its simplest form, it's where someone is perverted or influenced by bribery. Let me give you three instances, in the first of which it failed. My chum, Keith Taylor, was a uniformed police constable in 1968 when he received a call to a disturbance at a casino which receives a fuller description in Chapter 1. He was the front seat passenger in a Morris Commercial J2 police van, often described as a 'Black Maria'; many readers will recall that this van had sliding driver's and passenger's doors. As the van pulled up outside the casino, so the doorman emerged, slid the passenger's door open and said, "S all right mate, problem sorted', threw a fiver on to the lap of Taylor's greatcoat and made a motion of dismissal with his head. Taylor – a rather tough former member of 10 Para – was furious and threw the fiver back at the doorman. Since a constable's weekly wage at that time was £17 12s 8d, not every officer of his rank would have followed Taylor's example. As a matter of fact, I led a raid on that casino ten years later; the doorman was quickly overpowered to stop him giving the alarm to the occupants, and it is possible that whilst he was being restrained he suffered a little damage.

Well, you may say – so what? Taylor didn't accept the money, and was it really a bribe? More like a gratuity, perhaps. Maybe it was. But what Chum Taylor took objection to – as I did – was that someone closely aligned to the criminal classes thought that he could contemptuously dismiss a police officer who was doing his duty, rather like giving a tip to a waiter who had provided fair service in a restaurant.

OK – next example. I was having a drink with a group of CID officers one evening and during the course of the conversation I recounted the story of a repellent detective constable who had been asked by a criminal to obtain his file from Criminal Records Office at the Yard and sell it to him, for £25. This the officer duly did, and meeting the criminal under cover of darkness at the appointed time, he stretched out both hands; one holding the file, the other to accept his payment. It was a classic sting operation. Just as the transaction was about to be completed, there was a blinding flash coupled with the sudden 'pop!' of a photographer's flashbulb, owned by an employee of a now defunct national Sunday newspaper. The file and the pound notes went up in the air and the venal detective took to his heels. Not for long, though – he was sentenced to six months' imprisonment.

As I finished my recitation, I said to my audience, 'Can you believe it? Handing over a bloke's CRO file, his career gone, plus six months' porridge, all for the sake of twenty-five measly quid.'

Terry was an old-time Flying Squad officer who was anxious to point out the flaws in my story. 'No, no, no, Dick!' he cried. 'It's twenty-five quid a conviction; not for the whole fucking file!'

The third example was when I was having a drink with a senior CID officer – and here I really should point out that not all my time was spent drinking with colleagues – I did do some work, as well!

We were chatting about crime in general and I happened to mention that I thought it completely unacceptable to take money from a criminal under any circumstances. He nodded. 'Oh, I agree with you, Dick, absolutely', and then, after a short pause, added, 'Except for bail money, of course'.

I thought he was pulling my leg; when I realized he was serious, I was flabbergasted. '*Especially* for bail money!' I replied.

He frowned. 'Why on earth not?' he replied. 'You take a bloke to court on a straightforward charge, you know he's going to get bail but you just tell him that he's not. What's he want – a seven-day lay-down in a shitty dump like Brixton or to cough up twenty-five quid? So you don't object to bail – he'd have got it, anyway – and you're twenty-five quid better off.'

I expect he was waiting for the look of annoyance on my face to clear; when it didn't, he expostulated, 'Jesus! I'm only talking about routine cases – I wouldn't give bail to anyone charged with murder, for Christ's sake!'

Of course, that's just what several police officers did do, and the details are contained in this book.

Don't think I'm taking the moral high ground; I was a young detective, married with four kids, and having a nice few bob extra in my pocket during those days when CID officers didn't get paid overtime would have been welcome. But quite apart from the unlawful aspect of it, it's just that I couldn't bear to be in fief to some dirt-bag; if they wanted favours and I was able to grant them, they came at a price: information.

So let's take a look at police venality; it has happened in all police forces throughout the United Kingdom to a lesser or greater degree, but since the Metropolitan Police is the biggest force in the country it has had the biggest share of criminality within its ranks – so let's begin there.

★

I suppose what became known as 'The Trial of the Detectives' is as good a starting point as any. Two fraudsters, Harry Benson and William Kurr, were convicted of a racing scam and from their prison cells they began to talk about their arresting officers, who had a predilection for accepting large sums of money (and £100 was a very large amount of money indeed, in 1877) for providing tip-offs when arrests were imminent. It led to trial and two years' imprisonment for Chief Inspectors Nathanial Druscovitch and William Palmer and Inspector John Meiklejohn; the Attorney General declared that this was 'as a thunderclap to the community', and it also led to the abolition of the 'Detective Branch', which had been formed in 1842. The 197 detectives who were supervised by 20 sergeants had been pretty well much of a muchness; near-illiterate, bone-idle and incompetent. With the formation in 1878 of the Criminal Investigation Department, which was based on the French *Sûreté*, 280 officers (of whom 254 were based in Divisions) were now under the control of 'local inspectors' and were a much better motivated force.

'The Police and Public Vigilance Society' was a splinter group which accompanied a Royal Commission set up in 1906 to examine cases of police misconduct; one of its leading lights was Arthur Harding, a convicted and violent gang leader who loathed the police, and of the nineteen cases considered, nine officers were found guilty of misbehaviour and some were sent to prison. It was a pyrrhic victory for Harding; it earned him the enmity of Frederick Porter Wensley OBE, KPM, who apart from creating the Flying Squad and going on to be the Chief Constable of the CID, also ensured that justice finally caught up with Harding, five years later. Despite Harding's most valiant efforts to publicly threaten Wensley's life and that of his wife and children, he nevertheless went down for riot – twenty-one months' hard labour – and inflicting grievous bodily harm – three years' penal servitude – the sentences to run consecutively.

It was during 1928, whilst Wensley was in office as Chief Constable, that there were three near-catastrophic scandals. Two police constables, John Clayton and Charles Stevens, were each sentenced to eighteen months' imprisonment after trying to frame a young woman (she later admitted in court that she 'had often misconducted herself') who had repulsed their advances. Then there was the case of Station Sergeant George Goddard, who had accepted bribes on a breathtaking scale from Kate 'Ma' Meyrick, the owner of Soho's '43' club, to warn her of forthcoming police raids. At the time of his arrest, Goddard had paid for his house and car in cash, financed two betting shops and had a total of over £15,171 in various currencies, in safety deposit boxes and bank accounts under different names. On a weekly wage of £6 15s 0d, Goddard had some difficulty in explaining this away (especially after consecutively numbered £5 notes were traced right back to Mrs Meyrick) and he was sentenced to eighteen months' hard labour, fined £2,000 and ordered to pay the costs of the prosecution. Probably the worst scandal of 1928 was the arrest of Irene Savidge and Sir Leo Money MP for outraging public decency in Hyde Park. Although the case was thrown out of court, with Sir Leo demanding that the two arresting constables should be arrested for perjury, the officers had acted entirely properly – and Miss Savage and Sir Leo had not. The scandal arose from the way in which Miss Savidge was questioned by detectives; it led to a Parliamentary enquiry, in which three CID officers lied their heads off and were exonerated. But with Sir Leo still trumpeting his innocence as he had when he was arrested ('I'm not the usual riff-raff; I'm a man of substance. For God's sake let me go!'), the case had a bad smell to it; and by the time that Sir Leo was arrested and fined for molesting a young woman on a train five years later, the public had forgotten about him – they still believed the arresting officers were at fault.

After that, the Commissioner resigned, and although eight possible candidates were asked to fill his boots, none volunteered for the job. It was eventually filled after the ninth candidate was personally asked by His Majesty King George V to restore the Metropolitan Police to 'a happy family'.[1]

Not so happy was the celebrated fire-raiser, Leopold Harris, who in 1933 was sentenced to 14 years' penal servitude for offences including arson and conspiracy to defraud; when he complained from his prison cell that he had previously paid bribes to two Chief Constables, six superintendents and three chief inspectors for suppressing evidence and dropping charges, these matters were scrupulously investigated; but no one stood trial.

After the war, Joseph Grech, who was sentenced to three years' imprisonment for housebreaking, alleged that a Detective Sergeant Robert Robertson had been paid £150 to get a locksmith to manufacture a lock from the key of the burgled premises which had been found in his possession to fit Grech's front door, thereby showing that the whole business of his arrest had been a ghastly mistake. It was a clever ruse which should have worked, but didn't; and Robertson went away for two years. This led directly to an investigation involving allegations of corruption among the uniform officers at West End Central police station, some of whom were said to be accepting bribes of up to £60 per week for tipping off club owners of impending raids; but although an inspector, a station sergeant and a constable were disciplined, nobody gripped the rail at the Old Bailey.[2]

The same applied to Detective Sergeant Harry Challenor MM, who had planted half-bricks on people at a protest in 1963; he was found to be insane and was committed to a psychiatric hospital, whereas three of his aids to CID, for similar offences, were jailed for three years each.

It became known as 'The Challenor Affair', and apart from the court case there was a police internal investigation and a public enquiry; and with Challenor unable to defend himself, since by now he was raving in a psychiatric ward, it suddenly became fashionable for anyone found in possession of any item which they were unable to explain away satisfactorily to allege that the police had planted it on them.[3]

That was what actually happened in 1969, when Detective Inspector Bernard Robson pressed a package which supposedly contained gelignite into the hand of suspected safebreaker Michael Perry, in order to place his fingerprints on it. Robson and Detective Sergeants Gordon Harris and John Symonds had been obtaining money from Perry for sanitizing previous convictions at court, giving tip-offs of impending raids, offering help if he was arrested elsewhere and giving advice on where to secrete stolen goods. When Perry decided to covertly tape thirteen of their conversations and pass them to a newspaper, which in turn handed them to the Yard, it led to what became known as *The Times* Enquiry.

What had happened was bad enough; what was worse was the investigation. It was started off by Detective Chief

Superintendent Fred Lambert, an honourable man but one who was quite ill; he was quickly shouldered out of the running by Detective Chief Superintendent Bill Moody, who at that time was receiving eye-watering sums from Soho pornographers which would later fully justify his sentence of twelve years' imprisonment. Then, Her Majesty's Inspector of Constabulary, Frank Edgar Williamson QPM, was appointed as advisor to the enquiry. He had already inherited a hatred for the Met from his father; now it would intensify as matters were made as difficult as possible for him. The enquiry continued under Met control, and later Robson was sentenced to seven years' imprisonment, with Harris receiving six; Symonds, who had fled the country, was dealt with seven years later, when he was sentenced to two years' imprisonment.

Symonds had told Perry that if he was in trouble to let him know straight away, 'Because I'm in a little firm in a firm'. This would haunt the police for years to come; whenever an officer was accused of malpractice, the mantra 'You're a member of a firm within a firm, aren't you, officer?' would be brayed across the courtroom by the type of defence barrister who was often just as venal as his client.

No sooner were Robson and Harris weighed off than the trial of five members of the Yard's Drug Squad began; 1972 was a bad year for the Met. Three of the unit were convicted of conspiracy to pervert the course of justice; one went down for four years, the other two for eighteen months each.

All of these cases were bad; the worst was the prosecution of officers from the Obscene Publication Squad, aka 'The Dirty Squad', and the Flying Squad. The men of the Flying Squad, first formed in 1919, were portrayed by the press as hard-hitting, sometimes unconventional, granite-jawed, incorruptible detectives. Some of them were and some of them weren't.

The thread on the stocking began to unravel in 1972, when, as we know, the Met had more than enough on its plate. The *Sunday People* reported that Soho pornographer Jimmy Humphries and his wife, ex-stripper 'Rusty', had recently returned from a holiday in Cyprus with the commander of the Flying Squad, Ken Drury and his wife. Drury blustered: yes, he had been to Cyprus with Humphries, yes he had paid his share, and no, it had not been a holiday at all – he had been following up a lead on the whereabouts of escaped Train Robber, Ronnie Biggs.

It wasn't the most convincing of explanations; Drury was suspended, then he resigned and next he sold his own story to the *News of the World*, in which he named Humphries as his informant.

Knowing that being identified as a grass would cause a dent in his credibility as a major player in the Soho pornography scene, Humphries lost no time at all in repudiating this slur and made it clear that Drury had been enjoying the fruits of his illicit labours. The catalyst came when Humphries slashed his wife's former lover, then fled to Holland. Whilst he was awaiting extradition he began to talk. After he was sentenced at the Old Bailey to eight years' imprisonment he talked even more, and meticulously kept diaries were produced that gave details of which officers he had paid off, by how much, and when and where. It led to the arrest of twelve officers, including Drury and Moody, and a shocking picture emerged. Payments to operate porn shops were given to the police, pornographic material seized from one shop would be sold to another and there were further details of corruptly acquired holidays, social functions, clothing, cars and house improvements. It was Moody who had told a colleague that he was going to organize bribery 'as it had never been organized before', and another officer thrust money into the pockets of three honest officers in an effort to compromise them; they would become prosecution witnesses at the forthcoming trials. The same applied to honest officers who inadvertently became members of the Obscene Publications Squad; when they realized the high level of criminality that was going on and asked for a transfer, they were told that to engineer such a posting would cost them £500.

There were three separate trials. In the first, six officers stood trial, each accused on twenty counts of accepting £4,680 in bribes – five were found guilty and were sent to prison for a total of thirty-six years. At the second trial, six officers, also from the Dirty Squad, stood trial, accused on twenty-seven counts of accepting bribes of £87,485. During the proceedings it emerged that Moody had accepted the biggest single bribe of all – £14,000 – to help get a pornographer's manager off a criminal charge. Moody and Commander Virgo were each sentenced to twelve years' imprisonment (although Virgo's conviction was later quashed on appeal), and then others were sentenced to a total of twenty-four years. Lastly, there was the trial of three Flying Squad officers accused of accepting bribes from Humphries; one was acquitted, but Drury, accused of accepting bribes totalling £5,000, was sentenced to eight years' imprisonment (later reduced on appeal to five), and his co-defendant received four years.

The trials shook the Met to its very foundations. They led to sweeping changes brought in by the new Commissioner, Sir Robert

Mark GBE, QPM, who was determined to break the power of the CID. Instead of promoting some excellent, honest CID officers to fill the gaps left by the corrupt ones, he posted senior uniformed officers to replace them. The CID was now put under the control of the uniform branch. Interchange was introduced between the lower ranks of the uniform and CID. Career detectives would soon become a thing of the past. It led to a slippery slope from which the CID would never recover.[4] As I write this, an Assistant Commissioner at the Yard is writing to some 700 detectives ('of any rank') about to retire on pension, pleading with them to defer their retirement to stay on and act as mentors to the remaining officers. The 'remaining officers' are about to have their numbers increased by inexperienced special constables – volunteers, not warranted police officers – as detectives. This was a role which hitherto had required specialist teaching at the Detective Training School as well as years of practical experience; it does help when one's dealing with fairly serious crimes such as murder, rape and armed robbery. This concept was undoubtedly the product of an academic police officer, with his or her head safely in the clouds of make-belief land where anything might happen – and usually does.

Given the atrocious conditions in which those retiring detectives work, and piss-poor management, where selection for senior ranks is often based on gender, sexual orientation and ethnic origins rather than experience, it is quite likely that those CID officers who are looking with one eye at becoming fairly comfortably-off police pensioners or at the prospect of being rather elderly nursery nurses with the other, will bung in their resignations, grab their pensions and commutation and depart from the Met, quicker than shit through a goose.

However, since I was a career detective myself, you may consider my comments to be slightly biased.

*

I'm starting to drift from my original theme; that of corruption. It may appear from what you've read that the Met was an absolute hotbed of dishonesty; but bear in mind that over a very few pages I've dealt with just the limited number of cases – dramatic cases to be sure, but nevertheless, very few – which surfaced in just under 100 years. For example, in 1978, when the matters dealt with in this book got underway, there were 84 allegations of bribery – just one was proved. And in 1979 there were 85 similar allegations – and again, only one was substantiated.

Because, be in no doubt about it, during my quarter century in the Metropolitan Police, whilst I met some wrong 'uns, the vast majority of the people I worked with, men and women, in all of the various departments of the police, were committed, hard-working and brave.

This is as good a moment as any to introduce you to one of them, and his name is John Simmonds.

PART I

Coming

When Hilaire Belloc was asked by an impertinent reader if the verses contained in his *Cautionary Tales for Children* were true, this was his reply:

And is it True? It is not True.
And if it were it wouldn't do,
For people such as me and you
Who pretty nearly all day long
Are doing something rather wrong.

CHAPTER 1

Ever since he was a schoolboy John Simmonds had wanted to be a police officer, and after a spell in the police cadets he was sworn in as a Metropolitan Police constable at the age of nineteen, on 3 June 1957. As soon as possible he became an aid to CID; then he was appointed detective constable; and next, due to his extraordinary success at running informants, and at the age of twenty-two, he became the youngest officer with the shortest service ever to be posted to the legendary Flying Squad, which would be his home for the next four years. Promotion to second-class, then first-class sergeant followed, with secondment to the Regional Crime Squad (plus a full commitment to the Richardson Torture Gang investigation), then back once more to the Flying Squad. With his advancement to detective inspector came the Junior Command Course at Bramshill Police College, swiftly followed by promotion to detective chief inspector and a posting, in 1972, to A10, the newly-formed Police Complaints Department. Within a year came promotion to detective superintendent, and he was later posted to the London branch of the Regional Crime Squad (RCS). John Lock QPM was then the Commander of the Flying Squad and, as such, took command of the London RCS as well; he was an officer whom Simmonds trusted and liked very much. Simmonds was the youngest superintendent ever to attend the four-month residential Intermediate Command Course at Bramshill; and then it was back to the Flying Squad once more, working again with John Lock. With nineteen years service, and at thirty-eight years of age, after a career in which he had been showered with commendations, Simmonds was promoted to detective chief superintendent. One year later, in 1977, he took over command of the Yard's Serious Crime Squad.

A courageous, seasoned thief-taker, an expert handler of informants, a shrewd murder investigator, it seemed impossible that this posting would not act as a springboard to Simmonds' further promotion. Promotion to the rank of Commander, then Deputy Assistant Commissioner, was surely a foregone conclusion, and advancement to the highest echelons of the Metropolitan Police or any of the constabularies in the Home Counties was certainly not out of the question.

But it didn't happen. John Simmonds' career would be curtailed by his own fierce honesty – that and a web of corruption that he encountered which was so concentrated, and interpenetrated by Masonic influences, that it was utterly breathtaking.

★

The Serious Crime Squad (SCS) – 'The Gangbusters' – had been set up in the wake of the Richardson and Kray brothers' investigations. Their imprisonment had left a gap in the underworld, and there were many gangsters ready and willing to fill that void. The Dixon brothers and the Tibbs family, plus various other miscreants from the East End, had been wiped up, and the SCS now looked further afield for their targets; they found them in the form of the Maltese Syndicate in London's West End and in the Hungarian Circle – a gang of international fraudsters who, said a representative of the Chase Manhattan Bank at the gang's trial at the Old Bailey, 'had the ability to bankrupt a small European country'.[1]

There were always several operations being conducted simultaneously on the SCS, either in the planning, investigatory phase or the arrest stage (where everyone would be taken off their respective cases to assist), as well as those that were nearing or had actually reached court proceedings.

One such investigation in the planning stage was under the control of Detective Inspector Allan 'Charlie' Cheal, who was meticulously investigating the activities of a West End casino which was suspected of having heavy Mafia connections. Those concerned were a dangerous gang; just how dangerous became obvious when it was discovered that Cheal's main target wished to eliminate an individual who had become a threat to him. Various methods of how to dispose of the intended victim were discussed, and it was clear that the actual act of murder was imminent. There was no doubt that the information was 100 per cent accurate; it came from an intercept which had been placed on the target's telephone; incredibly, to make matters worse, the co-conspirators were detectives from the City of London Police.

A senior officer at the Yard was alerted, as was the Home Office, and the intended victim was moved to a place of safety without the source of the information being compromised. This was of paramount importance; in those days, telephone intercepts were seldom mentioned and officers under the rank of detective inspector were not supposed to know that they existed at all. In addition, then as now, telephone intercepts could not be used in court as evidence, and only very experienced officers could use them in the most circumspect way as a guide when interviewing a suspect, in order that the interviewee should have no inkling as to the source of the interviewer's information.

Now somebody in the City of London police had to be apprised of this matter, someone whose integrity was utterly beyond question – but who? John Simmonds told me:

> I went to my former Flying Squad Commander, John Lock; he was now the National Coordinator of the Regional Crime Squads. John had a Detective Chief Superintendent Hugh Moore, who was from the City of London Police, as his staff officer, and John vouched for his integrity and said I could talk safely to Hugh.
>
> I met up with Hugh Moore and told him the basics of our problem and identified the officers who were involved. I told him the risk of the individual now being harmed was gone but it concerned me that the detectives were even prepared to contemplate the actions that they had discussed with our target. Hugh assured me he would deal with the matter and isolate the detectives.

Simmonds did not disclose to Moore that the information had come from a telephone intercept, but in due course the message appeared to have got through and the City Police activity on the line ceased. It was not thought appropriate to take action against the City officers, to ensure the integrity of the intercept. In those days, rightly or wrongly, whenever police officers, whether in the Met or the constabularies, were compromised on an intercept, it was not actively followed up but discreet words of advice were issued and the officer concerned was moved or sidelined.

In the meantime, Cheal carried on with his investigations until he had compiled a report several hundred pages long, containing statements and surveillance notes regarding the casino's activities. Simmonds read it, considered that Cheal had done an excellent job and minuted the report, which he then forwarded to the Deputy Assistant Commissioner (Crime) (Operations); and this was where matters went badly wrong.

Until 1976, the DAC (C) (Ops) had been Ernie Bond OBE, QPM, a career detective and one much admired by the rank and file; a tough character, he had been David Stirling's sergeant with the wartime Special Air Service in the western desert. But, as he told me, 'On the day I got my thirty years in, I went!' – and he left behind him some very big boots to fill. They weren't. Bond's successor was David Powis OBE, QPM, who had spent the vast majority of his service in uniform. Following the pogroms of the Commissioner, Sir Robert Mark, who was determined to stamp out corruption in the Metropolitan Police's CID, as previously mentioned, many of that department's senior officers had been replaced with senior uniformed officers, whose experience, if they possessed any whatsoever, in investigatory matters was now no more than a dim, distant memory. This was particularly so in the case of Powis, whose investigative career had come to a halt twenty years previously.

Powis had published an unintentionally hilarious book entitled *The Signs of Crime*, supposedly a guide to catching criminals. He also had several nicknames, of which the most repeatable was 'Crazy Horse'. Curiously, he revelled in this; in the same way that Brigadier Mike Calvert DSO and Bar and Lieutenant Colonel Jack Churchill DSO and Bar, MC were known as 'Mad Mike' and 'Mad Jack' respectively, because of their keen disregard of danger, Powis really believed that 'Crazy Horse' meant he was held in the same high esteem by his subordinates as those wartime warriors were by their junior officers.

Sadly for Powis, this was put to the test when he chaired a selection board for promotion.

'Right, what's my nickname?' he roared to a luckless applicant.

The officer paled and stammered, 'I'd – er – rather not say, sir!'

'Nonsense!' bellowed Powis. 'Come on, man – out with it! What's my nickname?'

There were several more such exchanges, with the officer nervously declining to answer until finally, and probably realizing that due to his lack of forthrightness he'd failed the board in any event, he helplessly shrugged his shoulders and replied, 'Oh, all right – it's TCP!'

Since this was an acronym for 'That Cunt Powis' it also registered a blip on the career of the unfortunate candidate; but of such stuff are legends made.

Powis was a martinet who surrounded himself mainly with sycophants, many of whom were unformed officers instantly 'promoted' to the rank of detective. He devised unworkable rules, especially with regard to the meeting of informants on bail, and any detective who failed to sedulously observe every dot and comma contained in the myriad of forms and regulations which accompanied meeting a person on bail was destined to face a return to uniform – or worse. It was stipulated that the meet must be in a police station; I therefore reported, as directed, that I had met a man on bail in a Strathclyde police station and was duly rapped over the knuckles for this flagrant and unacceptable breach of the rules. You see, I had failed to read the small print, and Powis had specified in his nit-picking instructions that any such meets should be in a *Metropolitan* Police station. I was lucky to survive. Powis was hated and feared; he could return a detective to uniform on a whim – and he did. He revelled in minutiae, because to catch a detective out meant that he believed that he would be perceived as the far cleverer person, as John Simmonds and Charlie Cheal were about to find out.

★

There was little intimation of what was about to happen; it was close to midnight when Simmonds received a telephone call at home.

'Powis here!' roared a voice.

Simmonds immediately thought this must be a colleague winding him up, but those thoughts were dispersed when the voice continued, 'You – Cheal – my office, 10 o'clock, tomorrow!' – because Powis did indeed talk in that imbecile, telegraphic manner.

Thinking that Powis must have been as impressed with Cheal's report as he had been, Simmonds and Cheal entered Powis' office expecting to receive fulsome praise. Instead, Powis demanded to know the postal address of the casino, which was situated in a very long road, so long that it covered several postcodes. In the hundreds of pages contained in that report Charlie Cheal had made just one error – he had given the address of the casino as 'W1' instead of 'W2'.

It was all Powis needed to launch into a bellowing diatribe about attention to detail. Charlie Cheal was an excellent detective, a veteran of the Flying Squad and the Regional Crime Squad, but his temper possessed a very short fuse; and when it blew, it was advisable to don a steel helmet, shout 'Incoming!' and duck!

Cheal lost it, right now – it would cost him interview boards for two promotions; and what was more, after another later confrontation with Powis, Simmonds, too, knew that his own chances of advancement in the Metropolitan Police were at an end.

But then he received a telephone call from Hugh Moore, who was now a commander in the City of London Police. He referred to their previous conversation regarding the venal City Police officers and asked how reliable that information had been. Now that the investigation had been completed, Simmonds was able to tell him that the information had been 100 per cent, since the officers concerned had been overheard talking on the phone.

Simmonds asked why he had phoned, and Moore replied that there was a new Commissioner in the City, Peter Marshall QPM, and also a vacancy arising for the rank of detective chief superintendent; the incumbent, Sidney Hollis Smith, was retiring. When Moore stated that a Detective Superintendent Ernie Bransgrove was in line to be promoted to that position, Simmonds was astounded; Bransgrove had been one of the officers who had come up on the intercept. Clearly, little action had been taken since Simmonds' earlier contact, and he told Moore that he would sooner take the job than let Bransgrove get it.

As Simmonds told me, 'Moore asked if I was serious and with Powis stuck in my craw, I said yes.'

Following a meeting with the City Commissioner on a Friday afternoon, Simmonds was asked how soon he could start. Unencumbered with any fresh investigations, Simmonds replied that in theory he could start at 9 o'clock the following Monday morning. Marshall picked up the telephone, spoke to the Met's Commissioner, Sir David McNee, and as a result, having just celebrated his fortieth birthday, John Simmonds became head of the City of London's CID on Monday 5 June 1978.

Coincidentally, the No. 1 song at the top of the hit parade at that time, sung by John Travolta and Olivia Newton-John from the musical *Grease*, was 'You're the One That I Want'.

As Simmonds would shortly find out, there were a number of venal members of the City's Criminal Investigation Department who would discover that he was the very last person they wanted.

CHAPTER 2

Although the City of London is commonly known as 'The Square Mile', the description is only slightly inaccurate; to be pedantic, its area is 1.12 square miles. Its residents number 9,000, but its temporary population is huge – approximately 400,000 daily commuters, plus an unspecified number of tourists.

It is both a city and a county within London, comprised of twenty-five wards or sub-divisions, and it borders Westminster in the west, Islington and Hackney to the north, Tower Hamlets to the east and the River Thames in the south.

The City owns Smithfield and Leadenhall Markets; its single hospital is St Bartholomew's; it oversees the Barbican Centre; and Sir Christopher Wren's magnificent cathedral is situated in St Paul's Churchyard. It managed to survive the depredations of the Luftwaffe during the Second World War; in fact, the City has always been a survivor. During the Peasants' Revolt in 1381 the rebels took the City and the Tower of London, but not for long; and the City managed to endure the Great Plague of London. That commenced in 1665, and no sooner was it ended in 1666 than the conflagration which became known as the Great Fire of London was sent to disturb the City.

Above all, the Central Criminal Court – always known by the thoroughfare in which it reposes as 'The Old Bailey' – is where justice is often, but not always, dispensed.

The City is policed by England and Wales' tiniest police force; in medieval times it was patrolled by a day and night City Watch, under the control of two City sheriffs. In 1838 the two Watches were melded into one organization and the City of London Police Act 1839 was passed to field off attempts to amalgamate the fiercely independent institution with the Metropolitan Police, formed ten years previously.

Because of the number of banks and other financial institutions in the area, much of the reported crime – burglaries and frauds – was money-orientated. In 1946, the Metropolitan and City Police Company Fraud Department was set up. Known simply as 'the Fraud Squad' (or 'C6' Department at the Yard), it was the first fully integrated collaboration between the two forces. The City officers brought their expertise in complicated Stock Exchange matters and the Met supplied their detective and criminal intelligence resources.

The City Police headquarters is situated at Wood Street police station, and there are two other police stations, Bishopsgate and Snow Hill; the CID offices at each were under the command of a detective chief inspector. Traditionally, the uniform personnel, with their distinctive brass buttons and red and white chequered armlets and cap bands, are taller than the average police officer. This difference was emphasized at Snow Hill police station, which due to its close proximity to the Old Bailey was a favourite lunchtime spot for Met officers attending the court. In the canteen there were two rows of coat pegs; one, appreciably higher, was labelled 'City Police officers only', the second, far lower, was marked, 'Metropolitan Police officers and Traffic Wardens'. My Met contemporaries and I found this hilarious, although due to the sudden preponderance of officers suffering from hurt feelings, I've no doubt that this sign was removed long ago.

In 1978 – which is when we take up this story – there were approximately 830 taller police officers in the City as opposed to 22,197 in its much larger neighbour, the Met, which encircled it. The new City Commissioner had been in place since January of that year; he was much needed. He had succeeded Sir James Page CBE, QPM, whose lack of attention to discipline ('Call me Jim', he told his subordinates) had proved a disaster to morale and, unintentionally, had promoted some dubious practices.

*

Quite apart from the shady, fraudulent (and commonplace) dealings being investigated within the Square Mile, Simmonds found he had inherited a number of far more serious offences.

On 3 May 1976, four men, three of whom were wearing wigs and false beards, carrying sawn-off shotguns and pistols, had held up security and payroll staff on the third floor of the *Daily Express* building. Two of the gang were the 'inside men', who were in the cashier's office, in contact with the gang by telephone to a public call box. Two of the guards employed by Security Express saw what was happening, managed to barricade themselves in the office of David Aitken, the general manager, and were able to prevent the robbers from stealing £25,000. However, the raiders were able to exit through a back door, having robbed security guard Telwyn Roberts of seven bags, each containing £25,000, and escaped in a van which was found abandoned less than a mile away. A police spokesman believed that the thieves had possessed an accurate plan of the area where the £175,000 robbery had taken place. Perhaps they had. No arrests were made immediately; one year later, they were.

On 27 September 1977 seven men wearing balaclava helmets and brandishing sawn-off shotguns attacked three guards in a Securicor van carrying £1 million in wages for the Williams & Glyn's Bank in Birchin Lane. One of the guards was shot in the leg, and the gang made off with nine bags of cash, totalling £225,000. Their third getaway car was rammed in Upper Thames Street by a second security van, then they commandeered a fourth car after forcing the driver out into the road; it was later found abandoned. They were last seen getting into a taxi – 'We assume they hijacked it', said a police spokesman.

Suddenly, there was a breakthrough. Between 15 and 18 October 1977, four men – Francis Fraser Jr, James Fraser, George Copley and Allan Roberts – were arrested and charged with the Williams & Glyn's robbery. On 16 November Harry Wright and Tony White were arrested for the same offence. But then something odd happened. One by one, all of the accused were granted bail. Stranger still, thirty-six-year-old Allan Roberts, who was charged with attempted murder of the guard and who had a string of convictions and was on parole, having served half of a twelve-year sentence for armed robbery, had actually admitted being on the raid. Yet he, too, was granted bail.

Underworld sources later suggested that Roberts was in possession of £27,000 when he was arrested; yet the police declared finding only £13,000. This raised the question: had the police stolen the outstanding £14,000? If the sum of £27,000 was correct, yes, they might have done; either that, or it might have been handed over by Roberts for services soon to be rendered. Or it might just have been a rumour.

Whatever the truth of the matter, on 28 February 1978 Roberts vanished from police sight. That same evening, he was accidentally shot by John Hilton (who earlier that month had been released on licence for a murder committed in 1963) when the two of them carried out a £280,000 diamond robbery, during which a fifty-five-year-old jeweller was killed after being shot in the back with a sawn-off shotgun. Roberts bled to death; Hilton was eventually jailed for life for the jeweller's murder in 1991.

By May 1978, all the charges against the other five men had been dropped.

Within days, on 31 May 1978, two security guards drove their van into the loading bay at the *Daily Mirror* building in Fetter Lane to deliver pay packets to the newspaper's workers. Once inside, with the security door shut and padlocked, the guards assumed it would be safe to unload the wages, which totalled £197,000, on to a trolley. It was then that the two raiders, already inside the building posing as printers, struck; they smashed the padlock, opened the doors to allow entry to the third member of the gang driving a stolen Mercedes. One of the guards, thirty-eight-year-old Antonio Castro, fought back; he was shot in the chest at point-blank range with a service revolver which had been adapted to fire shotgun cartridges. Ignoring him, the robbers transferred the money into the car – and vanished. Castro (who two years previously had been shot in the ankle during a bank robbery) died on the way to St Bartholomew's Hospital; by a tragic coincidence, his wife worked there as a nurse.

And then, between 6 and 10 June 1978, there was another breakthrough. Tony White, just released from being charged with the Williams & Glyn's robbery and who had a number of convictions, including a twelve-year sentence for robbery, was arrested and charged with the murder at the *Daily Mirror*. Then it was the turn of Billy Tobin, a serial armed robber who at that time had been acquitted of robbery on four occasions, having, naturally, been framed by police. White was then released on bail; Tobin was later released in rather shocking circumstances.

But Simmonds saw there was something very wrong here. Eight men charged with armed robberies totalling £597,000, one where a custodian had been shot, the second where a guard had been murdered – and seven of the accused first being granted bail and then all eight having the charges dropped?

What the hell was going on?

CHAPTER 3

These misgivings were – for the time being – pushed to the back of Simmonds' mind; he had a new job in a new Force to contend with. He was shown around the headquarters by Ron Enston, his Divisional Office Sergeant. Many of the CID systems were archaic; asking why something was so, Simmonds was told that this was the way it had always been done. After a few weeks of this, Sergeant Enston's regular reply became, 'Stock answer, Sir!' Shown in the CID's current registry were files which were over sixty years old – in fact, the 1911 Siege of Sidney Street was still considered to be an existing enquiry. So this, plus other ancient processes, had to be addressed and updated.

Hugh Moore told Simmonds there were 'a few villains in the CID' and that between them they would clean them out.

Simmonds later said, 'He told me I would have to get around the ground and he would tip me off if he heard anything specific. I was appreciative of this and thought we would get on well. I was still conscious of John Lock's recommendation as to Hugh's integrity.'

It was an opinion shared by many; Hugh John Moore had been born in 1929 and following National Service with the RAF had joined the City Police in 1955. An active Freemason, he had risen fast through the ranks of the City's CID and had served with both the Fraud Squad and the Regional Crime Squad. He had been involved in many high-powered investigations and in 1982 he would go on to probe the mysterious (and Masonic-linked) death of Roberto Calvi ('The Pope's Banker'), who was found hanging under Blackfriars Bridge. Moore had been commended on eleven occasions and many of his contemporaries liked and admired him; then there were those who didn't.

Moore gave Simmonds a run-down on the detective inspectors and chief inspectors and categorized them as being either 'good' or 'OK', although there were two in particular, he said, who were not suitable CID material. This raised the question in Simmonds' mind: if they were unsuitable, why were they there and why should he be carrying passengers? He made his own discreet enquiries, but all he could ascertain was that these men were honest and had not been involved in corrupt practices. On the other hand, Moore rated highly another officer about whom Simmonds had no need to make discreet enquiries; he already knew him from his days as a detective inspector at Holborn. He had a poor opinion of him then, as he had now, but when he raised his concerns, Moore was very defensive. This raised another query: when Moore had told him he wanted to clean up the CID but had a down on officers who had declared themselves to be against corruption, how did this affect Moore's own integrity?

There was another concern. Moore had previously told him that the officers who had been named in the telephone intercept would be 'isolated'. But with the opening of an incident room at Bishopsgate police station it had been Detective Superintendent Ernest Bransgrove who headed the investigation into the *Daily Mirror* robbery, as he had the Williams & Glyn's and the *Daily Express* enquiries. Three high-level enquiries that were extremely controversial; and Simmonds lost no time at all in ensuring that Bransgrove was well and truly 'isolated' – with a transfer to the Fraud Squad.

Then there was the matter of Freemasonry. On the day of his joining the City Police, Simmonds had met the chief superintendent (administration) and had filled in all the necessary forms. That officer had told Simmonds that he did not wish to know if he was a Freemason or not but added that Freemasonry was 'not a good thing in the City at that time'. Simmonds passed no comment on that but later said:

> I had joined the Freemasons when I was a sergeant, and my reason for doing so was that I wanted a social life outside the police service without the fear of being compromised by persons of bad character. I believed Freemasons were just and upright people and that as a police officer I would not be at risk with my job by associating with such people. The lodge I joined was well-run, there was an equal mixture of Jews and Gentiles and they would not allow any one profession to gain control. I was informed that as I was the second police officer to join the lodge, they would not permit another. I was more than happy with that, because I did not want to be in a 'police' lodge.
>
> I kept Freemasonry separate from the job although I knew many officers who were 'on the Square' and did attend lodge meetings of friends, from time to time. As I went on in the service, I saw Freemasonry being abused both within the job and on the outside. So by the time I moved into the City, the fact that I was a Freemason was known to very few people and I intended to keep it that way.

I moved into the CID headquarters and from the outset, several people tested me out to see if I was 'on the
Square'. I blanked all approaches and it was generally
accepted that I was not 'one of them'.

From time to time, Moore would telephone Simmonds to suggest
that he should visit a certain pub at 8.00pm or a bar at 7.30pm,
and on each occasion there would be a convivial group of CID
officers in attendance, plus a few villains. At most of these meetings
one of the officers present was the detective chief inspector from
Bishopsgate. He had also been Ernie Bransgrove's second-in-com-
mand on the three City robbery investigations and his name was
Philip Anthony Cuthbert.

★

Simmonds had known Cuthbert from his time with the London
Regional Crime Squad. 'I found him to be a likeable person, very
enthusiastic, hard-working but also "Jack the Lad",' Simmonds
told me.

The expression 'Dandy Boy' refers to a well-groomed, well-
dressed man but often to one who is self-absorbed – and that was
how Dave 'Ginger' Dixon good-naturedly described Cuthbert to
me, adding, 'He was totally alien to anybody's idea of a City of
London copper.'

Liam Gillespie who, like Dixon, knew Cuthbert from their time
on the RCS told me, 'He was very popular, as were most of the
City officers who were attached to the Regional. However', he
added, 'he did have great trouble getting people to speak up for
him, later on.'

Cuthbert's rise through the ranks in the City had been rapid;
he had been promoted to detective inspector in 1970 aged twenty-eight, and six years later to detective chief inspector. He was
now thirty-six years of age, a proven thief-taker, had shown qual-
ities of leadership and had also exhibited considerable bravery on
several occasions which was reflected in his being commended on
eleven occasions.

After a couple of meetings in pubs when Cuthbert was present,
he commented to Simmonds that it was 'nerve-wracking' the way
that he (Simmonds) kept appearing right out of the blue and that
he must have had his ear to the ground. This Simmonds dismissed
by saying that he was simply getting round the ground and learning; but in fact, it was of course Moore who had suggested these
meetings. However, he dismissed this in turn by believing this was

down to Moore's deep knowledge of the City and obviously having good informants.

Some three months after Simmonds' arrival in the City, Cuthbert walked into his office to tell him that he had met a man who was the past Master of the Masonic lodge of which he, Cuthbert, was presently the current Master and who stated that Simmonds was in fact a Freemason. Simmonds agreed but made it quite clear to Cuthbert that he thought that Freemasonry and the police should be separate bedfellows and that he wanted it kept quiet that he was, indeed, 'on the Square'. All to no avail; in modern parlance, Simmonds had been 'outed', and the news went round the City like wildfire. Now that he was considered to be 'one of them', Simmonds became far more popular than previously with several of his contemporaries.

However, matters were unfolding 20 miles to the north of the City which would drastically change all that.

PART II

Arriving

'You don't know much', said the Duchess, 'and that's a fact.'

Lewis Carroll, *Alice in Wonderland*

CHAPTER 4

Neil Barrington Dickens (later Deputy Assistant Commissioner Dickens QPM) was a thirty-eight-year-old detective superintendent attached to No. 5 Regional Crime Squad in Hertfordshire. During his twenty years service with Hertfordshire Constabulary he had been commended on thirteen occasions for catching criminals and he was currently enjoying considerable successes running a number of 'supergrasses'. For those unaware of that particular term, a supergrass was a career criminal – inevitably an armed robber – who, having been caught bang to rights, volunteered (or was induced) to implicate every other criminal he had ever worked with, and who, having both given evidence against them and confessing all of the crimes which he himself had participated in, was given a reduced sentence, plus a new identity. Since – in the early stages, at least – that reduced sentence amounted to no more than five years' imprisonment, it was a very attractive bait to hook hardened crims who in ordinary circumstances could be staring twenty years in the face.

It was a system which worked very well in the 1970s and '80s. A check run in 1979 over a twelve-month period revealed that of the 200 prisoners committed for trial who had been confronted with the evidence obtained by the supergrasses, 92 per cent pleaded guilty. Other prisoners who had been 'supergrassed' sometimes became supergrasses themselves. Crimes were cleared up, property and weaponry was recovered and many worthwhile villains were put away. But eventually the system went the way of all things, a contributory factor being that some of the supergrasses were run by inexperienced officers who began to believe that their manipulative charges were really their friends and permitted them to run rings round them. The resultant (and often scandalous) publicity spelt the death-knell for the supergrass; a great pity. That's a very brief glimpse at supergrasses; we'll return to them a little later to evaluate their work and usefulness in depth.

However, in 1978 the trade in supergrasses was booming; and when Dickens received a request from a prisoner serving a sentence he went to visit him. Dickens had arrested the man, Geoffrey Simms, years before when he was a detective sergeant at Bishop's Stortford police station; he had nothing whatsoever to do with his present sentence. But Simms obviously had great faith in Dickens and believed that he was the complete antithesis of a crooked cop, because when he told him of corrupt practices by certain police officers, Dickens immediately informed his old boss from Hertfordshire, Ron Harvey, who was currently the commander of C11 (Criminal Intelligence) Department at the Yard.

Both officers went to the prison, where Simms made a detailed written statement in which names were named; being a provincial officer, Dickens had only heard of a few of them, and he and Harvey returned to the Yard, where the matter was discussed, as Dickens told me, 'at the highest level'.

The highest of the high at that time was the Commissioner, Sir David Blackstock McNee QPM; a devout Christian, he was now fifty-three years of age. He had become the head of the Met the previous year, having spent all of his previous thirty-one years' service in Scottish constabularies.

His deputy was a fellow Scot, Patrick Bernard Kavanagh CBE, QPM, who had seen wartime service with the Rifle Brigade and the Parachute Regiment. He had risen through the ranks of several constabularies, arriving at the Yard in 1974 as an assistant commissioner. In 1977 he had been appointed Deputy Commissioner; as such, fifty-five-year-old Kavanagh was responsible for organizing the investigation of complaints made in respect of Metropolitan Police officers and any disciplinary proceedings which might follow.

Gilbert James Kelland CBE, QPM was the Assistant Commissioner (Crime), being in command of all the detectives in London. This appointment came, like those of McNee and Kavanagh, in 1977, and it was probably a bit of a shock, since all of his preceding thirty-one years' of service had been spent in uniform.

So these were the three highest Met officers who were apprised of the situation at that time; in addition, Peter Marshall, the Commissioner of the City of London Police, was consulted, as was Her Majesty's Inspector of Constabulary, who referred the matter to the Home Office to decide who the investigating force should be. The allegations were immensely serious and potentially damaging – professional armed robbers had been paying colossal bribes, amounting to £60,000 or more, to venal City of London police officers, firstly for bail, then to have evidence diluted, then to get charges dropped altogether, in cases where one security guard had been shot and another murdered. If it were true, these police officers were every bit as crooked, cunning and experienced as those bribing them; in consequence, those who investigated these allegations would have to be as canny as their City of London

counterparts. Who should be chosen? What about the Met? That
was a non-starter; within a very short space of time, allegations
of impropriety were coming in from a different quarter – a supergrass run by the Flying Squad at Finchley was also naming names
and these included Metropolitan Police officers. These details were
passed to Don Neesham, the Commander of the Flying Squad, and
they were forwarded, upstairs, into the melting pot of allegations.

Who else then should head this investigation? Hard-bitten
detectives from Manchester, Birmingham or Liverpool – officers
who were well versed in understanding and tackling professional
criminals (and crooked cops), able to spot lies and duplicity from
a mile off?

So this can of worms was dumped in the lap of Merlyn Rees
PC, the Home Secretary. Prior to his appointment two years
previously, Rees' career had not been showered with accolades.
Previously, within a month of his appointment as Secretary of
State for Northern Ireland, he had lifted the proscription on the
murderous Ulster Volunteer Force (UVF), a heart-warming and
typically political piece of appeasement. Matters went badly wrong
one month later in May 1974, when the UVF were implicated in
the Dublin and Monaghan bombings which resulted in the deaths
of thirty-three civilians (including an unborn child) and injuries to
300 people.

With this track record of man-management, and with the experienced detectives of the country's major cities at his beck and
call, Rees eschewed the lot. Instead, he selected sleepy Dorset
Constabulary to spearhead the enquiry. They agreed. And to lead
this enquiry, Len Burt, the Force's Assistant Chief Constable
(ACC), was chosen.

It's necessary to examine the disparity between Dorset and the
Met. At that time, Dorset Constabulary's force of 1,092 officers
covered an area of 1,024 square miles which contained a population of 575,800; whereas the Met's force of 22,197 men and women
(including 3,250 CID officers) policed an area of 785 square miles
containing a wide ethnic mix of approximately 7 million people.

During 1977 Dorset investigated 25,186 indictable offences,
which included three homicides, one of which was classified as
manslaughter. The perpetrators gave themselves up. In the same
time-span in the Met's area, 568,952 indictable offences were
recorded; the number of homicides investigated was 142.

The Met policed several hundred marches, meetings and
demonstrations, which often degenerated into civil disorder;
Dorset Police's contribution to public order was an investigation

into a shopping trolley thrown from the top of a multi-storey car-park which struck a passer-by, fortunately not fatally.

The differences between the two forces, their respective environments and the way policing was carried out could scarcely have been more striking.

What follows is an account of that ill-fated investigation; ill-fated because what happened after the Home Secretary's calamitous decision would cause a former detective superintendent at Scotland Yard to tell me, forty years later, 'If I'd been sent down to Dorset to investigate cattle rustling, I'd have been out of my fucking depth, too'.

CHAPTER 5

On Friday, 8 September 1978, Cuthbert requested a lunchtime meeting with Simmonds. They met at Rakes Restaurant in Bishopsgate, where they sat at a table for two and Cuthbert asked if he could talk to Simmonds 'on the Square' – as one brother Freemason to another – and Simmonds, believing that Cuthbert was alluding to a personal problem, said he could. Cuthbert then asked if he was aware that an ACC from Dorset was looking into matters in the City; Simmonds was not at that time aware of any investigation, and said so. Cuthbert stated that three days previously, on Tuesday, 5 September, Commander Moore had told him that this was so, that he, Cuthbert, was the subject of this enquiry and that he should ensure that his finances were in order and that he could account for all his possessions and expenditure. Cuthbert said that he had been told that a man – 'Raymond' – who had been involved in a large theft at London Heathrow had been talking – and he was right.

He added that Moore had told him Burt was looking into allegations of corruption in respect of both the Williams & Glyn's and *Daily Mirror* robberies, but he told Simmonds that he, Cuthbert, had nothing to be worried about. However, he felt that since Moore had warned him, this was the only help he was going to get; but if things went wrong, he was 'not going to be the patsy' and he would 'put Moore in it' as well.

With this mixed message, not unnaturally, Simmonds wanted to know what Cuthbert meant; he replied that Moore had received money from the *Daily Express* robbery – 'not really villainy, it was £300 for bail'. However, although that sum was not correct, that was just the beginning; there was a lot more . . .

Simmonds told me what happened next:

> Many people have been critical of the way I handled this and as a result, I later resigned from the Freemasons. I was happy to speak to Phil on what I originally thought was going to be a private matter, but when he started talking about serious criminal acts and conspiracies among police officers, I chose to act as a police officer. People have said that as a Freemason I should have stopped Cuthbert talking, but what he was telling me was so serious that I believed that what I did was right.

The Commissioner was not available that afternoon, so I went home and my head was in a turmoil. I knew that I had inherited some corruption within the CID but nothing like Phil had told me. He said there was a wide circle of CID officers who were involved and it had gone right to the top, to Hugh. No wonder Hugh knew where to send me for the clandestine meetings that had been taking place and no wonder he had not wanted to do it himself. He was trying to be poacher turned gamekeeper.

On the Monday morning, I asked to see the Commissioner, Peter Marshall. I had mused over the weekend on what Phil had said and particularly the involvement of Hugh Moore. I decided to tell Peter so much, to test whether there was any truth in it before I told him the full story. I said I had had a discussion with an officer who had told me certain facts about an investigation that was about to be set up concerning the City and the Met. I then gave him details of the investigation as relayed by Phil.

Peter became very upset and demanded that I tell him who my informant was. He said that only three people could have known what I was telling him, the Assistant Commissioner of 'A' Department at New Scotland Yard, Hugh Moore and himself, because they were the only three people who had been involved in a conference in his office the previous week.

I then went through the whole story as detailed by Phil. Peter was obviously devastated. Phil Cuthbert was clearly privy to matters that had been discussed and Hugh Moore could be the only one to have leaked it. This supported Cuthbert's story to me and gave credence to the other matters he had alleged.

The Commissioner then called in Ernie Bright, the Assistant Commissioner, and we went through the details again. It was decided that I should attempt to corroborate what Phil had told me and I was to be fitted with a tape recorder and meet up with Phil to try to get him to repeat some of the things he had said. In the meantime, Peter Marshall advised me that there were certain documents that were in the CID Headquarters that it had been decided at the earlier meeting, attended by Hugh Moore, should be part of the investigation. The documents were in a combination-locked security cabinet in the detective superintendent's office and I was instructed to secure them.

The combination number was the same one that had always been on the cabinet, and at one time Hugh Moore had occupied that office. I took the papers and changed the combination on the cabinet. That night, the CID Headquarters was 'broken into', the office was entered and attempts had been made to force the security cabinet open. Only Peter Marshall, the AC(A) from the Met, and Hugh Moore knew of the significance of the contents of the cabinet until that Monday, when I removed them.

Matters were now not as secure as Simmonds would have wished. On 15 September, Chapman Pincher of the *Daily Express* telephoned to ask if it was correct that the Chief Constable of Dorset was making enquiries into the City Police; he was told that as far as the police were concerned, no such enquiry was taking place. Two days later, the same enquiry was made by Jack McEachran, the crime reporter from the *Daily Mirror*, who asked if it was true that the investigation was being conducted from Camberwell police station; Simmonds replied that he had no knowledge of any such enquiry being conducted. The following day, McEachran telephoned again, apologizing if his report had 'hit the fan' but saying he had discovered that the enquiries had centred around a chief inspector – why then was the investigating officer of so high a rank? Simmonds referred him to a press release issued earlier by the Commissioner and said that any further comment could prejudice enquiries. McEachran expressed disbelief and suggested that Simmonds was keeping matters back from him – and he was quite right. His sources of information were good; by now, Burt, plus twelve other officers from Dorset, had set up their headquarters in a portakabin at Camberwell police station.

Putting down the phone on the intrepid newshound, Simmonds immediately informed Assistant Commissioner Ernest William Bright QPM of the content of the conversation; the whole matter was about to be blown wide open – and Cuthbert's revelations had yet to be recorded on tape.

But it was not a matter which could be rushed; that would have alerted Cuthbert immediately. So it was not until Wednesday, 27 September that, having heard that Cuthbert was in the Ship public house in Artillery Row, Simmonds, who had been fitted with a covert National Panasonic Recorder with a Bovill body microphone, went to the pub and activated the recorder. There, amongst others, he saw Irvine Shine, a solicitor; he and Cuthbert were discussing a man named Stephen Raymond, who had made allegations against Cuthbert. Shine – who had defended Stephen

Raymond on a murder charge – claimed that he knew these allegations were false, and when Simmonds asked if he was prepared to say so to any enquiry, Shine replied that he was. Additionally, Shine mentioned that Raymond was manufacturing statements to help a friend on a robbery charge – and that was right.

It was clear that Cuthbert was concerned about what Stephen Raymond might have to say about him; he mentioned that Stephen's brother, Alan Raymond, had telephoned him the previous evening to say that he'd been seen by 'the funny people from Bournemouth'. Cuthbert also mentioned Burt, saying, 'He's a fucking real pig; God willing, he don't know fuck-all because he's a uniformed cunt, he's never done nothing, never been at court in his life and he's gonna come and throw loads of silly questions at us eventually, which we can answer completely . . .'

Simmonds and Cuthbert then went to Dirty Dick's public house (where the tape was changed over) and met Alan Raymond, the brother of Stephen, who told them of a meeting with the Dorset officers earlier that day. He stated that he had not told those officers everything regarding his dealings with Cuthbert, and Simmonds told him that the next time he saw those officers he should rectify matters.

Simmonds and Cuthbert left and walked along Middlesex Street before entering another pub. During the conversation Cuthbert alluded to his involvement in high-level corruption; all that and much more, including implicating Detective Sergeant John Leslie William Golbourn and naming a number of other officers, both in the City and the Metropolitan Police.

The tape was taken to Dorset Headquarters, where it was to be transcribed. A few days later, Simmonds had a call to say they were having difficulty with the conversations and ask if he could attend to assist with the transcription.

'I was appalled at the level of expertise that they were applying to the job', Simmonds later said. 'They had given the tape to an audio typist and expected her to just type it out as if it were a dictated tape. The fact that the conversations were from a body mike and were taken in a pub with music blaring had not been allowed for. They should have copied the tape and then using the duplicate, had it "cleaned up" in a tape laboratory. As it was, I took the tape, made a copy of it, then handed the original to the investigating officer and spent the next ten days at the Dorset Headquarters writing out the transcript by hand.'

The tape had lasted for three hours. The typescript would amount to 174 pages. It would eventually be exhibit No. 1 at an Old Bailey trial; but that day was not yet. A great many other things would occur before that happened.

CHAPTER 6

In the sixty-odd years of its existence, the Flying Squad (nick-named 'The Sweeney' – cockney rhyming slang for 'Sweeney Todd' – although, more prosaically, it was known at the Yard as C8 Department) had amassed a tremendous reputation for crimebusting; its successes included the Great Train Robbery Investigation, as well as the Bank of America robbery. The Squad concentrated on the activities of first division criminals, mainly armed robbers but also high-class burglars, receivers of stolen property and safe-blowers. The twelve squads at the Yard were each under the control of a detective inspector and No. 8 was known as 'The Dip squad'; these were officers who concentrated on the activities of pickpockets (a Squad priority since its formation in 1919) – and since 'Dips' were regarded as first-rate snouts or informants, this added to the rich flow of information coming into the Squad.

And then, on 10 July 1978, matters changed considerably. Leaving just four of its squads at the Yard, most of the Flying Squad was devolved: eight of the twelve squads, comprised of 110 officers, were inserted into offices situated in all four compass points around the capital – Rotherhithe, Barnes, Finchley and Walthamstow. They were renamed 'The Central Robbery Squad', and that was their brief: to collate information, investigate armed robberies to the exclusion of all other offences and to catch those responsible. They worked their quarter of London; and if the armed robbers, who, of course, knew no boundaries, ventured into another area, combined operations with other Squad offices (including the four remaining squads at the Yard) were launched, all under the control of the Flying Squad Commander.

This had been the brainchild of Detective Chief Inspector Tony Lundy, a Flying Squad officer who had flown to Canada to pick up a prisoner wanted for a London robbery. He had been highly impressed with the way that Montreal's Homicide and Robbery Squad collated the information on these offences and came to the conclusion that the Metropolitan Police could well do with such a dedicated unit. It was certainly needed; in 1978 robberies and violent thefts in London amounted to 12,180. The year following the formation of the Robbery Squad saw 74 shotguns and 44 handguns recovered from 2,286 prisoners, and cash and valuables in excess of £2 million seized.

Lundy had always known the value of informants and had achieved tremendous successes from running them; now, with Nos. 5 and 7 squads under his control at Finchley, he attained great success with supergrasses. In fact, it is fair to say that no other officer has ever achieved so much with that genre. Lundy was then thirty-six years of age and his work had been recognized by the award of twenty-three commendations.

There were two such supergrasses – Dave Smith and Billy Aimes – at Finchley police station, and quite apart from grassing their contemporaries in the world of armed robbery they were prepared to give information on serious misconduct by police officers.

Lundy required more personnel; in 1978 Detective Sergeant Mike Bucknole was a member of No. 6 squad at the Yard, and Commander Neesham posted him to Finchley. Upon his arrival, Lundy gave him carte blanche to 'tidy up some old jobs' from South London – a fertile area, since most of Lundy's work stemmed from North London. Bucknole got to work with fellow Squad officer, Ray Wood (the only detective constable ever to have been appointed OBE), and thanks to some top class information they arrested two serial robbers, Ray Fowles and Norman Jones – that was on 10 August 1978. They set about questioning them, and the following day Jones 'rolled over', saying he wanted help; by 15 August Fowles had similarly put his hands up. It was Fowles who told them that there was going to be a £180,000 armed robbery at Lambeth Town Hall the very next day; as a result, Peter Rose was arrested. Rose had only recently been released from a fourteen-year sentence for attempting to murder a police officer and possessing a Magnum revolver with intent to resist arrest;[1] and now, he too rolled over. All three were granted supergrass status, and since it was clear that Finchley was too small to accommodate five supergrasses, Lundy told Bucknole to find alternative accommodation for the last three. He found it at Whetstone police station, a mile or two away from Finchley.

Like their contemporaries at Finchley, as well as grassing armed robbers, Fowles, Rose and Jones were also able to provide information of police wrongdoing to the constabulary officers, although some of these allegations were mainly what other criminals had told them and were therefore hearsay.

However, there were three pitfalls awaiting the Dorset team, many of whom were uniform and traffic officers whose ranks had been upgraded and had had the soubriquet 'detective' plonked in front of them.

*

The first of these difficulties was the fact that few, if any, of these officers had ever previously dealt with informants. Informants (or 'snouts') are a detective's life-blood. From the earliest beginnings of a CID officer's career he or she is taught – or at least, they were at the time we're referring to – to cultivate informants, to discover who is doing what in the underworld, who is mixing with who, what crimes they've committed, the whereabouts of the proceeds of those crimes and, best of all, what crimes are in the planning stage to actually be carried out – by whom and when.

The cultivation of informants is a tricky business; they provide information for a variety of reasons: reward, revenge, to oust a rival criminal in order take over that particular piece of lawlessness or, on odd occasions, out of public spiritedness. It is the detective's job to evaluate the accuracy of the information as well as the who, the why and the wherefore of it. Sometimes, through sheer inexperience and the desire to 'make one's bones' as a detective, matters can go horribly wrong. It happened to me with my first 'informant' (who turned out to be nothing more than a cheap little con-man), and it resulted in my detective inspector acidly informing me that I had a great deal to learn about life in general and informants, in particular. But I did learn, and it never happened again.[2] During the whole of my career, in which informants featured to a large extent, I don't suppose I ran many more than thirty of them. Some – like the snout who gave me the thief of a £2½ million stolen Rembrandt – I used only once; others I ran for years.

The well-respected and well-informed Jack Slipper ('of the Yard') was on record as saying, 'The category of informants who give the most trouble are the ones who do it strictly for the money.' I don't agree; I much preferred that breed of informant, where money was paid for results, a straightforward business transaction, to those who requested 'favours' of one kind or another.

So the informant-handling detective was learning all the time: when to press hard for information and when to back off and give the impression that the information (and the informant) was of little consequence. Sometimes the information was such that – never mind background checks, no time to acquire a search warrant, impossible to carry out a measured, structured briefing – the job was going off *right now*! And in those circumstances the detective had to make a split-second judgement. Had he sufficient trust in the snout to, in police parlance, 'go in with his head down'? It was always a matter of experience and judgement – and sometimes it worked and sometimes it didn't. Often a plan had to be hastily worked out in the back of a Flying Squad car, speeding to the scene of goodness-knows-what. This would frequently be the case when a participating informant was one of the gang members, where everything depended on split-second timing, the circumstances were changing by the minute and anything might occur (and usually did).

So running informants was a skill that was developed by detectives on a day-to-day basis, over a period of years. It was not something which could be instantly instilled in police officers who had spent most of their careers spotting a worn tyre or reporting recalcitrant motorists for speeding. In the same way that donning a ten-gallon hat would not make the wearer an authentic cowboy, putting the title of 'detective' in front of these officers' inflated ranks changed absolutely nothing.

It was therefore essential for an officer engaged in this type of enquiry to have run informants – a Flying Squad officer was utterly dependent on snouts to bring in work to the Squad – before actually dealing with supergrasses. This was a serious deficiency on the part of the Dorset officers; and it brings me straight on to the second pitfall.

When they provide information to the police, supergrasses may or may not be telling the complete truth. Because they are seasoned criminals, lying has become second nature to them. If they are not actually being untruthful, they may embellish or belittle matters for whatever reason – inevitably to gain their own ends. But the overriding principle when dealing with one of their ilk is that independent corroboration must be obtained. Even if two – or more – supergrasses are saying the self-same thing about the guilt of a criminal, that, the courts say, is not corroboration; and if that's all there is, the prosecution will fail.

Let me give examples of authentication. If a supergrass states that he carried out a robbery on a certain date with 'Bill Smith' and that Smith's share of the proceeds was £5,000, and a search of Smith's bank account reveals that the day after the robbery that sum was paid into his account, then that is part-corroboration. And if Smith is arrested and is put up on an identification parade and a witness to the crime picks him out, that too is corroboration, as it is if when Smith is interviewed by police, he admits the offence.

So the process starts with experienced detectives talking to the potential supergrass to ascertain what he knows. Once the officer in charge is convinced (a) of the criminal's desire to confront, then give evidence against, his fellows, and (b) that the number of criminals that he can name and the number of offences that he can describe is substantial, then he will go to the office of the Director of Public Prosecutions to outline exactly what's on offer. It is only after – and not before – the Director has sanctioned the matter, that the criminal will receive Resident Informant – or supergrass – status. There would be absolutely no immunity from prosecution for any crimes which the criminal had committed; that was allowed only once, in the case of Derek Creighton Smalls (known to his fast diminishing number of friends as 'Bertie'). This gave rise to a storm in the Court of Appeal (Criminal Division), when although Lord Justice Lawton dismissed the appeals of the vast majority of those convicted by Smalls' testimony (their sentences totalling 308 years' imprisonment), he registered distaste that the DPP had entered into a written contact with a criminal allowing him to walk free after confessing involvement in a series of violent robberies and stated that 'it should not be allowed to happen again'.

The Director's initial reaction was to suggest that, Lord Justice or not, Lawton should mind his own bloody business; but he conceded he did have a point. If this became commonplace, it might well lead to public disquiet; and therefore he laid down the dictum that anyone wishing to 'do a Bertie' (as it became known) should first admit to every single crime they had committed. Nothing could be left out which had not been admitted and might at a later date be flung into the supergrass's face during courtroom cross-examination, thereby jeopardising the prosecution .

So after confessing all his misdeeds, the supergrass would plead guilty to three or four specific charges and ask the court to take into consideration the remainder of his transgressions when he was sentenced; which in the early days of supergrassing, as I've already stated, was usually (although not always) just five years' imprisonment.

It did not, of course, prevent allegations of impropriety being made. One supergrass was accused in cross-examination of giving untruthful evidence against a particular defendant in order to revenge himself for the breakup of their homosexual relationship. This conspicuously untrue allegation so incensed the fiercely heterosexual supergrass that he demanded a doctor be called immediately to the Old Bailey to carry out a rectal examination in the witness box, 'to prove that my arsehole ain't been punched!' This examination should be carried out, demanded the supergrass, in the interests of justice in full view of judge, jury, barristers, representatives of the press and a few not disinterested people in the public gallery. As can be imagined, this caused quite a furore in court, especially after an attempt was made to remove him from the witness box, because the supergrass offered to fight anyone who tried to do so. It was only after the allegation had been withdrawn (no pun intended) that equanimity at the Old Bailey reigned once more.

But even before receiving the Director's agreement, operations would be put in motion to arrest those referred to by the – potential – supergrass. Speed was of the essence, because the supergrass's contemporaries would be aware he had been arrested; and his failure to appear at the Magistrates' Court within a few days would carry ominous overtones. Had he been turned? Whilst those associates were prevaricating they had to be arrested, using the tried and tested crash-bang-wallop formula, and any evidence seized. And while they were being interviewed, the Director's authority would hopefully have been received and the supergrass's handlers' next step would be to take written statements in minute detail from the source, querying and questioning everything that had been told to them; eventually, when they were satisfied that every bit of minutiae had been covered, they would invite the supergrass to read carefully through the statement and then sign it as being correct. That's the first of two steps. Verification – from independent sources – would come next.

But in this case that was precisely what did not happen with the constabulary officers in many instances. Having told them what evidence they could give, the supergrasses often refused to provide a written statement – 'Nah, nah, Guv'nor, I mean, don't be rude, can't put nuffink down in writing 'til I've got me guarantees, can I?'

And instead of saying something along the lines of, 'In that case, don't waste my time; you're on your own', these officers sheepishly accepted the situation as dictated to them by low-life crims – but they did provide statements. The officers wrote them themselves, saying, 'Bill Smith told me . . .' and setting down all that Bill Smith had said, which might – or might not – have been useful intelligence but was of no evidential value whatsoever.

Nevertheless, Lundy permitted the constabulary officers full, unrestricted access to all of the supergrasses. It would have been a matter of politeness for the two officers from Dorset to have announced their arrival at Whetstone in 1979, rather than barging in, unannounced, to see Fowles and Jones; unfortunately, they did not.

'I blocked them from coming in', Mike Bucknole told me, 'but Superintendent Corbett was there and he said it was all right for the Countryman officers to see them. Apparently, the first thing they asked about was corruption, especially here at Whetstone, and the next thing I heard was Ray Fowles screaming, "Get these cunts out of here!" I don't know what information Fowles had about police corruption, but I did get the impression that it was third-hand.'

So that was the second of the pitfalls that I mentioned a few pages back; let's leave this lamentable state of affairs for now – there's plenty more of the same to come, I assure you – and go on to the third hazard.

The first principle of the celebrated Prussian general and tactician, Carl von Clausewitz was, 'Make your base secure; from there, one can proceed to freedom of movement'. Sound common sense. Although Burt had served with the Dorset Regiment during his National Service, it appeared that he may not have been a devotee of military history; had this been the case, he might – or might not – have heeded von Clausewitz' dictum. But he didn't; however, that was no excuse. Not having a clue as to how to proceed, he sought the advice of Frank Williamson, the former head of Her Majesty's Inspectorate of Constabularies, who, as you're aware, like his father before him, loathed the Met with a passion, having been badly thwarted during the scandalous *Times* enquiry in 1970. His advice to Burt was that, 'The first essential step in any corruption enquiry is to ensure that your office is secure.'

This, too, was prescient advice, but with an attempt having been made to retrieve important documentation from the security cabinet at the City of London's police headquarters (although this was understandably later hotly denied by Hugh Moore), Burt should not have been too surprised when his headquarters was apparently broken into and its records 'interfered with'. Since there was no security at night or any other time for the portakabin at Camberwell, which was as secure as a paper bag and for which the key was left with the duty sergeant, it was inevitable that desperate, lawless individuals would want to know precisely what was being stockpiled to the detriment of the Criminal Investigation Departments of two London police forces.

With the cooperation of Surrey Constabulary's Chief Constable, Sir Peter Jack Matthews CVO, OBE, DL – he had left the Met in 1965 and had never been a CID officer, thus distancing him from any 'taint' – the team moved to a fresh headquarters in Godalming. John O'Connor, who features largely in this tale later on, expressed surprise. 'Why didn't they go to Tintagel House or Wellington House?' he commented to me, and that would have made sense. However, perhaps the Dorset officers had considered these venues and thought the position untenable – these secure buildings were part of the Metropolitan Police establishment, and given the Camberwell portakabin fiasco it was a case of 'once bitten, twice shy'. However, the same fears did not extend to Peter Wright, the Chief Constable of South Yorkshire, just a few short years later when he arrived in London to undertake corruption enquiries into the Metropolitan Police. He and his team of twenty officers moved into the sixth floor accommodation in Wellington House and spent the next year there, without let or hindrance.

Tony Forward was the superintendent of Godalming sub-division at the time. He told me:

> My first floor office window looked out over the back yard and the exterior staircase leading to a row of flats, built to accommodate police officers and their families. Several of these were empty.
>
> At some time during my tenure, I was told from the chief constable's office that he had given permission for a team of officers investigating alleged criminal activity by Metropolitan Police officers to use the vacant flats as offices.
>
> The team duly arrived and I was introduced to the officer in charge, Assistant Chief Constable Leonard Burt from the Dorset Constabulary. He invited me to his office, the first flat from the staircase. It was furnished with a desk, chairs and a cabinet. A photograph of his wife in police uniform stood on top of the cabinet.
>
> He told me that his team had been using an office in a Met building but that someone had gained entry. I cannot remember whether he told me what the intruder had done but he did say that they could no longer operate there and were now running their operation from Godalming. He gave me no further details of this and I did not feel it was prudent to ask. I do not remember him talking about any opposition to his enquiry.
>
> He told me all statements, intelligence and information was being loaded into a computer and that there was a twin computer at a secret location so that should anyone interfere with the computer at Godalming, all the data would be saved on the twin computer. I did not ask him where the twin computer was located and assumed it was back in Dorset, where he came from. I did not see the computer, it was in another office.
>
> Computers for this purpose were rare in those days, certainly in my experience. He explained that if a statement was taken that mentioned a man in a red hat, the computer would immediately throw up details of any other mention of a man in a red hat.
>
> I did not meet any of the other members of his team but I understood that, because they came from Dorset, they were known as 'The Swedey'.
>
> A separate car park was used for the team's vehicles, out of my office view. I have no idea how many officers

were in the team, what ranks they held or what vehicles they were using.

Mr Burt was a friendly man, obviously very apprecia-tive of the accommodation afforded to him by the Surrey Constabulary. He invited me to visit his office at any time. If it was after 12 noon, he would offer me a glass of whisky from his cabinet. I visited his office probably twice a week.

Another, less frequent, visitor to Burt's accommodation was Sir Colin Philip Joseph Woods KCVO, CBE, QPM. After seeing war-time service with the King's Royal Rifle Corps and the Royal Ulster Rifles, he had joined the Metropolitan Police as a constable in 1946. He had shot up through the ranks and after thirty-one years' service was now Her Majesty's Chief Inspector of Constabulary for England and Wales. It was clear that, quite apart from the two Commissioners and the Home Secretary, a watchful eye was being kept on Burt's performance.

The constabulary team's accommodation was set above the car park at Godalming police station, where Geoff Todd was the chief inspector of communications with the Surrey constabulary. He told me:

They needed a secure and neutral base to operate from. Security of their new base was imperative and alarms were installed with a direct link to the Force HQ at Mount Browne, just a few miles away to the north of Godalming. I have only a vague memory, but alarms (Home Office ones, certainly) were fitted because of earlier problems.

*

Before we go any further, let me interject an allegorical story. Let's suppose that you, the reader, wanted to purchase a house, and an estate agent found one for you where a great deal of renovation was needed. On the plus side, the foundations were fine – good and solid. However, there was little else that was right. The roof leaked like a sieve, the floorboards were rotten, the plaster was coming off the walls, the plumbing and electrics were tragic and in between the bricks which hadn't actually blown, re-pointing was an abso-lute necessity.

Nevertheless, you still want the house, so what do you do? If you're a builder, you'd probably rub your hands with glee, hacking off the rotten plaster; and before you started inspecting the roof tiles, you'd check to ensure the rafters and battens were sound.

If, on the other hand, you were like me, fearful of getting an electric shock just from changing a torch battery, you would appoint a surveyor to determine exactly what had to be done and then hire competent plumbers, electricians, carpenters, roofers, brickies et al. – and tell them to get on with it. Bearing in mind that for the purposes of this story, money would be no object, I would do that because they, presumably, would know what they were doing, whilst I would not.

What I would *not* do is to stand in that ruin of a house and dreamily envisage what sort of wallpaper I should rush out to buy to immediately paste over those crumbling walls. But – metaphorically speaking – that's just what Burt and the Dorset officers did.

CHAPTER 7

Right, back to the reality of Godalming. So now we have the enquiry team safely ensconced in offices above a car park, albeit 48 miles from the City of London. That was a start. What was in their armoury? First, the evidence of John Simmonds' tape, which was backed up by independent evidence, and that was brilliant. This is what I figuratively referred to in the previous chapter as the sound foundations.

Next, the computer, which was certainly an innovative addition to a major enquiry at a time when few police forces possessed such a commodity. HOLMES (the Home Office Large Major Enquiry System) would not be launched until 1986, but in practice this was still light years away. Computers are all very well at accepting and storing information, but extracting same, especially in those early days, was a very different matter. Dorset's computer had been installed the previous year, but due to the unexpected complexities of the software programme it was unable to provide the reliability which was essential for full operational sustainability. Burt may have been happy with his 'man in the red hat' analogy, but in truth Dorset's computer had no systemized method of pulling out all of the statements relating to a particular allegation. It meant that the officers had to wade through masses of irrelevant data in order to locate what was pertinent.

But what else? Their evidence from supergrasses, much of which was second-hand and most of the remainder of which – if it was true – the offenders had declined to commit to paper. Next – surveillance? Not a chance; few, if any, of their officers were surveillance trained. Of course, they could have requested the services of C11's surveillance team, brilliant operatives trained to the highest standards who could move unobtrusively as well as seamlessly interchange with mobile surveillance – nondescript vans, cars, taxis and motorcycles – could follow on foot and into buildings and even meld into the countryside, using their covert radios; faceless men and women who could do their job and then fade away into the shadows whence they'd come.

Unfortunately not. They were 'Mets', weren't they? Tainted. Beyond the pale.

Ah – but what about electronic surveillance, then? 'Creeping' buildings and cars, in order to plant listening devices, using tall buildings, telegraph poles and lampposts to attach long-range microphones and cameras, the use of briefcase and handbag cameras? Well – afraid not. Dorset didn't have any of that equipment. But – hang on a minute – C11(2) Department at the Yard did, together with the personnel to install, activate and use it. It required a written order from a high ranking officer to use that equipment – and with his ACC's rank, that could have been Burt – but once again, it was 'The Mets' who'd be supplying the merchandise, and who could trust them? Not Dorset, that's for sure.

Wait a minute – here was a breakthrough. What about telephone intercepts? That way the enquiry team would know exactly what was going on. Intercepts were not, of course permissible in court, but nonetheless, the Dorset officers would see this as irrefutable evidence.

So let's take a closer look at telephone interception, which had been in use by the Metropolitan Police's Special Branch since before the First World War. Please put out of your mind the picture of rather seedy looking coves in cellars attaching jubilee clips to telephone wires; it looks exciting and plausible in detective films, particularly of the American variety, but the truth of the matter, in dear old Blighty, is rather different.

For a police officer to obtain a warrant to intercept someone's telephone calls is incredibly difficult. There are two reasons: it has to be proved that it has been unsuccessfully attempted to obtain evidence from all other conventional sources, and then the matter must be serious enough (and in the public interest) to necessitate the Home Secretary personally – or if he or she is out of the country or in any other way inaccessible, for their deputy – to sign the warrant. So would a case such as this – where massive bribes had allegedly been paid to senior police officers – have been suitable for telephone calls to be intercepted? Certainly. It was the Home Secretary (the estate agent previously, symbolically, referred to) who had personally authorized the enquiry in the first place; it was in the public interest to get to the bottom of it.

However, the second of the two reasons is that at that time there was an absolute maximum of twenty 'crime' lines – or intercepts – for the Met (Special Branch and Customs & Excise had their own arrangements) at any one time. There were ten more, for the whole of England and Wales. All of them were strictly and regularly reviewed by a senior civil servant and also a high ranking Yard official. Any intercept which was not revealing pertinent and valid information within an inflexible time limit was taken off. It was stringently enforced; appeals – 'Just another week, Guv!'– were generally useless.

Dorset could have applied for such a warrant – and, as I say, would almost certainly have been granted one – but all of the produce arising from the intercept would have been channelled through C11's 'Confi' Section, as were all the Met and constabulary intercepts; those were the regulations. As far as Dorset was concerned, it was a 'Catch 22' situation.

There was one other way: to apply for a 'rocker', which did not require anything like the high standards required for an intercept. A successful application would mean that a record was kept of every number calling or called by a target's telephone, plus how long the call lasted. The name and address of the subscriber making or receiving the call was also supplied – unless, as so often was the case, a telephone box was used. It was a useful intelligence-gathering exercise to see who was speaking to whom; and as far as Dorset was concerned (had they been aware of, and enquired after this facility) it would have been excellent news, because it was not monitored by C11.

However, on the downside, of course nobody would have had a clue as to what the parties were talking about. On the other hand, it was possible to deduce, from the time and the frequency of the calls, that one party was going to meet another, and therefore surveillance teams could be put in place to monitor the movements of the sender or receiver of the telephone calls, or both. So Dorset could have utilized that option – if they'd had a surveillance team, of course.

But let's take this as a possible scenario. Let's say that Dorset had put an intercept on, and let's go further and suggest that they had obtained C11's services – a top-notch surveillance team and all the technical support they required. One more thing remained – how to 'read the line'.

It's a sad fact of life that people on intercept do not generally use the received pronunciation based on the educated speech of southern England which is widely accepted as standard. Sometimes they don't use English at all. I once wanted to have an intercept put on the telephone of a Triad gangster, and although most of the conversations were carried out in Mandarin or Cantonese, that was not particularly a problem. The difficulty arose because much of his conversation was peppered with slang derived from Taiwanese Hokkien, and we didn't have an interpreter with a high enough security clearance to read the line.

So the line reader must be savvy enough to interpret what's been said. One caller said, 'I've got a load of kettles wot are kosher – see yer tomorrow.'

The superintendent who picked up the message had spent much of his career in the West End. 'Right, get on to Property

Index', he told me. 'See if a lorry-load of electric kettles belonging to a Jewish wholesaler have been stolen.'

The person on the line was an East Ender like myself, so I was able to say, 'Guv'nor, what he's saying is that he's got a load of watches which are worth having.'

The following day, the target turned up at the meeting place, where he handed over a briefcase containing a large number of stolen gold watches. If the superintendent had had his way, the briefcase would have been ignored, with the surveillance team waiting for a pantechnicon (or a van, at least) to turn up.

So reading a line could sometimes be difficult, and without wishing to unnecessarily denigrate the rural officers, given the jargon that many Met and City police officers use it might well have been impossible for them to comprehend what on earth was going on.

'Did they have a line on?' I asked John Simmonds.

'I don't know', he replied. 'I would have done.'

But, of course, he wasn't a Dorset officer.

It rather left them in that house with solid foundations but needing a great deal of TLC and in which, despite an abundance of expenditure – in the end the cost to the taxpayer amounted to £4 million – they were unwilling or unable to invest. Instead, they chose the emblematic wallpaper by chasing shadows created for them by their 'informants' and concentrated on disciplinary offences, when by hiring the proper workmen they could have brought the whole rotten pack of cards tumbling down.

The most ridiculous aspects of the Dorset officers' distrust of the Met was that the head of C11 Department was Commander Ron Harvey, who was as straight as a die and who had been responsible for bringing the allegations of corruption to the attention of the Home Secretary and HM Inspector of Constabulary in the first place. It had been the head of the Flying Squad, Commander Don Neesham, in the second place who had similarly forwarded the same allegations, in respect of his own men, to the same officials.

Perhaps Dorset should have had rather more faith in the Met. Distrust was one thing; but they progressed to being rather like small, round-eyed children, frightened out of their wits by an alarming fairy story, and – look behind you! – paranoia was just around the corner.

*

The move to Surrey was seen as an incredible waste of time; John Newman, a Police Federation representative, told me that he had later defended one of the rural team on a disciplinary matter who was scathing about how the enquiry was run: 'He commented that practically all day, each Monday, was utilized filling out the group's football pools and collecting the money, and no work was done on Friday afternoons as everyone was heading back to their homes.'

From outlying Surrey the team had to travel into the capital (and elsewhere) to conduct their enquiries. To start with, there was a mood of optimism – in fact a couple of the officers that Bryan Martin met were euphoric.

He told me, 'They said that after they'd been on the enquiry for six to nine months they'd been promised a new car and promotion.'

It sounded rather reminiscent of the freshly liberated black slaves who, following the end of the American Civil War, were assured that (depending on which political party they voted for) each of them would receive 'an acre of land and a mule'. But then, paranoia crept in. The personnel were told never to park their cars close to the police stations they visited. Drinks, even coffee, had to be paid for, as did telephone calls. Mistrust spilt over into hysteria when the officers were told not to visit supermarkets, since the security staff were all ex-police 'and they could fit you up with shoplifting'.

In order to provide themselves with an identity, they informed the popular press that they were to be known as 'Operation Countryman'. Why they should have done so is debatable; internal investigations had never been given a code name before. But this was not adopted by the Met; previously, some of the officers in outlying constabularies had been mockingly referred to as 'Carrots', 'Turnips' or 'Swedes'.

However, taking into account Countryman's apparent lack of awareness in dealing with criminals, and their susceptibility to big city life, the Met decided upon a more crushing nickname for them. As a counterpart to the Flying Squad – 'The Sweeney' – they decided to dub the Countryman officers 'The Swedey', as a tribute to their parochial origins.

And if this was considered to be nothing more than good humoured banter (which it quite conspicuously was not), matters came to a head when T-shirts were printed showing the logo 'Mets are Magic – Countryman are Tragic' and were distributed at a Police Federation conference at Scarborough. In the same way that early members of the wartime Special Air Service donned white berets which led to fights in the Cairo bars, this too was considered to be slightly provocative. One of the London representatives was tackled by a provincial officer in a public lavatory and feared that a confrontation was looming. Not a bit of it; the provincial chap thought the emblem on the T-shirt didn't go far enough; he told the London officer that he knew the operational head of the enquiry and that the logo should have read 'I know the cunt in Countryman'.

That was bad enough; and as tales of the Countryman officers' ineptitude and gullibility spread, the Home Office put rather more thought into a suitable epithet for them. From behind closed doors in Whitehall, away from the ears of the tabloid press, they referred to Countryman as 'Malice in Blunderland'.

PART III

Searching

I will do such things –
What they are yet I know not; but they shall be
The terror of the earth.

Shakespeare, *King Lear*

CHAPTER 8

Now that Countryman had begun their investigations in the City, more oddities were being uncovered. The former City of London cop who writes under the pen name of 'Harvey Yates' told me that on the morning of the *Daily Mirror* robbery he was on patrol in an armed response van. The crew had been told that 'A job was going to go down in the City'; for a week or so they had been brought on three hours early to provide cover and whilst they were on that particular detail the unit was permanently armed.

But on this particular morning they were told to report to Wood Street police station; the sergeant in charge of the van demurred, saying they were on a job on the orders of their superintendent. However, control stated that the orders superseded those of a mere superintendent – they came from the Commander, Hugh Moore.

And curiously, it was not only the crew of the armed van who attended Wood Street – all the other City vehicles did, as well as all of the CID. The reason given was a lecture on the preservation of items at the scene of a crime. But nobody was paying attention.

As Yates told me, 'There was the air of a party, some officers laughing. The impression I got, even before I knew about the murder/robbery, was that something corrupt was going on. All the good guys were sulking. All the bent ones were enjoying themselves.'

After half an hour an officer walked into the hall and handed Moore a slip of paper. He told the room, 'It seems there's been an armed robbery at the *Daily Mirror*.' Then he smiled.

One of the getaway cars, a Mercedes, had been found abandoned, but when Yates discovered that the four occupants had run off into the nearby Bourne Estate – which was odd because it would have meant they would be on foot for some time, thereby leaving themselves unnecessarily vulnerable – he looked around for another change-over vehicle. He discovered it: a red Volvo V6 estate. For one thing, the Volvo's plates did not correspond with the car tax; for another, the 'S' suffix plates had new screws, but the bumpers on the car were of the type which had only been used, at the latest, on cars with 'R' registrations. A market worker told him that the Volvo had been there since 6.00 that morning, but because it was blocking the access of some of the larger vans in the market, he and his fellow workers had decided to move it out of the way; this they had done with ease, since it was unlocked. When the Mercedes arrived, following the robbery, the Volvo was boxed in by another van waiting to unload; hence the gang's enforced dispersal through the Bourne estate.

Yates now takes up the tale:

> Two senior detectives came into the square from the direction of Leather Lane – one at least a Lodge member, so viewed as dangerous.
> 'Go back to the Mercedes', one of them said. 'That car's been checked.'
> 'I don't think it has, Sir. I've been here all the time and I'm the first person to come over to it', I replied.
> 'Don't argue. Just fuck off.'

Yates then said to me, 'One question that went through my mind at the time was, what was such a senior officer doing wandering around the backstreets? He didn't approach the getaway car – the Mercedes – just the Volvo. Shouldn't he have been at the scene?'

Yates also mentioned the arrival of a SOCO (Scenes of Crime Officer), who upon hearing of the strictures of the two senior officers refused to go near the car, advising Yates, 'And I suggest you don't, either.'

Just to reinforce matters, one of the senior officers suddenly reappeared, telling Yates, 'If I see you near this car again, you're in the shit. Do you understand?'

But this prescient advice was ignored. Summoning a senior, uniform officer, Yates explained his misgivings. When the boot was opened there was a flap, which when raised revealed extra floor space. It also revealed a Metropolitan Police sergeant's uniform.

As the SOCO commented in shocked tones, 'Now look what you've done!'

A Major Incident Room was set up and, as Yates explains:

> Money was seemingly no object and fortunes were made from the overtime and other means of supplementing income. It was the sort of police work that most recruits consider a target when they join, although the joy of such a unit had worn off on me, especially as one of the senior detectives on the team was the one who warned me off checking on the Volvo. One of the lads off my unit did volunteer to go on it despite my advice, left one day and, oddly enough, returned the next. He said he found a sealed brown envelope in the drawer of his desk and had

given it to the detective in charge of the room. After a discussion as to whether the envelope should be opened and the contents examined, our lad returned to his desk and the following day was returned to our unit.

There were rumours that such envelopes contained £35, the weekly backhander for those of constable rank, but the thing with rumours is that you can never source them. The only thing that was certain was that the PC volunteered because of keenness, yet came back a day later, depressed. A little later, he transferred to the Metropolitan Police, taking our sergeant with him.

Two prisoners had been arrested and charged with the murder and robbery at the *Daily Mirror* building. Yates accompanied one of the accused in a high security van from Brixton to the Mansion House Justice Rooms, and on one occasion only, en route, the prisoner had the first of two very short conversations with Yates.

He told him, 'Don't worry lad. You can have an early day today, 'cause I won't be coming back', adding, 'My brief's got it all arranged – I'm getting bail.'

This, thought Yates, was highly improbable, if not impossible; nobody got bail on charges such as these. And yet, when a senior CID officer got into the witness box he didn't even try to post objections; it threw the magistrates and the clerk of the court into some confusion, but eventually they remanded the prisoner in custody again. On the return journey the second of the two exchanges between prisoner and escort occurred.

'I thought you were going on a holiday', said Yates.

The prisoner seemed unfazed by his predicament. 'Don't you worry, I'll be out next week' was his reply – and what was more, he was.

By now Yates was getting extremely concerned for his wellbeing. He had been sent with a colleague on a house-to-house enquiry in a housing estate in connection with the *Daily Mirror* robbery; within a very short space of time, a Mercedes containing three heavies was patrolling the estate and, as he discovered later, had been looking for them. Had they been set up? It seemed more than a possibility.

Now Countryman had descended on the City; everybody, it seemed was being interviewed. Two days before Yates' interview he was approached by a certain detective, known for his Masonic connections, who told him he should be careful about what he said to Countryman, adding that someone with a family had a lot to lose. But despite that, Yates resolved that he would answer truthfully any questions he was asked.

When the detective superintendent from Countryman and his chief inspector started their interview, Yates fully expected to be asked about the finding of the Volvo, particularly so because, whilst he had been waiting, he had shared the waiting room with the Met sergeant whose Volvo had been stolen. When the sergeant was told by Yates that it was he who had found the stolen car, he became extremely excitable and started looking under tables and in light sockets.

'This place has got to be wired,' he exclaimed. 'That's why they've put us together!'

But it wasn't. Yates was questioned about an arrest carried out by another officer where the prisoner had been taken in the van to the police station. The vehicle log showed that Yates was on the van all day. In fact he hadn't been; he'd been on foot carrying out PNC (Police National Computer) checks, and he explained that the log hadn't been filled in properly. He was bemused – as he said, 'The interview seemed very weird to me.' These officers were investigating the biggest ever corruption probe in the police – certainly in the City Police – and yet here they were talking about a prisoner being transported to the police station.

Shortly afterwards he received a note through the internal dispatch congratulating him on his good sense in keeping his mouth shut – but shut about what? His family had been threatened, but to whom could he complain? He approached a specific senior officer, one he felt he could trust completely – he described him as being 'straighter than a plumb line' – who engineered a two-year posting to a District Police Training Centre. At the end of that period, Yates put in a request to transfer to a county force. As he stated in his memoirs:

> I resented the fact that so many of the obviously corrupt officers were not prosecuted and were, instead, allowed to retire and accept other jobs, but I could see the reasoning. The legal system was just as corrupt as the service, all the work the decent lawyers put in being negated by the greedy, unprincipled and dishonest ones. There was no way those high up in the Firm with their connections and influence would have been convicted. The policy of enforced retirements resulted in a much more trustworthy police service, but the real bastards got away with it.
>
> All the fun had gone out of the City. It was a good time to be leaving. As far as I was concerned, the corrupt side of the Force had beaten me.

★

Rumours and speculation were by now flashing around the City; and how much of it reached the ears of the Countryman personnel was debatable.

There was, for instance, the theft of a large amount of cash over a Bank Holiday period during the early 1970s from the branch of Lloyd's Bank at St Andrew's Hill, Holborn Circus. After the branch had closed on the Thursday afternoon, none of the staff re-entered the bank until the Tuesday morning, and that included Lloyd's own security; but quite obviously, somebody had. Registered keys for the bank had been kept at the local police station, Snow Hill, and should they have been needed to enter the bank, a 'premises report' would have been completed. But in the investigation which followed, no such report had been submitted; what was more, there was no sign of the keys, nor of the handsome wooden box in which they had once reposed. There was a cartoon by JAK (Raymond Jackson) – who contributed to the *Evening Standard* and *Mail on Sunday* as well as the *Daily* and *Sunday Express* – who was unable to resist adding the title to his latest work: 'There's only one police force that could have done it!'

JAK, I know, was terribly pro-police, but it could be he had a point.

There was also the matter of the Williams & Glyn's robbery where not all the money in the security van had been stolen. It was taken from the van by uniformed officers to be transported to Bishopsgate police station for safe keeping until a senior CID officer had it transferred to his car for even safer keeping. It was never seen again – by honest eyes, that is. The CID officer in question (John Simmonds told me, 'His reputation stank') denied the incident had ever happened.

One story that grew in popularity concerned the previous City Commissioner, Colonel Sir Arthur Edwin Young KBE, CVO, CMG, OStJ, KPM. Seconded to Northern Ireland in 1969 to become the province's last Inspector-General and the Royal Ulster Constabulary's first Chief Constable, he took with him a sidearm drawn from the armoury at Bishopsgate police station. When Sir Arthur returned to the City in 1971, because the armoury was closed, the weapon was handed in at the station's front counter but had never been booked in. There was no trace of it until the robbery at the *Daily Mirror*, when it was said that a pistol found at the scene had been the one issued to the former Commissioner. True or false? Sir Arthur died on 20 January 1979, several months after the Countryman enquiry had commenced. Did Countryman hear of this rumour? Did they mercilessly interrogate the guiltless seventy-one-year-old veteran? Was it a classic piece of disinformation? Who can say?

On 18 October – the day after he had finished transcribing the covert tape recording – Simmonds was present at the City Headquarters when Countryman officers Detective Superintendent Tony Conway and Detective Sergeant John Crow requested that he set up a meeting between them and two City detective constables – Raymond Symmons and Tony Wallis.

When he asked the nature of the interview, it was implied to Simmonds that Countryman had evidence that the officers had interfered with exhibits in a particular case, and that if they denied doing so they would be liable to prosecution.

What was alleged was this: following the murder/robbery at the *Daily Mirror* building on 31 May 1978, the gang had escaped in a fawn Mercedes and – being thwarted in their make of change-over vehicle, because the stolen Volvo had been boxed in – had transferred to a white Rover, which had been found abandoned in South London. Billy Tobin had been arrested and three keys were found in his possession. These opened lock-up garages, and in one of them was found a stolen Daimler, with five sawn-off shotguns, two loaded revolvers and a mask in the boot. In a nearby garage an incriminating rent book and other items were found. It was said that Detective Inspector James Jolly of the City Police had suggested that the two officers should state that the rent book and other items had been found in the Rover, thereby establishing a link between Tobin and the crime. This the officers refused to do, and they made no report of it at the time; except, perhaps, that one of them did so in an oblique way.

'I recalled DC Symmons expressing concern to me, within days of my arrival in this Force, when he took my photograph, that he hoped now I had arrived there would be a more professional approach to the job', said Simmonds, 'and although I pressed him at the time to expand upon this, he declined to do so. It was nevertheless apparent to me that he was expressing concern over aspects of his job in Scenes of Crime.'

Simmonds voiced the opinion to the Countryman officers that it was highly probable that initially both officers would deny the allegation, and so it might be better if he were to interview the officers first. He was given authority to tell the officers that if they were truthful they would be granted immunity from any criminal or disciplinary proceedings. Both officers stated that Jolly had asked them to change the location where the items had been found; both said they thought Jolly's request had been real and not a joke; and the two officers were provided with written proof of their indemnities.

Having ascertained the facts, Simmonds handed the officers over to the Countryman personnel to obtain their written statements. But then Superintendent Conway saw Simmonds and showed him the statement of Wallis, who had gone back on what he had told Simmonds. He spoke to Wallis once more, telling him that nobody wanted him to tell anything but the truth and pointing out that earlier he had provided a version of events which was quite different to that contained in his statement. Simmonds told Wallis to consider his position and to make up his mind as to what actually happened. Wallis obviously did so, and returned with Conway to rewrite part of his statement.

So that was Countryman's first City scalp. What happened next?

This allegation was strenuously denied by DI Jolly, and he repeated his denial when he appeared at the Old Bailey two and a half years later on 22 April 1981, charged with attempting to pervert the course of justice. The jury obviously did not accept the word of the two young detectives; it is possible that the rewritten statement may have played a significant part in their decision. They did, however, accept Jolly's word when he told them, 'I would not do that. I would not ever make any suggestion that evidence should be planted', and he was acquitted.

Nor was he the only one to be freed; strenuous efforts had been made to release Billy Tobin following his arrest for the *Daily Mirror* robbery, with Cuthbert handing his solicitor a helpful 'question and answer' brief during an unsuccessful bail application; but one month after making their statements, both Symmons and Wallis were called to give evidence at the Old Bailey in Tobin's defence. He, too, was acquitted. Having made a down payment for bail in the sum of £3,000, Tobin angrily demanded it back; he got it. He then went on to commit further robberies.

By 7 November 1978, Cuthbert – variously described by his colleagues as everything from 'slightly flashy' to 'a lovely bloke' – had been suspended from duty. Simmonds voiced his opinion to Countryman then – and he still adheres to this view – that had Moore (and others) also been suspended there and then, Cuthbert would have given Queen's Evidence and the whole rotten house of cards would have come tumbling down. But Moore – though questioned – never was suspended from duty.

As Simmonds told me, 'Countryman wanted to get the facts before they "attacked". Hugh Moore was, in my opinion, the lynch pin, and as long as he stayed in office, the bent ones gained strength from this. Through naïvety they [the Countryman officers] thought they would steam into the City and the CID lads who had been on the take would roll over and cough up. History shows this was not the case.'

This was backed up when on 22 November Simmonds saw a detective constable who had been an exhibits officer on one of the robbery enquiries. Simmonds told him that he had been given an assurance from Countryman that if an officer right on the edge of the enquiry had been given small sums of money by venal officers, then that officer would be granted immunity from prosecution provided that he was absolutely honest about it. Simmonds told him that if he had received any payments at all, he would have expected it to be in the region of £50. Bearing in mind that it was being said that payments of between £60,000 and £90,000 were being talked about, was it right for him to protect those officers, all for the sake of £50?

After some heart searching, the officer admitted taking £50.

'One payment?' asked Simmonds.

'No, three lots', was the reply.

'Who from?'

'Mr Cuthbert.'

This dovetailed exactly with what Phil Cuthbert had told Simmonds about handing out 'silly fifties'. By drawing junior officers into his web, by paying them what, to him, was a pittance, he was ensuring their silence, working on the assumption that in committing a criminal act themselves they could never implicate anybody else. Well, Cuthbert was wrong.

And so, in their way, were Countryman. Simmonds now wanted to interview other detectives who, he believed, had been ensnared by Cuthbert, but Countryman, seeing Simmonds' success, obviously thought this was going to be easy. However, as Simmonds said:

> I had been a CID officer for over eighteen years and had the unfortunate experience of investigating many police officers. I learnt that a bent cop knows all the rules and if you are going to catch one, you have to be subtle about it. Bent coppers are not frightened of an inexperienced police officer, no matter what his rank is. Very few of them were career detectives and even fewer, if any at all of them, had the experience I had in dealing with corrupt police officers. It's alleged that they then went crashing into young detectives, asking them to hand over their warrant cards, saying that was how easy it was to suspend them. They then were told to admit that they had received money from Cuthbert and his cohorts. The tactics were a complete failure, and no other officer came forward.

The young officer who had confessed to Simmonds suffered badly at the hands of his contemporaries. He was ostracised, abuse was hurled at him, and the sad, even illogical aspect of it was that many of the officers involved in this vilification were basically honest men, of junior and senior rank, who had not in any way been implicated in the corruption enquiry; yet they obviously felt it their duty to malign him. However, he survived it and went on to have a productive career elsewhere in the police.

Simmonds was in much the same position now it was known that he was responsible for Cuthbert's suspension, although his senior rank protected him from much of the abuse. As Simmonds told me:

> My Admin Sergeant, Ron Enston, was a very loyal and honest officer who gave me incredible support when things were at their worst. He was, like many others, very honest and was appalled at the way a minor group had taken over what was once a very proud and efficient CID unit. My CID was split down the middle, those who recognized that it was about time that something was done and those who were either part of the villainy or for misplaced loyalty, despite being potentially honest themselves, did not like police reporting police.

Hugh Moore was in a different position. He hated Simmonds and did everything he could to undermine him; this extended to hounding those who supported Simmonds as well. What was more, he still had a few tricks up his sleeve. But before we deal with those matters, we must travel a few miles to the west, to New Scotland Yard, where any possible cooperation between the Met and Countryman was disappearing, faster than a politician's promise.

CHAPTER 9

Now that Countryman were ensconced in their new headquarters at Godalming and had demanded a computer – albeit one which was not the be-all and end-all of information retrieval – they also requested a staff increase to bring their strength up to thirty-five, and they got that, too.

Uniform officers Sergeant Kevin Pengelly and Inspector John Cobbett were two of the four Surrey officers who were seconded to the enquiry. They were given detective status and stayed for under a year before their Chief Constable pulled them back.

'Peter Matthews was old school; a good man but old-fashioned', Kevin Pengelly told me. 'He said Countryman were not operating as per their remit and he was right. In fact, Dorset were not only investigating complaints reported to them, they were investigating crimes as well.'

Pengelly went on to say:

> The ordinary Dorset cops were OK but they really didn't trust us – some of us (including John Cobbett) had done jobs with the Met in the past. We did nine to fives, no nights, no weekends.
>
> Burt didn't know his arse from his elbow. He brought with him a load of officers who'd never been in CID; they were mainly traffic. The officer in charge of our mini-squad was a superintendent who'd come from traffic – no CID experience at all. He didn't have a clue. When he wanted to interview somebody, I'd say, 'Let's do some homework first – let's do some background', but he'd say, 'No, we're going to talk to them.' Well, you can't argue with a superintendent.
>
> I went into the City with John Cobbett; we wanted the diaries of the officers who were on some sort of mini-squad. We were told they didn't know where those diaries were. We got great assistance from DCS John Simmonds. He came into the room and told them, 'Get that locker open!' They said they didn't know where the key was – Simmonds went and got a screwdriver and forced it open, and there were the diaries. We discovered the officers had

been falsifying expenses, overtime and mileage claims; they were claiming for hundreds of miles in the City, which is only one mile square! I did do some work on Cuthbert and Golbourn; I didn't know they got convicted.

The Met were a cagy lot; I interviewed a commander there. He said, 'Aren't you going to caution me?'

I replied, 'No, Sir. All I want is a witness statement. If you were going to be cautioned, I'd have to be of assistant chief constable rank.'

When I returned to Surrey, my old post had been filled; I finished up at Woking.

Pengelly told me that everything they did was recorded in statements: where they went, what they did, who they saw, where they had their refreshments. 'There must have been thousands', he told me.

When I told him that when Peter Matthews took over the enquiry in March 1980, 2,000 statements were handed over, his response was, 'I'm not surprised.'

*

Burt had been appointed under the provisions of Section 49, Police Act 1964, and his terms of reference, agreed by both the City of London Commissioner and the Met's Deputy Commissioner, were to investigate certain allegations of criminal malpractice in both Forces. But Countryman received many complaints from criminals about police officers which were nothing to do with the incidents under investigation; consequently, these matters should have been referred to the named officers' respective Forces for investigation.

However, Burt kept these allegations 'in house', and since Kavanagh was mindful of the furore which had followed Williamson's ill-fated investigation into the *Times* enquiry eight years earlier because of the Met's interference, he decided to let matters slide. It was a mistake. 'Appeasement', growled Churchill, almost 40 years previously, 'never works' – and he was right.

The Commander of the Flying Squad, Don Neesham, was furious. Six weeks previously, he had initialled a complaint about Countryman's dealings with one of the Squad's supergrasses, Keith Warne, who was having soft options dangled in front of him when about to become an important witness in a major robbery trial. And that wasn't all. It appeared that the Countryman team were willing to attend court to 'put a good word in' for criminals who had provided information, even on the flimsiest of evidence – or upon matters which, with even with a modicum of investigation, would prove to have no basis in fact at all. Mick Dunn, who was a South London detective sergeant for 23 years, was still furious when he spoke to me of his involvement with Countryman, even almost 40 years after the event:

> I'd arrested a well-known South London villain for a series of major burglaries and the case went to the Bailey. He didn't give evidence, but his brief stood up and told the judge that his client was giving evidence for Countryman. The judge demanded that the Countryman officers should attend court, and a DCI and a DI turned up and produced a 992 [a voluntary statement under caution] consisting of one and a half pages, in which the prisoner admitted a number of burglaries and robberies. Not one offence was identified, nor when they were committed – this was the only statement. He got eighteen months, suspended.

No wonder Dunn was annoyed. The prisoner had told Countryman that he had details of twenty-two Met officers with whom money had changed hands. He was quite correct; it had. However, these turned out to be authorized payments from the Yard's Informants' Fund. Very few police forces apart from the Met had a similar fund; even fewer had any idea that such a fund existed at the Yard. What initially was thought to be a thrilling breakthrough concerning money illicitly changing hands between 'tec and crim was nothing of the kind – and the prisoner declined to take his allegations any further.

So that was one example of being too eager to accept that a properly legal transaction was a corrupt one; another was when the criminals told their unworldly interrogators that detectives had handed them statements in respect of offences they had committed. That had been sufficient to send them into transports of delight – first-hand evidence of police corruption! Except, of course, that it wasn't.

What the officers had handed to the criminals were what was known as 'Section One' statements, which they were perfectly – and legally – entitled to do. These statements were provided prior to their appearance at the Magistrates' Court in order to commit them to the Crown Court for trial – and without service of those papers there could be no committal. It was a chore carried out on a weekly, sometimes a daily basis by the Met officers who had copied and prepared the statement bundles. This was something not done by constabulary officers, who had their own solicitors to do it for them.

It was as simple as that; and since Burt was playing his cards so close to his chest, and because Kavanagh was being denied details of the allegations against his officers, and since very few reports were being submitted by Countryman to the DPP, it was hardly surprising that Countryman were gleefully expounding about the number of officers being accused of corruption when they were accepting that utter tosh, such as this, was 22 carat evidence of wrongdoing. One such enquiry went on for eighteen months, until it was passed on to Met officers, who promptly wet themselves laughing. Mick Carter, a much commended East End detective sergeant, had put a pair of villains – well known for making reckless allegations against police since the 1960s – away for twelve and eight years respectively for conspiracy to commit burglary.

Following their release, Carter met up with one of them and later told me, 'He said, "Mick – we had a visit from Countryman while we was doing our bird, asking about the investigation and wanting to know if we wanted to complain that we'd been stitched up – we told them to bugger off!"'

And to reinforce this absence of malice, one of the villains survived to take a convivial glass or two with Carter at a detective's funeral in 2016.

Not all crims were as forthcoming as Carter's prisoners, as will be seen when we examine the case where Countryman claimed their first Met scalp.

CHAPTER 10

Having joined the Metropolitan Police in 1963 at the age of nineteen, it appeared that John O'Connor's success was assured. He was well educated, he was quickly appointed to the CID and in 1968 he passed the examination for sergeant and was transferred to the Flying Squad – but not for long. He was informed that he had been selected for the twelve-month residential Special Course at Bramshill, the National Police College, and that if he passed the examinations at the end of the course – and he did – he could confidently expect in the fullness of time to be promoted up to and possibly beyond the rank of deputy assistant commissioner.

There was one substantial difference between O'Connor and many of the other successful candidates: they were purely academics, while O'Connor was a hands-on cop with a number of spectacular successes to his name, achieved by intelligent policing, telephone intercepts and the use of highly placed informants. It had led to a number of commendations for smart police work and, in 1975, to appointment as a detective chief inspector on the Flying Squad, where success followed success.

As we already know, on 27 September 1977 the robbery occurred at William & Glyn's Bank, Birchin Lane, where a guard was shot in the leg and £255,000 was stolen. Since this was being dealt with by the City of London police, it was not a matter which concerned the Met, until an 'All Ports' warning was issued in *Police Gazette*. This confidential police publication was distributed nationwide, circulating details of persons wanted for various offences. In this instance the publication gave details of two of the men suspected of involvement, namely Anthony White and Henry 'Harry the Rat' Wright, and one of O'Connor's informants provided information which led to an address at Angmering-on-Sea, Sussex. There was a joint operation between the Flying Squad, Robbery Squad and the Brighton Regional Crime Squad, and as a matter of courtesy, since he had provided the information, O'Connor was included in the raid. On 16 November 1977, White, Wright and some other people at the house, including two women, were arrested – but not before the whole scenario had developed into broad farce. During the dawn raid a Flying Squad driver accidentally tripped the two-tone sirens on a Squad car; in the ensuing rush the wrong house was searched – it belonged to a magistrate – and when the right address was entered, a locked interior door was kicked in, resulting in a slight impact to the head of one of the lady occupants. Asked by a concerned custody sergeant how she had come by this injury, she replied, 'I was 'aving a shit and the door fell in on me.' No other questions were put, nor answers demanded, of the prisoners, who were handed over to the City of London Police.

In July 1978 O'Connor was asked to set up, then run the No. 1 Area Robbery Squad, which was comprised of two Flying Squad teams. He was asked by the late Detective Superintendent (later Commander) Phil Corbett QPM to go to Whetstone police station, where three supergrasses, Ray Fowles, Peter Rose and Norman Jones, had collectively named 198 criminals involved in 640 offences. Amongst those identified were Charles Canavan, Joe Beveridge and David Henry Shaw, alleged to have committed armed robberies. On 6 September, Canavan and Beveridge were arrested by O'Connor's officers, and Shaw's address was searched, but he was not there; his brother Peter was, and he was arrested.

Through an intermediary, O'Connor received a telephone call from David Shaw, whom he had never met – and in fact, never would meet. O'Connor tried to lure him into surrendering, promising him fair treatment, but when Shaw asked him about bail, O'Connor replied that whilst he could not make any promises, since he was not the officer in the case, Shaw would certainly stand a better chance of bail if he voluntarily surrendered at Chiswick police station. This conversation was reported to Superintendent Corbett.

Several weeks went by without hearing anything further, and by now, on 13 October 1978, O'Connor had his hands full dealing with the murder of John Potter, a security guard shot during a £5,685 armed robbery at Northfields Underground Station.

But when a meet was arranged to arrest Shaw when he arrived at the Hilton Hotel, Park Lane at 6.00pm on 26 October 1978, O'Connor took the precaution of having a surveillance vehicle nearby to photograph Shaw, as well as his own Flying Squad driver waiting to convey him and Shaw to the nearest police station. He had received permission to keep the meet from the operational head of the Squad, DCS Sewell, and had informed Superintendent Corbett and Detective Inspector Derek Ramsay from Whetstone police station. In addition, details of this venture were entered in the Squad's occurrence book; everything that should have been done had been done.

But by 6.30 Shaw had not turned up; the surveillance operative was stood down, and O'Connor and his driver headed back to
Acton. When O'Connor then received a radio call to say that Shaw
had now arrived at the Hilton, traffic was heavy in Park Lane; he
was convinced that Shaw was 'mucking him about', and apart from
this he had other important engagements in connection with the
murder investigation, so he told his driver to continue to Acton.

In November O'Connor received another phone call from Shaw
saying he wished to meet him in order to surrender. As O'Connor
said, 'By this time, I was completely bored by the whole Shaw saga
and could not have cared less whether I arrested Shaw or not.'

Nevertheless, having informed the same officers as before and
having secured permission for the meet, on 2 November O'Connor
went with an intermediary to Fino's wine bar in Mount Street, W1.
He did not request any back-up because he did not believe that
Shaw would turn up, although if he did, he was confident of his
own ability to talk Shaw into accompanying him. There was no
sign of Shaw in the bar and after fifteen minutes the intermediary
left to make or receive a phone call; when he returned he said that
Shaw would not be keeping the meet since he had seen police officers entering the bar. The two men left and, as always, a report was
made to O'Connor's senior officers.

What O'Connor was unaware of was that Detective
Superintendent George Bosley and other officers from Countryman
were in the bar; also a man named Christopher Yarnold. It was
clear that Shaw had told the officers that the reason for his presence was a corrupt meeting with O'Connor.

A few days later, O'Connor received a telephone call from
Detective Chief Inspector (later Detective Chief Superintendent)
Bill Peters at Whetstone, who told him that he had information that
Shaw was trying to set him up. O'Connor laughed at the suggestion and disregarded it. But the same suggestion was made when
the intermediary telephoned O'Connor on 8 January 1979 to tell
him that Shaw had made allegations of corruption; as O'Connor
put it, 'Once again, I was mildly amused.' And on the following
day, O'Connor was told by the same man that Shaw had made his
allegations to the Dorset police on the promise of a reduced sentence or immunity from prosecution.

The next day, 10 January, O'Connor arrived at Sutton police
station (which was where he had recently been transferred to) and
was asked to see Chief Superintendent Trew. In Trew's office he
was confronted by Detective Superintendent Bosley of Dorset
police, together with a sergeant, a police constable and Detective
Superintendent Martin from CIB2. They went to O'Connor's

office, where his official and desk diaries were seized, as was his police pocket book, and put into bin liners; he was then asked to accompany these officers to Scotland Yard.

O'Connor told me, 'I was thinking, "this is a load of bollocks"', but in front of his staff he was unceremoniously escorted out of the police station and into a car in which, with the Countryman officers either side of him, he was conveyed to Scotland Yard. There he was taken to the office of CIB2's detective chief superintendent for an interview.

Prior to Countryman, Bosley had been the uniform superintendent in charge of Dorset's Christchurch sub-division, where 30 per cent of the town's 35,000 population were aged sixty-five and over. Now, with his transition to 'detective', Bosley and the sergeant produced a prepared questionnaire. The first question was, 'You know David Henry Shaw?'

When O'Connor replied, 'No, I don't', this, he told me, 'Completely threw them. They'd worked on the assumption that I'd say "yes" and this messed up the rest of their questionnaire. I told them, "I don't know him, I've heard of him".'

O'Connor was told that he had been accused by Shaw and his brother Peter of meeting David Shaw and obtaining £2,500 from him in respect of a statement made by the Whetstone supergrass, Peter Francis Rose, which implicated Shaw in a robbery at Redhill, Surrey on 16 July 1978, a statement which he (O'Connor) had supposedly stolen and copied. This, he was told, had happened in August 1978.

'When – early or late August?' asked O'Connor, adding that he had been on holiday for three weeks that August – but although Rose had made that statement on 22 August 1978, it appeared that Shaw or Bosley didn't know.

O'Connor then demanded to know the whereabouts of the allegedly purloined statement – only to be told that Shaw had told the Countryman officers that it was 'so incriminating' he had torn it up.

Similarly, it was said that O'Connor would be paid a further £2,500 once he had passed over further statements to Shaw. This first transaction had taken place at a West End wine bar on a date unknown. He was also accused of tipping off Shaw prior to the search of his premises on 6 September and of receiving £500 from an informant to assist his case at the Old Bailey. Regarding this last matter, O'Connor had provided evidence of the informant's sizeable input of information by means of a written letter to the trial judge, Edward Clarke QC, when the informant pleaded guilty to fraud charges. For a police officer to do this meant that

authorization had had to come from right at the top of Scotland
Yard's CID hierarchy. O'Connor had secured that – everything was
completely documented. In fact, since the offences by the informant had been committed in Surrey, Sir Peter Mathews, the county's Chief Constable, had also been informed of the intention to
submit a letter to the judge.

O'Connor could give the informant no guarantees as to his
sentence; fortunately, the judge imposed a suspended sentence,
which left the informant free to carry on providing information to
O'Connor; but to preserve his credibility to his contemporaries he
stated to them that his freedom was due to the payment of £500 'to
a bent friend in the police'. This is a cover which has been used for
years; in fact, John Gosling, one of the leading lights in the post-
war (and highly secretive) Ghost Squad, used to tell his informants
– who to the surprise of their associates had been granted bail – to
use just that story.

This was the substance of the allegations; plus, he was also (and
rather ridiculously) accused of being responsible for tripping the
Squad car's two-tone switch at the raid at Angmering-on-Sea, in
order to alert the occupants and permit them to escape.

Furthermore, an associate of Shaw's claimed that he had been
arrested and had been put under pressure to implicate Shaw in
various crimes. He told Countryman:

> The detective sergeant explained to me that it wasn't me
> that they wanted to put away, but David Shaw that they
> wanted to put away for a long time, because David Shaw
> had been getting two colleagues into trouble. He kept
> repeating himself about David Shaw and that was all he
> seemed to be interested in.
>
> Whilst I was in custody, I saw a detective chief inspec-
> tor. He asked me to make a statement admitting the
> offence and implicating Shaw. I gave him the same reply .
> . . He said, 'He's getting or trying to get police officers into
> trouble.' I told him it was no business of mine. He replied,
> 'I'm making it your business.'

O'Connor knew he was completely innocent of these charges and
that he had nothing to fear; he answered every question and signed
authorities for his bank and savings accounts to be scrutinized. At
the conclusion of the interview, which had lasted from 10.00am
until 5.00pm, he was told he could return to duty.

At 1.00am the following morning O'Connor received a telephone call from the informant from whom he had allegedly received

money, to say that he had been held all day at Redhill police station and had only just arrived home. He stated that he had been offered immunity if he would incriminate O'Connor. It was clear that Bosley was totally unaware of the relationship between O'Connor and the informant; working on the assumption that his phone calls were intercepted, O'Connor took the opportunity to fire a volley of abuse of Bosley down the phone .

Later that day, O'Connor went to work as usual. Commander Patterson of 'Z' Division had told O'Connor's senior officer that the Director of the Complaints Bureau had informed him that O'Connor was completely in the clear, and this message was passed on to him. This makes it all the more strange that at 5.30pm that day he was summoned to Commander Patterson's office; the commander apologized on behalf of the Deputy Commissioner for the behaviour of the Dorset officers regarding the manner of his arrest – and then suspended him from duty.

And now the waters become rather muddied. Detective Inspector Derek Ramsay was one of the officers with whom O'Connor had constantly liaised when he was endeavouring to get Shaw to surrender. O'Connor was not aware of the fact that at the time of his interview Ramsay had arrested an armed robber named Richard Ross Shackleton, who had become a supergrass. Shackleton said that he wanted to speak to a senior officer; this was Detective Chief Inspector Bill Peters. In December 1978 Peters obtained a statement from Shackleton; it was vague and it recounted an overheard conversation between David and Peter Shaw saying that they intended to 'set the police at one another'; the officer who was going to be fitted up was 'Connor' or 'O'Connor', but no clue was given as to how the fit-up was going to take place. At that time, nobody – outside of Countryman – had any idea that O'Connor was under suspicion. The statement had been obtained on the direct orders of Commander Neesham, but after consultation with the Yard's legal department it was decided to file it away for future reference, though not before Neesham – 'An absolutely 100 per cent honest man; as good as gold', Peters told me – had sent a copy to the Countryman offices.

However, Ramsay was decidedly unhappy; he felt that somehow this matter was connected to Operation Countryman. That evening, he telephoned their office at Godalming and asked for the only name he knew – Detective Superintendent Bosley. The call was taken by a sergeant, who stated that Bosley was unavailable, so Ramsay outlined the contents of Shackleton's statement and the sergeant agreed to check their files for a detective by the name of Connor or O'Connor. Back came the answer – that nobody by either of those names featured in Countryman's records. Since the Countryman detectives had placed O'Connor under observation six weeks earlier at Fino's wine bar, the sergeant was being, in the late Alan Clark's words, more than a little 'economical with the *actualité*'.

Ramsay was still dissatisfied; he asked the sergeant to inform Bosley of their conversation and requested that the superintendent telephone him at Whetstone as soon as possible. The following morning, Bosley did just that – this was recorded in Whetstone's telephone message book – and Ramsay formed the impression that Countryman weren't interested in the Shackleton statement so he let the matter drop. But Countryman didn't. On 10 January Ramsay was told to report to the Yard; no reason for the summons was given, but he was assured that his visit would last no longer than an hour. He arrived at 11.00am and was taken to the general office of CIB2 on the ninth floor. There he was informed by a sergeant from Countryman that Superintendent Bosley wanted to question him but that Bosley was currently interviewing somebody else. Unknown to Ramsay, the 'somebody else' was, of course, John O'Connor.

After forty-five minutes Ramsay asked what was going on. The sergeant made it plain to him that he was under arrest, together with three other Metropolitan Police officers, on suspicion of corruption. Ramsay was furious, and when he stated he wanted to lunch in the canteen, this was refused. It was not until 6.00pm – seven hours after his arrival at the Yard – that Ramsay was seen by Bosley. Ramsay protested about his treatment; Bosley stated that he was not under arrest at all. In fact, said Bosley, he would be required as a prosecution witness, but he did not say what he was supposed to be a witness to.

Ramsay told me, 'Bosley started to dictate a statement to his detective sergeant. When I complained, he informed me he was tired, having been up for nearly three days. I mentioned my call to his office regarding O'Connor and his subsequent return call to Whetstone. He became very angry and said I was lying.'

In fact, it was implied to Ramsay that (a) he had concocted the statement himself, (b) Shackleton had been coerced into making the statement, and, since this had been done to protect O'Connor, (c) every police officer who knew of the Shackleton statement – up to and including Commander Neesham – was part of a conspiracy to protect a fellow officer. But if that was the case, astonishingly, Neesham was never questioned by Countryman about the Shackleton statement.

And as O'Connor told me, 'Don Neesham was a real leader of men. If I'd been bent, he wouldn't have lifted a finger to help me.'

His sentiments were echoed by Ramsay, who told me, 'I knew John well, and Commander Neesham and Phil Corbett were my bosses. I completely vouch for the honesty of all three.'

Putting two and two together, it was now clear that Shackleton's statement (plus Ramsay's testimony) clearly exonerated O'Connor, and Ramsay, furious, told me, 'I refused to leave the office until Bosley arranged to inspect the uniform message log at Whetstone police station.'

However, Bosley terminated the interview; Ramsay's statement was never completed. Why was this? O'Connor had heard that Shaw had made a deal with Countryman and that promises had been given as to the reduced sentence he would receive if he would give evidence against certain police officers; and O'Connor had heard that Shaw had also made allegations of corruption against two City of London police officers.

Whether these allegations were true or not he had no idea – but he had to consider the following. It was no secret that Derek Ramsay had submitted his resignation to the Metropolitan Police (which became effective on 28 February 1979) in order to set up a business in the Philippines. O'Connor believed that Ramsay's statement had deliberately been delayed in order for him to go abroad so that his evidence would be lost. Because if Ramsay proved beyond all doubt that the accusations against O'Connor were trumped up charges, then Shaw's testimony against the City of London officers would be worthless. O'Connor's fear was that he would be suspended until after Shaw had given evidence against the City of London officers – and although neither he, nor anybody, else was aware of it, the trial of those officers would not start for another three and a half years.

Bill Peters was one of the other officers interviewed by Countryman. 'I told them they should have spoken to Shackleton about this, but as far as I know, they didn't', he told me. His opinion of the enquiry team? 'I regarded them as clowns – country bumpkins and completely out of their depth.'

CHAPTER 11

By now, O'Connor had been suspended for three weeks; he was advised to go on the offensive, and he did. He sent a letter of complaint to Mr R. V. Andrews, the Under Secretary of State (Home Office Police Department) in respect of Burt and other Countryman officers, voicing his fears and mentioning all of these matters – and there was more.

No attempts had been made by Countryman to authenticate O'Connor's story. The Flying Squad Occurrence Book, which listed his actions regarding the proposed meetings with Shaw, had not been seized by Countryman. There were the officers named in that book, whom O'Connor had kept informed and who had sanctioned his actions. Commander Neesham, the head of the Flying Squad, and his deputy, DCS Sewell, had not been seen. The C11 photographer and O'Connor's driver who could have authenticated their reason for being at the proposed meeting had not yet been seen.

Incompetence – or deliberate obstruction? The intermediary who had arranged the proposed meetings between Shaw and O'Connor now contacted O'Connor; he told him that Shaw wanted him to corroborate the allegations against O'Connor, which he admitted were false, and wanted to meet him to tell him what to say. He offered to meet Shaw wearing a covert tape recorder and also to record the telephone conversation which he would have with Shaw. O'Connor immediately passed this information on to Commander Neesham, who submitted a report to the Director of the Complaints Bureau.

Had this offer been taken up it would have provided irrefutable evidence of O'Connor's innocence – and of course, Shaw's worthlessness as a witness. But it wasn't. In fact, the intermediary was seen by Countryman and warned to stay away from Shaw.

One week after O'Connor's arrest and suspension, Superintendent Bosley and a sergeant arrived at Christopher Yarnold's address for the purpose of obtaining a statement from him in respect of the meeting at Fino's wine bar the previous November, when O'Connor had arrived in an attempt to arrest Shaw. Nothing wrong with that – although purists would question why a statement should be delayed for over two months, after which time a witness's memory might have become slightly hazy.

But it was what happened thereafter which makes matters questionable.

Having completed the statement, the officers were taken by Yarnold and his wife to Les Ambassadeurs, a private members' club in Mayfair, where the bill – in excess of £60 (not much now, but quite a lump in 1979) – was paid by Yarnold, using an American Express card. They then returned to Yarnold's flat, where the two officers were supplied with more drinks. Bosley then decided to pay his part of the bill and handed Yarnold a cheque drawn on his own account.

It is debatable whether or not the Countryman officers were aware that a warrant for Yarnold's arrest had been issued on a charge of conspiracy to defraud. Did they check at Criminal Records Office before the meetings, either at Fino's wine bar or the cosy tête-à-tête at the Mayfair Club? If they didn't, they should have done – after all, they had had two and a half months in which to do it – and then they would have discovered that, quite apart from anything else, Yarnold had previous convictions and had served terms of imprisonment.

And the outcome was this: here was a convicted criminal involved in an investigation of police corruption during which a senior police officer had been suspended on the words of two other criminals, socializing with and in possession of a cheque drawn on the account of the very officer who had been appointed to investigate that corruption. Blimey.

*

'I know that David Shaw made an allegation of corruption against John O'Connor', Mike Bucknole told me, 'but it was unsubstantiated. Although I was seldom in the office, because Ray Wood and I were out getting corroboration about what the supergrasses had told us, as far as I know, John O'Connor never made an appearance at Whetstone.'

There were still matters which required resolution and, it seems, were not addressed. The Rose statement had been kept in the safe at Whetstone; the combination was known to just four officers – O'Connor was not one of them. Details of the operation to arrest Shaw and the others were known only to Ramsay, his senior officer and the Surrey CID officer – not O'Connor. Therefore he could not have tipped off Shaw the day before the raid. But even supposing that somehow O'Connor *had* tipped off Shaw, it is simply unimaginable that Shaw would not have informed his brother, who was arrested at the address the following morning. Most telling of all was that David Shaw had no reason to pay O'Connor, or anybody else, for sight of Rose's statement. Shaw's brother Peter, who had been arrested and charged on Rose's evidence, would, as a matter of procedure, have had Rose's statement served on him prior to his committal proceedings; he could have informed his brother of the evidence against him. And why would Shaw have torn up the statement for which he had allegedly paid £2,500? That Shaw could have produced the copy statement would not, in itself, have incriminated O'Connor, but it would have been proof positive that the copy existed.

There was one other matter: if Shaw had wanted to meet O'Connor at Fino's wine bar on 2 November for a corrupt purpose, why did he not arrive? Shaw was aware that the bar was full of Countryman personnel ready to pounce on a corrupt cop, so if that was the case, why not arrive and spring the trap? The short answer was because Shaw knew that O'Connor was not corrupt – and more ominously to the point, so did Countryman. The whole set of allegations was as leaky as a sieve.

These were amongst the many thoughts which went round and round inside O'Connor's head. He was unable to take another job due to disciplinary regulations, which also provided for segregation from his serving colleagues; his miserable Christmas of 1979 passed into 1980 – and by late January, a year having elapsed since his suspension, nothing – not one word – had been passed by Countryman to the office of the Director of Public Prosecutions. There were cars in the street near to his house bearing Dorset number plates, there to ensure that if he met with any of his colleagues or attempted to get a job, this would be noted and acted upon. He was living in a vacuum.

'I always wondered why John O'Connor never contacted me when I returned from Manila to give evidence in outstanding cases at the Old Bailey', Derek Ramsay told me. 'Typical John, I guess, not wanting to involve others, knowing he was under surveillance.'

'It affected my wife', O'Connor told me. 'They went through all our savings accounts. It was the subject of comment that I held four building society accounts – this was because you couldn't get a mortgage unless you had an account with the building society in question. We wanted to buy a house round the corner – it fell through.'

But the Home Office report had brought some results. Commander Patterson handed O'Connor a crumpled letter signed by the Chief Constable of Dorset, Arthur Hambleton, and saying in scrawled handwriting, 'The allegations against my officers will be investigated when your investigation is finished.'

Perhaps that investigation included an attempt to discredit Derek Ramsay's probity by instigating a newspaper article which inaccurately suggested that Ramsay was now living in the lap of luxury in the Philippines, the owner of a large hospital. This so upset Ramsay's mother that she wished to take legal action on her son's behalf; she was eventually dissuaded from this course of action after her Member of Parliament suggested that to do so would merely prolong unwanted press coverage.

Meanwhile, on 26 July 1979, David Shaw had been sentenced for robbery at the Old Bailey in somewhat curious circumstances. You see, the robbery for which he was sentenced was not the one which had been carried out in Redhill, Surrey on 16 July 1978 and for which he had been circulated – remember, it was this robbery where he frantically wanted to see Peter Rose's statement and for which he had been willing to pay John O'Connor £2,500 to obtain it, then had torn it up.

Oh, no. This was a £10,000 robbery in the City of London in 1972. He had been arrested for it at the time, had not been picked out on an identification parade and within a couple of months had paid £2,000 to two City of London police officers for dropping the case. Shortly afterwards, he had been sentenced to seven years' imprisonment for conspiracy to rob, at which time he could have asked for that offence to be taken into consideration, but didn't. So when he was released on licence, as Edwin Glasgow defending him told the court, 'His past caught up with him.' Three supergrasses all named him as participating in that robbery, but now, Mr Glasgow unctuously told the irascible (and obviously disbelieving) Judge Edward Clarke QC, his client had severed all connections with his criminal associates and was living 'an honest and industrious life'.

Superintendent Bosley, possibly making his début at the Old Bailey, proudly told the court that Shaw had given the Countryman enquiry 'valuable assistance'. He went on to say, 'Since December 1978, Shaw has made four statements to me, personally, in relation to police corruption. In relation to the 1972 robbery, for which he is now to be sentenced, he has named names. As a result of that, my enquiries are proceeding in relation to certain officers and those enquiries have not yet been concluded.'

Perhaps Bosley was referring to the allegedly corrupt City of London police officers, perhaps not, but if he was, this was obviously not made clear to Judge Clarke, who, it appears, was not impressed.

'You made £2,250 out of that robbery', he snapped at Shaw, 'and I don't care a row of pins whether you gave it to a policeman, a postman or your wife.'

He then sentenced Shaw to eighteen months' imprisonment, suspended for two years, fined him £2,500 to be paid within six months or nine months' imprisonment in default and ordered him to pay £500 costs.

But not a word about O'Connor, who was by now in his sixth month of suspension and was unimpressed by Shaw's sentence.

As was Richard Ross Shackleton, who had named thirty-three of his associates and who two days earlier had admitted shooting a prison officer in the legs, two robberies involving a total of £25,000 and asked for eighteen other offences to be taken into consideration. He was sentenced to eight years' imprisonment – instead of the normal five-year tariff for supergrasses – and from his cell demanded to speak to police officers – proper ones, he emphasized, not those from Dorset. He had quite a lot to say, and as a result, Shaw was arrested once more and was charged by Surrey officers for the original offence at Redhill for which O'Connor had sought to arrest him. This time he was committed in custody from Highgate Magistrates' Court to the Old Bailey. It was there, on 22 February 1980, that Shaw made an application for bail. Surrey police objected – but Detective Superintendent John McLaren from Countryman supported the application.

Let me stop here for a moment and say that during all my attendances at courts – both Magistrates' and Crown – throughout my career, which a lot of the time included the Old Bailey, never did I hear of anything like that happening.

Well, there you are – on that occasion, it did. After McLaren said that Shaw 'was assisting them considerably with their enquiries', Mr Justice Hodgson not unnaturally wanted to know how important it was that Shaw should be available.

'It is very, very important', said McLaren, earnestly. 'It is the type of Countryman evidence we cannot obtain without him being with us.'

He was absolutely right about it being the 'type of Countryman evidence' because it was certainly par for the course; and after he was bailed, he vanished.

So, from the scene, did Bosley. He was now replaced by Chief Superintendent Steve Whitby. Like Burt, Whitby had spent all of his twenty-six years' service in Dorset. He had been promoted to sergeant in 1966 after eighteen months' service with the Regional Crime Squad and since then had been a chief inspector in the Eastern Division's Control Room as well as being a staff officer there, before becoming head of the CID in 1975. In 1979 he had received his promotion to detective chief superintendent and had been seconded to Countryman.

'Because I was innocent, I was not intimidated and showed them no respect', O'Connor told me. 'His [Whitby's] attempts to intimidate me were met with a resounding lecture on sex and travel.'

Now it was early 1980, and O'Connor had just about had enough. When Steve Chambers from ITN decided to expose the shortcomings of the Countryman investigation in a programme entitled *Bang to Rights – or Fitted Up?*, O'Connor was enthusiastic about the project, especially since Chambers had gone to great lengths to include in the script every bit of information pertaining to the case. He took the script to the Yard to show it to Deputy Assistant Commissioner Peter Neivens OBE, QPM, the Director of Information. Prior to that, Neivens had been Director of Complaints and Investigations Department, and it appeared that some of the poison spread by Countryman had seeped through to him, because without even reading the script he remarked, 'That little crook will never hold a warrant card in his greasy hand again.' Chambers replied that he would be pleased to include that quote in the programme, whereupon Neivens paled visibly and begged him not to.

Neivens was clearly unhappy about the proposed programme, and so, it appears, was the Commissioner.

'I remember clearly trying to contact the Commissioner of the Met, to inform him ITN had approached me to discuss John's suspension', Derek Ramsay told me. 'I was messed around with "not available" and "out of town" and eventually asked to meet Commander [*sic*] Neivens in his office. Upon arrival, I noticed my life's files on his desk. He requested, on behalf of the Commissioner, that I decline the offer of ITN.'

But the programme was never shown; it was halted at O'Connor's request after he received a telephone call from CIB2 on 7 March 1980 – two weeks after Shaw's successful bail application – asking him to go to the Yard. 'It's in your interests to do so', he was told. As a spoiler, on the train journey there was a piece in the *Daily Mail* headed, 'Yard Man Cleared'.

At the Yard he saw Kelland, Powis and Ronald Steventon.

'Kelland told me, "We didn't know what was going on",' O'Connor told me, 'and I replied, "Well, you should have done".'

Rather nastily, Deputy Assistant Commissioner Steventon said, 'Any reason why I shouldn't put you back in uniform?'

This was a reference to an inaccurate diary entry – in fact his Form 163 (a form detailing allegations of misconduct) cited seventeen assertions of breaches of the regulations, on which no action whatsoever was taken.

He was reinstated, although he told me, 'All this affected me – I wondered, was it all worth it?'

I suppose it depends on one's point of view. Within seven years he was promoted three times and with the rank of commander he headed the Flying Squad – not the rank and posting which one would normally associate with, as DAC Neivens put it, 'a little crook'.

Neivens' description also failed to accord with the opinion of Detective Sergeant Brian Crouch, who had worked with O'Connor on the Flying Squad: 'John was one of the good guys.'

David Shaw, in common with a number of other criminals, had led Countryman around by the nose until he got what he wanted. He never intended to give evidence against the City of London officers. The Chief Constable of Dorset, Arthur Hambleton, later – much, much later – agreed that it had been wrong for Countryman to have supported Shaw's bail application; but by then, it was far too late.

Two other matters are worth mentioning. Some time after being reinstated, O'Connor was having a drink in a pub in Queen Anne's Gate, close to the office of the Director of Public Prosecutions. A stranger approached him and enquired if he was John O'Connor; the man introduced himself as Michael Chance and he had been on the staff of the Director's office. He told O'Connor that he was very sorry about the way he had been treated, given the lengthy period of suspension he had faced.

'I was assigned to Countryman', he said, 'and I told them I wanted to see the file of John O'Connor. I saw it. I was able to report to the DPP that there was no worthwhile evidence. The Director was so concerned when I reported the position to him that he arranged for us to meet the Commissioner straight away to put him in the picture.'

As a result, O'Connor had been reinstated, immediately; but Countryman had left their mark on him.

He told me, 'I am still astonished after all these years about their utter incompetence and vindictiveness.'

Derek Ramsay took matters a little further when he told me, 'What amazes me is why John was never compensated, when the powers that be realized he was totally innocent.'

The second matter was that three men were arrested, and two of them had been interviewed by O'Connor, in respect of the mur-der/robbery at Northfields Underground Station in October 1978 which O'Connor was investigating. They had made certain admissions. The men were charged and were eventually committed to the Old Bailey for trial. O'Connor was not called by the prosecution due to his having been suspended from duty on spurious charges. However, his pocket book contained notes of the interviews and this had been countersigned by an officer who had been present; therefore, in law, that officer could refer to those notes whilst giving evidence. However, the pocket book had been one of many items seized by Countryman at the time of O'Connor's suspension. They refused to release it.

It came as no surprise to anybody that the three men, after two trials in November 1979, walked free from court. The name of one of the men was David Lawson Ewin. Like many unpleasant substances, he rose to the surface again, details of which may be found in Chapter 23.

And now it's time to concentrate on other armed robberies; and what befell the police officers who investigated them.

CHAPTER 12

When an £18,000 armed robbery by masked raiders went off at the National Westminster Bank, Bayswater Road, Paddington on 19 October 1977, it was not too long before two men – Patrick Carpenter and John Twomey – were arrested. Born in 1948, Twomey grew up in Paddington, had several brushes with the law and was sentenced to Borstal Training. In 1971 he was one of a team of seven men who held up the employees of a Westminster City Council building at gunpoint and stole £27,000. Twomey's share was £2,000, and five years' imprisonment.

In 1975 he was sentenced to twelve months' imprisonment for an attack on a taxi driver and the following year to two months for possessing an offensive weapon. In between times, he stood trial for a wages robbery at St Mary's Hospital, Paddington, which had occurred in 1969; but although supergrass Maurice O'Mahoney gave evidence against Twomey and three other men, all of them, to the accompaniment of cheers and clapping from the public gallery, were acquitted.

So at the time of his arrest, Twomey was the proud possessor of thirteen previous convictions – and one or two acquittals.

The police evidence for the Paddington bank raid was this: the investigation was carried out under the control of Detective Inspector Terry Babbidge at Paddington police station. Within a short space of time, Detective Sergeant John David Ross BEM (an award for gallantry, having disarmed a gunman some ten years previously), attached to the Flying Squad, received information as to the perpetrators and he, together with his younger brother, Detective Constable Michael Bradley Ross (who in 1972, in an incident quite separate from his brother's award, received the Queen's Commendation for Brave Conduct for arresting an armed man), Detective Constable Paul Rextrew from Paddington, Detective Constable Derek Watts and Detective Sergeant Tony Russell, searched premises in London. At one house two sawn-off shotguns and money from the robbery was found, in another, component parts of the guns were found and Twomey and Carpenter were arrested; during their interviews incriminating admissions were recorded, and both were charged and remanded in custody.

Terry Babbidge told me, 'When the money was found, it was shown to the teller at the bank. Most of it couldn't be identified but she pointed out a £10 note. She told me, "It had my initials on the top, right-hand corner and the date, which was also my birthday. My pen was smashed in the robbery and never used again".'

So far, so good. However, matters which cast a shadow over this case started at Lambeth Magistrates' Court on 12 March 1979 at the committal proceedings to the Old Bailey of one John Arthur Bindon. Since the age of eleven Bindon had been in trouble with the law, and in the years that followed he had been convicted of malicious damage, possessing ammunition, stealing a car and grievous bodily harm. A psychotic, third-rate gangster, Bindon was a sometime television actor and friend of Her Royal Highness Princess Margaret, due, it was said, to his possession of a twelve-inch appendage, upon which he could hang several half-pint beer jugs. This, we must assume, could only be done when he was in a state of mild excitement.

Now he appeared at court on a charge of murdering John Arthur Darke. Nor was Darke a shrinking violet; he had escaped from custody on four occasions and had convictions for unlawful wounding, conspiracy to rob, possession of firearms and armed robbery. Darke had been hacked to death with a machete; a contract killing for £10,000, it was said, but the charge was not substantiated, because in November Bindon walked free from court. South London gangster Joey Pyle, who had been charged with being an accessory to murder, accompanied him on his walk to freedom. After some more brushes with the law, including several charges of possessing offensive weapons, Bindon sadly passed away in October 1993.

Darke – who in 1976 had been acquitted of murder – was a police informant and he had been paid £850 from the Informants' Fund in respect of the arrest of Carpenter and Twomey. Coincidentally, it was Twomey who was said to have put up the contract on Darke; something then, as now, which he strenuously denied. It was the perfect opportunity for Twomey, a witness at Bindon's committal proceedings, to allege that police had come to his home and planted two sawn-off shotguns – two days later, Twomey and Patrick Carpenter's trial commenced at the Old Bailey.

But not for long. On the day the trial started, the prosecution requested an adjournment after the production by the defence of covert tape recordings.

Stating that 'This case really smelled', Twomey's lawyer, Lord Gifford QC, told the court, 'It has been the defence's case from the outset that there has been a massive fabrication of evidence by a number of police officers. The defence has been responsible for bringing these tape recordings forward and assert that the recordings are proof positive of corrupt behaviour by some of those officers in the context of this case.'

Having represented members of the Guildford Four and the Birmingham Six, and later involved in the Broadwater Farm and Bloody Sunday enquiries, Lord Gifford could be described as a lawyer who was not particularly prosecution-minded.

This complaint was taken up by Countryman. On 27 March Rextrew had just been posted to the Flying Squad and partnered with Detective Sergeant Brian Crouch.

But, as Crouch told me, 'We never had a chance to work together because as soon as he arrived, he was suspended.'

Similarly suspended from duty was Michael Ross, from 'L' Division, and the news spread around the Middle Temple like wildfire; unfortunately, it was a case of 'Chinese Whispers', and the more predictably left-wing barristers erroneously deduced that it was *John* Ross who had been suspended. In fact, he would not be suspended from duty until over a year later, in June 1980.

John Ross and Detective Sergeant Charlie Scott from the Flying Squad had enjoyed several successes, one of which was arresting a robbery team from Dagenham. Scott – who described John Ross as 'a good egg' – told me:

> As the trial was underway at the Old Bailey, the defence demanded the attendance of John Ross, mistaken in their belief that it was he who had been suspended. They went pale when he presented himself as my corroborating officer!
>
> They – the defence – still thought he was suspended, and John offered to show them his warrant card. Red faces all round, and the judge was cross with the defence. John was offered up for cross-examination and declined to say anything until he had had sight of both his pocket book and diary, which had been taken by Countryman. They refused to hand them over; there was a stand-off, and the Countryman observer at the back of the court was ordered by the judge to give them up, which at first he refused to do. When the judge mentioned 'contempt' and the prospect of a couple of days in the cells, they were handed over.
>
> At this stage, Countryman were making themselves busy checking the mileage claims of those on the Squad who were authorized to drive their own motors – heady stuff!

On another job with John we nicked some robbers and recovered some cash; Countryman were soon on the scene demanding to take custody of the recovered money, which would be taken by them, to be slept with in a police cell overnight.

When Twomey and Carpenter's trial recommenced on 3 April 1979, Paul Purnell QC for the prosecution offered no evidence against both men, and the Recorder of London, Sir James Miskin QC, not unnaturally stated, 'I think the public are entitled to know why.'

'At present, because an enquiry has begun, the officers are suspended, and as a result of information which has been provided to counsel in the case, it is clear the enquiry will take some considerable length of time,' replied Purnell, adding, 'Without there being any reflection on the officers, it is not the prosecution's intention to call officers under suspicion.'

The charges of robbery and possessing firearms against the two men – as well as an additional charge against Carpenter for possessing cannabis resin – were dropped, and legal costs, estimated at £35,000, were ordered to be paid from public funds.

Outside the court, Twomey aired his grievances. 'It started out as a personal grudge but then it snowballed', he told reporters. 'All I can say is that we were framed by having guns planted on us, and then the threat was used against seven other people I know, that if they didn't pay money, the same would happen to them.'

Eight months after the Twomey/Carpenter case collapsed, Babbidge (who recalls it was on Christmas Eve 1979, although in fact, it was 19 December), Russell and Watts were suspended. The Countryman investigation was now well under way. Frank Pillinger had been a detective constable at Paddington, and while Detective Sergeant Chris Wilson went to the scene of the robbery at the National Westminster Bank, Pillinger arranged for the Scenes of Crime Officer to attend also. Later, Pillinger was posted to Staines police station. He told me:

> One Saturday, whilst at home, I received a phone call asking me the following day to attend 'CO' [Scotland Yard] to be interviewed by a superintendent from Countryman; no reason. I duly arrived at 'the big house', where I was interviewed by a DI and a DS from Countryman. I was interviewed about the blag, my movements that day. I asked them if they had my diary for reference which they did not, so I did my best to recollect what had happened.

Their tack changed, wanting to know my opinion of Terry
Babbidge, DC Paul Rextrew and a DC Ross. I felt the
whole interview was very amateurish and I then left with
their thanks. I went into work at Staines on the Monday
morning, only to be told there was a rumour I had been
arrested. Chinese whispers put me in the frame; anyway,
I managed to persuade people I had not been lifted and
got on with life.

Chris Wilson, who had been a detective sergeant on the Flying
Squad's 4 Squad before being transferred to Paddington, did
indeed go to the bank. He recalled:

> I know Twomey was arrested; I may have been involved
> in the arrests and I seem to remember searching a prem-
> ises at Fulham. I was summonsed to 'CO' – I believe the
> day before my holiday. I went into the canteen; there were
> 2–3 other people there. I remember Derek Watts and Tony
> Russell were there.
>
> The interview by Countryman was not very friendly;
> the officer in charge was a ginger-haired man, I think a
> chief superintendent. I can't recall exactly what was said,
> but I do remember they went about it the wrong way.
> While I was there, I was shadowed by two officers wher-
> ever I went, even to the loo. I wasn't called at the trial of
> Babbidge & Co.

Now under suspension, Babbidge believed his phone was tapped,
and he told me, 'I was followed and colleagues didn't dare come
near me. My wife was very worried and we moved to Bournemouth.'

In fact, as will be seen in due course, Mr and Mrs Babbidge had
good reason to be concerned; hence the move to the south coast.

One month later, Michael Ross and Rextrew were taken
to Godalming, where they were kept for two days before being
charged with accepting inducements of £1,500 and demanding
the same amount with menaces.

Rextrew told me, 'Superintendent Murdoch from
Gloucestershire – part of Operation Countryman – dealt with us
very fairly; they were doing their job.'

The two men appeared at Bow Street Magistrates' Court on 21
January 1980. There they were remanded into police custody for
three days; on 24 January bail was granted in the sum of £10,000
each and they were ordered to surrender their passports.

Almost one year passed. On 15 January 1981 the Ross brothers, Rextrew, Russell, Watts and Babbidge were all charged at Bow Street Magistrates' Court with conspiracy to pervert the course of justice; again, they were remanded on bail.

Another year went by. On 1 February 1982 the trial of the Ross brothers, Babbidge and Rextrew got underway at the Old Bailey before his Honour Judge Robert Lymbery. Having seen active wartime service as a tank commander, Lymbery was discharged with the rank of major and read for the Bar. After serving as a Circuit Judge, he had now arrived at the Old Bailey; this was one of his first cases.

John Christopher Calthorpe Blofeld QC (later the Honourable Mr Justice Blofeld) led for the prosecution and told the jury, rather sarcastically, that the detectives appeared to be having 'the luckiest day of their lives' when they allegedly found the items at the homes of the former prisoners. All four officers were charged with planting evidence, Babbidge with making a false statement in respect of Twomey, Rextrew and Michael Ross with demanding and receiving £1,500 from a James Stephens and they and John Ross with similar charges in respect of a Thomas Green – to which all four pleaded not guilty.

Babbidge told me that a police constable who had gone to live in Ireland had made a statement saying that he had sold one of the shotguns found at Twomey's address to Rextrew. 'But at the trial, he denied the truthfulness of the statement, saying he had made it because he was under so much pressure.'

Perhaps that was the witness that Blofeld was referring to when he told the jury, 'There might be police witnesses among whom there could be those who will be less than entirely wholehearted in his desire to tell you all they know' – or perhaps not.

As to the covert tape recordings, Rextrew told me, 'There was a meeting in a pub – the Eight Bells on Putney Bridge – between me, Michael Ross and two other men. This was recorded and the tape was handed to solicitor James Saunders. There was no disclosure and on the first day of the trial the prosecution served transcripts of the tape on us.'

The meeting had taken place between 8.00 and 8.30pm. But when the tape was examined by an acoustics expert – seventy-six-year-old Derek Faraday, a former BBC engineer – it was revealed that in the background the licensee calling 'Last orders' could be heard; the tape could not have been made at the time alleged.

And that begs these questions: since these recordings had allegedly been made, in respect of James Stephens on 8 November 1977 and Thomas Green on 23 November 1977, why had it taken

so long – over four years – for them to surface? When were they
handed to Twomey's solicitor, James Saunders? When did he hand
them to the police? Why wait until sixteen months had elapsed with
his client in custody before making these revelations? At the time
of the trial collapsing, Lord Gifford had said, 'There are sharply
conflicting versions of when this investigation should have been
started.' Right.

After an application from the defence on 11 March, the judge
(who, it was said, 'dispensed justice with outstanding impartiality
and consistent soundness') discharged the jury from returning verdicts in respect of the Ross brothers and Rextrew receiving corrupt
payments of £1,500.

Messrs Twomey, Carpenter, Stephens and Green gave evidence, although not before, with masterly understatement, Blofeld
had told the court, 'It is possible that people with convictions will
have no love for the police.'

Babbidge recalled Twomey giving evidence at the trial. 'The
first time, he was "booted & suited", tearful and distressed. But
then a Jiffy bottle, used in a robbery, was found with his thumb-
print on it – Burt wanted nothing done but Powis overruled him
and he was charged. The next time in court, Twomey showed his
true colours.'

Next, it was the turn of Babbidge, who was formally acquitted
of making a false statement. And then, on 22 March, all of the
four defendants were acquitted by the jury of all of the remaining
charges.

Russell and Watts had had their charges thrown out at the
Magistrates' Court; nevertheless, they were still committed to the
Old Bailey on a separate indictment. As the other four officers were
acquitted, so Russell and Watts were arraigned and had no evidence offered against them.

During the trial, one of the defence counsel compared the difficulties of policing London with those facing the rural forces who
had taken part in Countryman. London officers, he said, were dealing with incidents of armed robbery every hour, whilst policemen
in Dorset had little more to worry about than the theft of invalid
carriages. These were comments which, according to the listener's
disposition, were either quite amusing or, in the opinion of Judge
Lymbery, cruel and inaccurate; the judge felt impelled to react to
'the nasty little stories and innuendos' that Countryman officers
did not understand the problems of policing London and added
that, 'Anybody who thought the standards of London policemen
should be different from those of policemen anywhere else should
examine his conscience.'

But whether or not those remarks were 'cruel and inaccurate', the fact remained that during the year that this robbery took place, Dorset Police investigated 66 robberies. During the same time-span, the number of robberies and violent thefts dealt with by the Metropolitan Police amounted to 12,415.

★

I have always said that the police disciplinary code covers everything between being born and dying; there are few working coppers who'd disagree with me.

There was a detective superintendent who was offered a massive £15,000 bribe, which he refused. But he was put on a police disciplinary board for failing to report that he'd been offered the bribe.

'Don't I get any credit for not accepting it?' he indignantly asked the board members, but he didn't, and back to uniform he went.

I bore this in mind when, having arrested a burglary team for stealing a huge amount of expensive designer clothing, the receiver approached me in an alarmingly oily manner and suggested that I could become suddenly richer if I dropped him out of the proceedings. I impolitely rebuffed his offer, made a note in my pocket book to that effect and informed my detective inspector of our discourse. Unfortunately, this gentleman had been born without a spine and this deformity was added to when, upon receipt of my information, his arsehole dropped out.

'Don't tell *me*!' he cried. 'I don't want to know!'

You will not be too surprised to discover that he was later promoted to the rank of superintendent.

So I telephoned CIB2 and imparted my information to a very distrustful detective sergeant.

'Why're you telling me this?' he asked.

'Because GO (*General Orders* – the policeman's Bible) says so', I replied.

'Yeah – but why? I mean, what's your angle?' he persisted.

We went backwards and forwards, and in the end I gave up. It seemed to me that whether or not you wanted to take the correct form of action, if the hierarchy wanted to stuff you, they would. Although the receiver – he was sentenced to twenty-one months' imprisonment – didn't make a complaint, had he done so, do you think that my pusillanimous inspector or the doubting sergeant at CIB2 would have recalled our conversations? No, I don't think so, either.

★

The Ross brothers were put on discipline boards. Michael Ross was found guilty of disobeying an order by meeting men against whom he knew criminal proceedings were pending. He appealed against the finding but lost and was dismissed from the Force in July 1982. His brother John was similarly dismissed four months later, and together they set up a wine bar. Rextrew, who had told reporters that the charges were 'monstrous and should never have been brought', resigned. He told me that the effect on his family had been 'dreadful'; his father, Ken, had been a successful Flying Squad officer, whose list of commendations had commenced after he was awarded £15 from the Bow Street Reward Fund for relieving a dangerous criminal of a loaded pistol. For his mother, Coral, happily the date of her son's acquittal coincided with her fifty-third birthday.

Babbidge appeared on a disciplinary board before Powis; he was accused of moving to Bournemouth without first having been given permission. Babbidge explained why he had moved. He told Powis that he had no option to go without informing anybody because he had received utterly reliable information that a man well known to him – and to the Ross brothers, Rextrew, Watts and Russell, as well – had taken out a contract on his life and that of his family with a certain notorious and murderous South London family. Powis demanded to know the source of the information, and Babbidge told him. With that, Powis got up and left the room. When he returned, Babbidge's information had been verified beyond doubt; it had been the result of a telephone intercept. Then, as now, it was not a matter that could be admitted in evidence. Babbidge's unlawful move was dealt with by means of a caution.

Babbidge was later promoted to chief inspector; before he retired, in 1992, he was also awarded the Queen's Police Medal for distinguished service. His opinion of Countryman? 'I thought they took too much on board; they were out of their depth.'

Whenever it was that the tape in the Twomey/Carpenter case came into Countryman's possession, it appeared that Burt had not learned the lessons from John Simmonds' handing over of the tape of his conversation with Cuthbert, containing all the attendant pub noises. A magazine article claimed that the tape had been 'authenticated' by Countryman, but if by that it was meant that the tape was genuine, it appeared this was not the case. Or did Burt know of the background noises which proved the recording could not have been made when it was said to have been? Was his desire to see police officers convicted – whom he perceived to be corrupt – so great that he was willing to overlook this glaring discrepancy? He was frantic to stop Twomey being arrested again whilst he was giving evidence. It also appeared that he was willing to permit John O'Connor to hang out to dry in the hope that David Shaw's credibility would be intact to give evidence at the trial of the City of London officers – when there was irrefutable evidence that Shaw's evidence was lies and that O'Connor was innocent. All rather disturbing; and anybody reading this may put their own interpretation on his motives.

However, consider this. Outside the court, a mysterious visitor had sat for the whole of the trial. It transpired he was a detective superintendent from South Wales Police and part of the Countryman enquiry. His task, during the whole of the seven-week trial, was to remain there, ready to give the officers' past history should they be found guilty. Thankfully, before he could take root, somebody came along to tell him that they had not been.

CHAPTER 13

Babbidge and Co were not the only Met officers to stand trial.

On 22 January 1980 – the same day that Deputy Commissioner Kavanagh of the Met and Commissioner Marshall of the City announced that Sir Peter Mathews, the Chief Constable of Surrey Constabulary, had been appointed 'advisor' to the Countryman enquiry – Detective Sergeant Brian O'Leary and Detective Constable Roy William Leavers, both attached to the Flying Squad's 9 squad at Rotherhithe (and who had been suspended from duty for the previous 12 months), were arrested by Countryman. The following day, they appeared at Bow Street Magistrates' Court charged with stealing £14,790, the property of the Receiver of the Metropolitan Police on 16 October 1977, conspiring to pervert the course of justice by arranging for one Leonard Roberts to make a false confession under caution and theft or suppression of material evidence. In addition, O'Leary was charged with making a statement in evidence against Roberts which he knew to be false or did not believe to be true. Both officers were remanded, having been granted bail in the sum of £10,000 each, and both were ordered to surrender their passports.

The allegations were that when making an arrest nearly three weeks after the Williams & Glyn's robbery the officers had discovered £30,000 hidden in a vacuum cleaner belonging to Roberts. Allegedly taking a large percentage of the cash, they had apparently told Roberts they would only charge him with receiving £12,000. At their trial, eighteen months later, Kenneth Richardson for the prosecution warned the jury to examine Roberts' evidence 'with very great care'. The jury did just that, and on 9 June 1981 they acquitted O'Leary and Leavers of all charges.

Former Flying Squad officer Eddy Cherry provides an interesting insight into these matters:

> At that time, armed robbers had been ripping the City of London apart. Nine squad, having gathered intelligence and evidence, traced and arrested a number of those responsible and . . . found identifiable bank notes . . . but were precluded from completing the investigations

because of the City claiming jurisdiction. The villains then
walked free, and there is no doubt in my mind that had
it been left to 9 squad they would at the very least have
stood trial.

Like all of my South London Robbery Squad colleagues, I was (and still am) extremely bitter about the
way in which, having been tasked with investigating allegations against City of London officers, they [Countryman]
actively and openly extended their remit and canvassed
violent criminals who were awaiting trial or serving long
terms of imprisonment to make baseless allegations
against Met officers who had often spent months of pains-
taking investigative work to bring about their arrest and
charge. The villains of course jumped on the bandwagon,
hoping to use it as a way of avoiding trial or getting convictions quashed.

The . . . irony is that had Countryman approached
the Robbery Squad for information, rather than trying to
tar them with the same brush as the City officers, they
would have got immediate cooperation, as we were royally
hacked off with the way the City had 'mishandled' the
investigations.

Just six weeks had passed since Leavers and O'Leary were acquitted. They were reinstated, and O'Leary took a three-week refresher
course, necessary since he had been returned to uniform and the
duties of uniform and detective sergeants vary so immeasurably.
He then reported for duty at St Mary Cray police station.

Then, on 20 August 1981, *World in Action*'s programme, 'A
Conflict of Evidence', was televised. In it, Leavers was said to have
been forewarned that he was going to be questioned by Countryman
– something that he strongly denied. But far worse was the emer-
gence of a covertly taped conversation between O'Leary and a man
on bail for robbery and firearms offences, in the course of which
O'Leary allegedly said, 'Now, I can't promise you anything but I'm
certain I can come up with one or two things because there's got to
be one or two mistakes.' This had taken place in a South London
wine bar in February, at a time when O'Leary was on bail awaiting
trial for the offences of which he was subsequently acquitted.

The TV audience was informed that 'The criminal was being
offered a measure of assistance and . . . both were familiar with
arrangements where money changed hands in exchange for
favours'; not only was this prejudging the issue, it was a classic
case of 'trial by television'.

Following its transmission, Deputy Commissioner Kavanagh said, 'The *World in Action* programme has not been very helpful. Granada Television were requested to let us hear the tapes, so we could assess their evidential value. They declined. We repeat our request and ask for their cooperation.'

A spokesman for Granada said that it would 'consider the question of the tapes', but according to his contemporaries O'Leary was 'stitched-up' after he met an informant. The tape was apparently heavily edited, I was told, 'so much so that when full access to the tape was requested, it was refused, which tells you a lot.'

O'Leary was suspended once more; by the time he gave an interview to the *Sunday Express* he had been suspended for another eighteen months which, with a very brief period of re-training and a similarly brief posting to a suburban police station, brought up his period of suspension to four years.

'I want to know the outcome', said O'Leary. 'I'm not looking to resign until then. All I can do is sit back and wait.'

O'Leary was not alone in his misgivings; Leslie Curtis, the Chairman of the Police Federation added his voice to the situation, saying, 'We have made representations to the Home Office about these long suspensions. There should be a limit of, say, six months. And the officer concerned should be kept informed of progress made in the enquiry.'

'Even if I got my job back, it would not be the same', said O'Leary, and he was right. At his discipline board he protested that he had been unaware that the informant was on bail; but he was, and since O'Leary did not have permission to meet him he was required to resign.

Roy Leavers spent the rest of his career in uniform; he was said to be deeply embittered by the investigation.

He wasn't the only one to be upset; what affected a constable also disturbed a commander.

CHAPTER 14

Don Neesham had been the commander of the Flying Squad since 1976. He was hugely liked and respected – by working detectives, that is. This was his fifth posting with the Flying Squad and would account for ten of his thirty-three years' service. His was a career filled with commendations: 'for persistence and ability in effecting the arrest of a team of violent criminals'; 'for ability and determination in arresting three dangerous criminals for robbery with violence'; 'for the conviction of five dangerous criminals for conspiracy to rob'; for displaying 'courage and devotion to duty in effecting the arrest of three vicious criminals for malicious wounding, one of whom was in possession of a loaded firearm'. This was a cross-section of the plaudits bestowed on him, quite apart from the award of the Queen's Police Medal in the 1977 Birthday Honours List.

At fifty-five years of age, Neesham had served in the Flying Squad in the ranks of detective constable, detective sergeant (first class), detective inspector and detective chief superintendent. Now the Squad's commander, he knew Flying Squad's work inside out – but he was not a happy man.

One of the reasons was Countryman's conduct. The supergrass Ray Fowles, who had spoken to Countryman regarding allegations of corruption involving police officers, was giving evidence in an important Flying Squad robbery trial concerning two serial robbers, Alf Berkeley and Danny Gowan; officers from Countryman attended the trial. Detective Chief Inspector Tony Lundy knew that there was a possibility that Fowles might react unpredictably if he saw those officers in court; and given Fowles' reaction when the two Countryman officers had barged into Whetstone, these were not fanciful suspicions. Although neither Lundy nor any of his officers was the subject of Countryman enquiries, it was possible that Fowles might blurt out his dealings with those officers during his evidence; and the sensational headlines that Countryman was attracting might well inaccurately suggest to the jury that it was Lundy's investigation team who were the subject of those enquiries, thereby prejudicing the outcome of the case.

Countryman was asked by the Yard to keep out of the court; Neesham followed this up by contacting the Director of Public

Prosecutions' office with the same request. However, this was seen by Countryman as a conspiracy between the Met and the DPP to frustrate their enquiries. This begs the question, how? By requesting that the Countryman officers stay away from the court?

However, more was to come. In an attempt to negate Fowles' testimony, the defence called Stephen Raymond to rebut his evidence. It will be recalled that Raymond and his brother had already featured early in this matter with regard to Cuthbert.

It's time to pause for a moment and take a closer look at Stephen Patrick Raymond, who was born in 1945 in Stoke Newington. Whilst he was serving a six-year sentence for robbery he struck up a correspondence with the highly questionable MP, Tom Driberg, who would come in very handy in 1970 when South London gangster Eddie Coleman was shot dead and Raymond supplied a chest to dispose of the body. The killers fled to Scotland, and Raymond posed as Tom Driberg on a train when he joined them, but then rather spoilt things by using the MP's stolen credit card and was arrested. Raymond and two others were charged with the murder, but the manipulative crook called Driberg, former Solicitor General Sir Dingle Foot and his MP brother, Michael, to say that on the night of the murder all four of them had dined at The Gay Hussar Restaurant. Raymond was acquitted of the murder but went down for three years for obstructing justice. He escaped from prison, was recaptured and then, in 1976, involved in the spectacular theft at Heathrow Airport in which Stanley Houghton – see Chapters 18 and 23 – was similarly concerned. Raymond fled to Switzerland but came to grief when he ostentatiously delved into a briefcase swollen with stolen money to purchase a silk shirt and an observant salesgirl phoned the police. He was sentenced to ten years' imprisonment and now he needed help – a lot of it.

Raymond had told the court that the Deputy DPP had given him immunity from prosecution in return for providing Countryman with evidence of corrupt police officers – which was blatantly untrue. But when Lundy requested that Countryman come forward to prove that Raymond was lying, even though those officers had proof that Raymond's evidence was untrue, they refused to do so. This behaviour was nothing short of atrocious. It had been revealed on Simmonds' covert tape recording, when the fact that Raymond had manufactured false statements for this case was discussed with Raymond's solicitor. Countryman were in possession of the tape, they were fully aware of the contents and still they did nothing. It led to the Deputy DPP being called to court.

And added to that, when Lundy and his officers arrested a robbery team ('on the pavement') for a £16,000 robbery, during which

shots were fired and three cashiers were hit across the face with an
iron bar, the gang's leader, one Joey Maybur, who had already served
eleven years for an armed robbery, approached Countryman and
agreed to assist them. Maybur then applied for bail, and his application was supported by a letter from Countryman to the judge
stating that he was assisting them with their enquiries. It is almost
impossible to comprehend Countryman's jaw-dropping arrogance
– or naïvety. Bail was refused, but then Maybur pleaded guilty; the
rest of the gang, who stated they were pleading not guilty, were
remanded to be tried at a later date; that was usual practice. But
what was not normal was that Maybur's defence team asked for
him to be sentenced immediately; in ordinary circumstances, the
rest of the gang would have been tried and, if found guilty, would
have been sentenced at the same time as their leader, once the
judge was in full possession of the facts – as to who did what, to
whom and when.

Of course, the judge was aware of this, and said so – but then
the defence barrister stated that Maybur was assisting Countryman
regarding 'serious matters', and this was confirmed when a representative from Countryman got into the witness box and added his
voice to the mitigation. So Maybur – who by rights, being the possessor of sixteen previous convictions, should have received twenty
years' imprisonment – was sentenced, once again, to eleven years.
The following week, the rest of the gang appeared in court once
more; now they all pleaded guilty, but since their self-confessed
leader had received eleven years, it would have been manifestly
unfair for them to receive the same sentence when they were lesser
lights. They were, like many a good Nazi general, 'only following
orders', and it was only right and proper that they should receive
reduced sentences of between two and a half and eight years.

But never mind, Countryman still had Maybur, ready and willing to give evidence against those corrupt police officers; only,
of course, they didn't. Now that he was free of the toils, having
received a sentence which was approximately one-half of what he
deserved, Maybur told Countryman to 'get stuffed'.

How their poor little faces must have dropped when they
received that news – and yet detectives, experienced in the ways
of criminals' chicanery, saw it coming from a country mile away.
Countryman, with their inexperience and their gullibility in believing anything told them by wily criminals, discovered – and not for
the first time – that they had been royally shafted.

Matters were not improved after Burt had attempted to inter-
fere in the trial at which Twomey and Carpenter gave evidence;
but now there would be a twist in the tale because of simperingly

weak man-management on the part of senior police officers at the Yard that would cost the Met dear – them, the Flying Squad and particularly Don Neesham.

★

Gwyn Waters, who had served several tours with the Flying Squad, told me:

> Don Neesham was a great administrator, organizer and operator, with many informants. He was very popular and a great defender of the CID. I was the detective chief superintendent on the Squad. I'd been promoted to DCS in 1974 and had served on 'S', then 'C' Divisions and came to C8 on 4 January 1977, as deputy to Don.
>
> Don was on holiday when Jock Morrison [the commander of C1 Department at the Yard] told me I was in Friday's *Police Orders* to be transferred to C1 on 19 September 1977. I went upstairs and saw Steventon [then Deputy Assistant Commissioner 'C' Department (Admin)] who said it was to help promote my career. He also later said he knew I had a job to go to, which wasn't true. I asked which of the two it was – to further my career or because I was going to leave the job? When Don came back from holiday and found out, he went berserk. I retired in October 1977.
>
> Steventon was determined to break the hierarchy in the CID. He and Kelland were Freemasons at the St James' Lodge and they wanted to promote their protégés – fellow Masons – to fill the senior posts in the CID. We were blocking them; I was a Freemason but as far as I know, Don wasn't.

On 30 April 1979 a calamitous decision was reached: in the words of the Commissioner, in his memoirs, *McNee's Law*, 'In order, once again to avoid any accusation of obstruction to the Countryman enquiry, it was decided to move Neesham to other duties. When told of this, however, he exercised his right to retire on pension.'

Since the 'other duties' meant he was going to be transferred to a uniform post, Neesham had resigned on the spot. Fiercely protective of his men, he had complained that some of his officers had been disciplined and fined for failing to notify Thames Valley Police that they had searched premises in their area. It was an omission of which many active officers had been guilty; that included Neesham himself, who in 1963 had been reprimanded for travelling out of the Metropolitan Police District in his private car without permission and failing to record these matters in his official CID diary. So perhaps that had a bearing on his support of his officers in similar circumstances, fifteen years later.

The official reason for Neesham's departure was a toss-up between 'voluntary retirement' and 'health grounds'. His service record originally showed the reason was 'Service and age'; then 'and age' was hurriedly scrubbed out, because commanders were entitled to soldier on for a few more years. Just as hastily written was his length of service – it was shown as '30+ years'; it looked as though he couldn't be got rid of quickly enough. Neesham would later say the reasons for his resignation were, firstly, because of Countryman: that they regarded him as being part of a conspiracy to pervert the course of justice, that they had circulated stories in the press alleging that the web of corruption included at least one commander and, by inference, that commander was him; secondly, because of what he considered 'idiocy' on the part of the likes of Kelland and Powis, whom he regarded as being intent on destroying the detective force. This slotted in with what Gwyn Waters had told me; additionally, Bill Peters told me that in his retirement Neesham had warned him about certain Masons in the police.

So was Neesham's transfer made knowing that he would never willingly accept it and would resign? Was it, in effect, a 'double-whammy' – a simpering sop to placate Countryman and, at the same time, to get Neesham out of his position as head of the Flying Squad in order to clear the way, as Gwyn Waters stated, 'to break the hierarchy of the CID'? Many old-time CID officers refuse to believe anything else.

Neesham had served his country well: after three years' wartime service with the RAF and thirty-three years' distinguished service with the Metropolitan Police, he went to work for the Tobacco Advisory Council; an extremely embittered man (with considerable justification), he refused to communicate in any way with the press. His widow told me that when he died on 12 June 1996, it was 'because he was broken-hearted'.

CHAPTER 15

S o what have we got so far? One City of London officer and eight Metropolitan Police officers acquitted; another Met officer suspended for fourteen months when the head of the investigation knew he was innocent. In addition, any number of professional criminals running rings around a bunch of unworldly individuals who, as one officer put it, 'knew as much about criminal investigation as my arsehole knows about steam navigation'.

But we're getting ahead of ourselves. Let's go back a couple of years, in this Fantasy Island of investigation, and see, following Neesham's demise, what was going on.

*

By July 1979 Dorset had brought out their big gun: the Chief Constable, Arthur Hambleton. Born in 1915, Hambleton joined the West Riding Police Force in 1937; in 1942 he volunteered for the Royal Marines and as a company commander demonstrated exemplary bravery. Having been severely wounded, he was mentioned in dispatches and awarded the Military Cross. Demobilized in 1946 with the rank of captain, he rejoined the police and enjoyed a meteoric rise through the ranks – from constable to Chief Constable of Dorset in just sixteen years. He was appointed OBE, advanced to CBE and awarded the Queen's Police Medal.

Hambleton presented a dossier to Deputy Commissioner Kavanagh and Assistant Commissioners Bright and Kelland; it contained details of allegations of 209 cases of corruption in respect of a total of 78 police officers both in the Met and the City of London – up to and including commander rank. These were specified as follows: three Met and one City commanders, three Met and two City detective chief superintendents, six Met and one City detective superintendents, eight Met and three City detective chief inspectors, seven Met and two City detective inspectors, twenty-seven Met and three City detective sergeants and six Met and six City detective constables.

And what had they allegedly been up to? Of the four commanders, one had received money in respect of a major crime enquiry which resulted in none of the witnesses making an appearance.

Another had received part of a total of £40,000 paid to officers in respect of a bank robbery investigation, had arranged early parole for criminals for payment and had been paid £2,000 for assisting criminals. A third had received money in respect of a theft; and the last was accused of corruption, perjury and conspiracy. Those last allegations also referred to one of the detective chief superintendents, and it was said that both of them 'were likely to be charged'. They weren't.

Neither was the detective superintendent who was said to have received part of £20,000 paid over by criminals following a robbery, offered assistance to a prisoner for £15,000, corruptly received part of a £40,000 bribe following another robbery and received £6,000 for supplying information. Not only was he not charged, he wasn't suspended either.

Names of detective constables who had taken part in burglaries and dealt in drugs were itemized, as was that of a detective sergeant who helped a prisoner to escape. Another sergeant had received £2,000 to assist a prisoner on an identification parade, and yet another, who had by now retired, had assisted criminals in carrying out robberies for payment.

So far, Countryman had consisted of some forty officers from Dorset, Avon and Somerset, South Wales and Sussex; now Hambleton demanded (and got) a substantial increase in personnel. Officers were brought in from Gloucestershire and Northamptonshire, and Countryman now boasted a strength of ninety-two, made up of officers from thirteen provincial constabularies.

The Met had offered to deal with any complaints which Countryman might wish to pass on to them; this offer was refused, with Countryman stating that the information which they had accrued had been passed to them in confidence.

The commander of CIB2, Tony Lampard QPM, told me, 'I said to Ray Anning [Deputy Assistant Commissioner Anning CBE, QPM], "Do you think we ought to offer them some help?" and he replied, "Yes" – but they refused on two occasions.'

In addition, it was clear to experienced officers in the Met that criminals were being encouraged by Countryman to make these allegations to trade their way out of heavy prison sentences. One internal police report concluded with the words:

> This force should endeavour to establish a formal policy with the Chief Constable of Dorset to ensure that the zealousness of his officers to gain evidence in respect of their enquiries does not lead them to lose an overall perspective of police duties.

Veiled hints of obstruction were made by Countryman, who, it appeared, had no faith at all in the higher echelons of the Met, or in the Attorney General or the DPP. This, it appeared, was a two-way street; by now, the DPP, Major Sir Thomas Chalmers Hetherington KCB, CBE, QC, TD, had called on Sir David McNee to express his concern about (a) the expertise of the investigators, and (b) the length of time these enquiries were taking.

The Police Federation was concerned, too. Their chairman, Jim Jardine, stated, 'I do detest anybody who is crooked, but I do think some of the enquiries have taken a long time.'

On 8 July 1979 the *News of the World* reported, 'When it first began nine months ago, enquires were expected to last no more than two months; but now the investigation is likely to take two years.'

The *NoW* didn't know the half of it.

*

It was Thames Valley Police officers in charge of 'Operation Julie' (named after one of the 800 officers recruited from ten different police forces) who broke up one of the world's biggest manufacturers of the hallucinogenic drug LSD in the late 1970s. In March 1978 the fifteen-strong gang were jailed at Bristol Crown Court, where sentences of between two and thirteen years' imprisonment were imposed. When the syndicate was arrested, the officers found accounts of the manufacturing process which revealed a shortfall of two million 'tabs' of the drug; they were told that the discrepancy was as a result of manufacturing failure. Now some members of the jailed syndicate alleged that they had bribed members of the Met's Drugs Squad, and in August 1979 this led to two of the serving prisoners taking Countryman officers, plus those from Bedfordshire Constabulary, known as 'Operation Craig' (named after the son of one of the officers), to Steppingly Woods, near Flitwick, Bedfordshire. There, in glass jars buried 3ft below the surface to protect them from frost and temperature variation, were found one million 'tabs', with an estimated street value of £5–8 million in the UK (and possibly as much as £15 million in other parts of the world). The tabs had originally sold for £1 each; however, due to the initial seizure, their value had risen dramatically.

Leonard Burt confidentially told the press that the find resulted from 'information from the most delicate but reliable sources'. But what did it prove? Nothing, except that the 'Julie' officers had been lied to regarding the manufacturing shortfall and that, knowing the precise location, the gang members had buried them there as a nest-egg for when they were finally released. Then perhaps, not liking prison one bit had forced this disclosure, in the hope of a little early parole. And if the syndicate members had lied to the 'Julie' officers, had they also lied to the Countryman officers? Corrupt Drugs Squad officers? This was strongly denied by the Met's Commissioner, but if they were crooked, certainly nobody was convicted, charged or even suspended.

*

By October 1979 Deputy Commissioner Kavanagh wanted to know which direction the Countryman enquiry was taking; Burt responded by saying that the DPP was taking too long to make a decision on a report which he had submitted five months previously, although McNee would later say that he had been told that this was due to inadequacies contained in the report.

It was pointed out to Burt that he had launched enquiries which far exceeded his original brief and that he was hoarding information regarding officers accused of misconduct. This Burt denied. Kavanagh reminded Burt that under the provisions of the 1964 Police Act (from which the enquiry had commenced) he (Kavanagh) was fully entitled to be kept informed of matters which affected discipline within his Force; and Hambleton, who was also present, saw the wisdom of this and agreed that that course should be taken.

But another month went by and still no such information was received at the Yard. McNee, furious, wrote to Hambleton demanding details of allegations made against his officers and stating that if he, Hambleton, or Burt felt that they were being obstructed in any way in their investigations they should let him know, and he would deal with it.

Later the same month, there was a meeting at the Yard; present were McNee, Kavanagh, the DPP, Burt and Hambleton, the latter bringing with him some of the information which had been requested. Hambleton told McNee the rest of the details would follow shortly and that thereafter there would be a steady flow of information. He also agreed that no further branches of the enquiry would commence without prior consultation. So there was a little, fairly satisfactory horse-trading going on which was considerably assisted when the DPP offered Countryman a full-time member of his staff, an offer which was accepted.

It was a prudent move. It would not have been needed in the Met, where officers, apart from attending courses at the Detective Training School to keep up to speed with current legislation and criminal case law, were also attending courts on a very regular basis, something their constabulary counterparts – if they were real detectives at all – were not. Additionally, Met officers knew how to prepare comprehensive reports for the DPP, knew what was relevant information and what was not. If all of the information was not available to be included in the initial report, i.e. additional statements, photographs, exhibits, plans, then this would be mentioned in the report, with the assurance that these other important matters would be included in supplementary reports, and in this way the DPP would be kept up to speed as to what was happening with the enquiry.

Therefore, since the provincial officers did not have this expertise, the DPP's representative would be in a position to guide Countryman as to what were, and what were not, pertinent lines of enquiry, as well as what were or were not acceptable levels of evidence necessary to secure convictions.

But it was not such a smooth ride as one would have hoped. Kenneth Dowling, a representative of the DPP, refused permission for a Countryman superintendent to interview a prisoner on remand at Brixton prison; the officer went anyway. The furious DPP wrote to Hambleton, 'I find this cavalier treatment of Treasury Counsel and my department quite unacceptable.' This was followed by a report in the *Sunday Times* in which Burt stated he was angry at the way both the Met and the DPP were obstructing his enquiries.

This was a jaw-dropping and unprecedented suggestion to make: that the Director of Public Prosecutions, whose office at 4–12 Queen Anne's Gate was responsible for dealing with all serious offences in the United Kingdom (plus the British Dominions beyond the seas), was actually obstructing enquiries into criminal investigations; in fact, nothing comparable would be heard for almost another forty years, when the President-elect of the United States, Donald Trump, stated that his intelligence agencies had leaked salacious information about him.

If Burt was angry, McNee was furious and the DPP was incandescent with rage. On 7 December 1979 a meeting was called at the Yard. Present were Hambleton, Ernie Bright, the City's Assistant Commissioner, the DPP and Kavanagh. A detailed press statement was prepared which read as follows:

OPERATION COUNTRYMAN

1. This press statement is issued to explain the current position and to correct some of the misleading reports which have appeared in recent weeks about Operation Countryman.

2. In August 1978, H.M. Chief Inspector of Constabulary following a request by the Commissioner of the City of London Police, asked the Chief Constable of Dorset to provide a senior officer to investigate alleged irregularities by detectives of the City of London Force. At the same time, the Deputy Commissioner of the Metropolitan Police asked that associated allegations about Metropolitan Police officers be included in the investigation. I, Leonard Burt, the Assistant Chief Constable of Dorset, was appointed with a number of detectives.

3. As enquiries progressed, it became necessary to augment the team and a total of 80 detectives with supporting clerical staff are now engaged. This does not mean that the allegations against police officers received by Operation Countryman have dramatically increased, indeed some of the complaints received have been investigated and proved unfounded.

4. Five officers of the Metropolitan police have been suspended from duty and files have been submitted to the Director of Public Prosecutions for proceedings against four of these officers. A City of London officer has been charged, appeared at court and will be dealt with in the future.

5. During the whole of the enquiry, constant consultations have taken place with the staff of the Director of Public Prosecutions and on several occasions have sought the advice of the Director. Additionally, on two occasions, advice has been obtained from the Attorney-General and the Director jointly.

6. Suggestions that the Countryman investigations have been obstructed are completely without truth. I and my officers have received the fullest cooperation and every assistance from the Director and the two Commissioners. In particular, the Director has acceded to a request I made concerning the giving of certain limited undertakings to persons helping our enquiries, and I unhesitatingly accept that, when criminal proceedings against police officers are being considered, there can be no departure from the evidential requirements which apply to civilian suspects.

7. Recently, the Director of Public Prosecutions has made available a senior member of his legal staff to advise me and my senior officers and he now occupies an office at Godalming police station in the Countryman suite.

8. My detectives are working extremely hard, they are dedicated and have the will to succeed; they are undaunted by some reports that have appeared in the press and other media. Events in the future will prove that the Countryman team have been more than adequate for its task and that any difficulties they have encountered have been overcome.

9. This statement has been seen by the Commissioners of the Metropolitan and the City of London Police and the Director of the Public Prosecutions.

This was what many would consider to be what is colloquially known as 'a whitewash'. Hambleton was asked to get Burt to append his signature to it but was initially unwilling to do so. However, Hambleton later stated, the DPP pointed out to him that if this press statement was not released, he – the DPP, not Hambleton – would have to resign. Precisely why it would have been necessary for the Director to tender his resignation in those circumstances is not entirely clear, but in any event, this was later absolutely, categorically denied by the Director. Be that as it may, since Hambleton himself was due to resign from the police within a matter of months, this might well have adversely affected the prospect of any half-promised knighthood. In danger of being crushed between a rock and a hard place, Hambleton (who would later state, 'Reluctantly, I approved the statement to keep the operation together') telephoned Burt at home and read him the text of the statement. Burt refused to sign, at least until he had read it himself, so Hambleton drove down to see him the same day with the statement. It's not known what blandishments Hambleton used to get Burt to sign the document (which was then circulated to the press) – perhaps the promise of appointment as Chief Constable of Dorset? But whatever happened, Burt never did become Chief Constable of Dorset or anywhere else; and although Hambleton subsequently became a Knight of the Order of St John, that was nice but not quite as nice as being tapped on the shoulder with a ceremonial sword by Her Majesty.

In his memoirs, as previously mentioned, McNee had stated that at that meeting on 7 December Hambleton had told Kavanagh that Don Neesham had been unhelpful to the Countryman team and that as a result, 'It was decided to move Neesham to other duties. When told of this, however, he exercised his right to retire on pension.'

However, this was quite wrong. We already know that Neesham had retired over six months previously, on 30 April; and that is a matter of record. This, in part was corroborated by Hambleton, when he later appeared in a *World in Action* television programme: Kavanagh had disputed any obstruction by police and Hambleton had replied, 'What about this man Neesham? He obstructed us', and Kavanagh had replied, 'Well, we moved Neesham for you.' In the same programme, both the DPP and Kavanagh denied that Neesham had been discussed.

Well, well. A real can of worms; and yet it was the Met and the City detectives who were supposed to be up to no good.

The Times was of the opinion that 'If Countryman suffers the slings and arrows of criticism and speculation, the Metropolitan Police must feel like an encircled wagon train.' Morale was under attack; one rumour circulating was that senior officers at the Yard wanted nothing better than mass resignations from the CID; and even though that piece of gossip was unlikely and unrealistic, as a rumour it was damaging. One matter which was circulated and was far more believable was that even when the Met chalked up a success with spectacular arrests in a high profile case, it was submerged by fresh reports and allegations from Countryman.

For years, the Yard and the press had enjoyed a harmonious relationship. During the post-war years, Reggie Spooner, the head of the Flying Squad, would meet reporters and journalists in the snug bar of the Red Lion pub, next to the Yard, each evening. There he would tell them which stories to publish – and more importantly, what not to publish, asking them to hold back until he could give them the go-ahead to publish something really sensational. It worked well. In later years, journalists would pass on allegations of misconduct to CIB2 rather than publish them first, and this, too, worked well.

But now things had changed. In late 1979, police periodicals (not *The Job,* the Met's in-house newspaper, which was regarded by most as being sycophantic trash) such as *Police Review* were going on the offensive and attacking some newspapers for their pro-Countryman content; and there was increasing concern that an atmosphere of distrust was growing between police and the press which in turn would affect public confidence.

Now it's time to leave the high politics of this matter and return to see what business was being conducted in the City of London – and I assure you, much of it was monkey.

CHAPTER 16

Eleven months had passed since John Simmonds had covertly taped Cuthbert, and the tension towards him in the City Police was rising, palpably. He received a telephone call from a friend in the Met who told him that a fellow police officer was running him (Simmonds) down, saying that he was a grass and 'to watch out for him'.

One of Simmonds' detectives told him that he had been stopped in the street by an unknown man who told the officer to tell Simmonds to watch out because certain people were after him and were going to 'fit him up'. Simmonds told me:

> The credibility of the story did not hold up but I knew this officer; he was in my opinion one of many who had been caught up in the corruption, against his will. He knew about, or was even party to, the discussions that had taken place, and it was more than he could take – and this was the only way he could warn me. I had other threats and I always said if anyone were to do anything to me, they should do it properly, because otherwise I would come back with vengeance at them.

Simmonds was telephoned by a man who provided only his first name; and Simmonds recognized neither the name nor his voice. But he saw the man in his office and identified him as being someone he had met during the Richardson 'Torture Trial' enquiry, some twelve years previously. During the conversation it became clear that the man was involved on the fringes of a fraud enquiry, and more importantly, he had been in the company of three City detectives in a public house when the conversation had turned to Simmonds. They had asked the man if he could provide incriminating information about Simmonds, since they were going to try to find something either to put Simmonds away or to fit him up. These detectives were working for a man whom they referred to as 'Hughie', and Simmonds' contact believed his surname was 'Moore'.

'In one of his outbursts at me, Moore threatened he would get me', Simmonds told me, 'and obviously they were digging deep.'

Just how deep was demonstrated next.

Simmonds' wife, Barbara, received a parcel in the post at their home in Hertfordshire. Her name and address were correct, although the postcode was hopelessly wrong. She was not expecting a parcel, so she put it in the garage and telephoned her husband.

When the package was opened, it revealed a ladies' gold watch and an invoice numbered 295062, together with a complimentary slip from the Customer Service Department of Timex Corporation, Dundee, Scotland. The slip read as follows:

> Reference your watch recently returned with complaint. Enclosed please find a replacement watch, which we trust you will find to your complete satisfaction. With apologies for the inconvenience caused.

This was a handsome apology and a generous gesture on behalf of Timex, except for one matter – Barbara Simmonds had never sent Timex a gold watch for repair; in fact, she had never owned one.

Simmonds spoke to the Customer Service Department, who agreed that they had indeed received a watch from a 'Mrs Simmonds' but said that it was not their policy to repair watches; it was far simpler, said a Mr McGregor, to send the aggrieved customer a new one instead. The watch that Timex had received? They had simply recovered the gold case and scrapped the rest.

Simmonds sent the following letter, dated 23 August 1979, to Timex:

Dear Mr McGregor,

I refer to our telephone conversation on Tuesday 21 August 1979, respecting the watch delivered to my wife.

My wife thanks you for your offer regarding the watch, but nevertheless feels that it would be right to return it to you in the hope that it may be forwarded to the rightful owner.

We have exhausted our enquiries of friends and relatives who may have possibly sent the original watch to you for repair, and in returning it to you, I ask that should you possibly find the answer, that you be so kind as to let us know.

Thanking you once again,

Yours faithfully,
J.J. Simmonds

As Simmonds told me:

> I could see the sinister aspect of this; a stolen watch had
> obviously been sent for repair in my wife's name. The
> sender was relying upon us thinking it was our lucky day
> and keeping it when it was sent back. Obviously, at some
> stage, an 'anonymous' tip-off would be made to some
> police agency and the watch would be 'found'. The men-
> tality of this scam had all the hallmarks of a particular
> detective that I knew, but I was never going to be able to
> prove it. I immediately rang the ACC, Ernie Bright, to log
> yet another 'attack'. I handed in the watch and let it be
> known that I had done so, just to prevent some innocent
> police agency being caught up in this dirty war.

Before we go on to the next chapter in the City of London Police
Force's criminality – as was claimed by Countryman – we have
to pause to seek the assistance of one Peter Miller who, thanks to
keeping a number of very old diaries, was able to cobble together
some interesting data regarding the Countryman enquiry.

*

On 24 November 1977, Miller – then a detective sergeant (and also
the senior CID officer) at Hatfield police station, Hertfordshire
Constabulary – was at Springhill Prison in the Thames Valley
Police area interviewing an inmate, when one of his detective constables contacted him saying that City of London officers, including DCI Cuthbert, had requested local assistance. A search was
being conducted at a transport café on the A1 trunk road run by
one Charlie Ackerman, who was subsequently arrested and taken,
with property which had been seized, to Hatfield police station.

By the time Miller had finished his interview at the prison and
returned to Hatfield, Ackerman had been bailed for one month,
the City officers had gone and Miller was left to deal with identi-
fying the property.

There was some crockery – identified as being part of the
Timothy Whites collection – and also some of the popular Fabergé's
Brut shaving cream. Miller told me:

> On the bottom of the box was the number 1457,
> which referred to the branch of Boots the Chemists at
> Waltham Cross. This had been in Boots' possession until
> 6 September 1977, but they didn't know when it had

disappeared. From memory, I think they had cages of mixed products for transportation to branches. I recall having a security chap down from Nottingham to identify it, but unfortunately, whilst they could say it was theirs, they were unable to prove it was stolen. I had a closing interview with Ackerman when he surrendered to bail on 22 December 1977. He stated he believed it was bankrupt stock. As we couldn't prove a theft, it followed we couldn't charge handling, so he was released. I can't be 100 per cent sure on the property but I think we may have invited him to disclaim it and it went back to Boots. A file was submitted to our headquarters, as was the case in those days.

And that was the end of that; a fairly no-account case, which had been properly investigated but had failed to produce a charge.

But almost two years later, on Tuesday, 11 September 1979, the case was resurrected when Miller was interviewed at Welwyn Garden between 2.15pm and 4.15pm by Detective Superintendent McLaren from Avon and Somerset Police who was then part of the Countryman team. As Miller recalls:

The opening of the interview was him asking me if I was a Freemason. I replied that I was not, and McLaren said he would check it out and find out if I was. I did think that if this was important, he should have done his homework before my interview. His attitude put me in the suspect category, although I was not formerly cautioned. The interview revolved around the search at Ackerman's, and the accusation was that Cuthbert had said that the purpose of the search was to recover a firearm. This was the first I'd heard of it; had there been a suggestion that there had been a firearm on the premises, I should have contacted a senior officer so that a proper operation could have been mounted. There was also a suggestion that we, the local CID, had conspired with Ackerman in some form to ensure there was no prosecution. This, of course, was quite untrue, but that was what I was suspected of. There is another issue that I always felt was connected in some way. On the very large forefront of Ackerman's café was a large trailer, where fresh veg was sold on a daily basis. We established on a previous occasion that the guy running the veg sales came from Brixton. I can't recall his name. I had my suspicions that he was connected to

robberies, as we occasionally recovered vehicles that had
been stolen from Brixton and used in crime. Around this
time I submitted an intelligence report on my suspicions,
hoping that someone had the capacity to do some work
on it, and I often wondered if the two matters were connected. I wasn't made any the wiser by the Countryman
interviews, although I'm sure I told them of this.

The following day, I was again interviewed by two
Countryman officers between 5.00pm & 8.30pm regarding the same matters, during which time they took a statement from me.

On 1 November 1979 I was attending the advanced
CID course at Hendon. I was recalled to force and
between 4.30pm and 6.30pm that day I went to Hatfield
police station for a further interview with Detective
Superintendent McLaren; during this time, we made a
tour of the transport cafes on the A1 and I again made a
statement.

On 22 November 1979 I was recalled once more from
the course and between 2.00pm and 5.20pm I was interviewed by Detective Sergeant Rice from Countryman.
Again, I made a statement. By coincidence, there was a
detective sergeant from the City of London attending the
same course and he was interviewed about the same time
as me. It was about this time that Countryman arrested
Ackerman and, without additional evidence, charged him
with receiving stolen property. When the case got to court
it was discontinued, because no theft could be proved; I
had told them that, several times.

Finally, on 30 November 1982, I was seen by a
Countryman officer who wanted to take a witness statement from me, I was told, to be used in connection with
disciplinary proceedings against Cuthbert. I remember
commenting that by this action I was no longer a suspect,
but I got no response.

Well, that was interesting. By that date, Cuthbert was four months
into his three-year prison sentence, so it's debatable as to how or
why disciplinary proceedings could be instituted against him. But
it appears the whole matter as far as Miller was concerned was
dealt with in a cack-handed manner. Four interviews as a suspect,
without being cautioned, where the same matters were dealt with
over and over again – two of them taking place not only when
Miller was attending a course, very important to his career, but

also at a time guaranteed to cause him the maximum embarrassment with his classmates and instructors.

Miller's views on Countryman?

> Their interviews were more formal than anything, except
> for the initial contact by McLaren when he was referring to
> Freemasonry; that was more aggressive. I got the impression
> that they didn't believe me or were looking for something
> that they had knowledge of, which they didn't share with me.
> As the ranks of the interviewing officers reduced, they were
> a little less formal but not friendly. From my short time with
> them I got the impression that they were somewhat naïve.
> Working on the Met borders, there were occasions when our
> investigations were frustrated in one way or another and you
> felt you had to keep your cards close to your chest. I don't
> think Countryman were switched on to the sort of things
> that they may have been confronted with. They didn't seem
> to understand the law, i.e. if you couldn't prove theft, then
> you couldn't prove handling stolen property. This was shown
> clearly when without additional evidence they charged
> Ackerman and the prosecution subsequently collapsed.

I have seen a copy of the witness statement taken from Miller to prove disciplinary matters against Cuthbert; it did nothing of the kind. It was not timed or dated, nor was it countersigned by the officer writing it; in fact, it was badly scrawled gibberish. Somehow, this did not surprise me in the slightest.

It appeared that round about that time Countryman were making themselves busy in the county of Hertfordshire. One City officer told me:

> I was told to come to headquarters at Old Jewry regard-
> ing a football meeting. Since this was on a Saturday, I
> thought this was a bit odd, but I went because I wanted to
> be selected to play for the team the following week. There
> was no football meeting. Instead, I was interviewed by
> Countryman regarding a firearm which had been found
> in Hertfordshire – I think it might have been to do with
> the robbery at the Williams & Glyn's bank. I knew nothing
> about it. But their questioning was repetitive; they asked
> the same questions over and over.

It appeared that Countryman were unable to profit from their past mistakes; blundering questions in respect of Peter Miller which

City of London Police:
(*Above left*) DCS John Simmonds. (*Above right*) DS John Golbourn and DCI Phil Cuthbert.
(*Below*) Wood Street police station.

The Men in the Know about the Dorset Enquiry:
(*Above left*) Commissioner Peter Marshall.
(*Above right*) Commander Hugh Moore.
(*Right*) Assistant Commissioner Wilford Gibson.

The Law Administrators:
(*Above left*) The DPP Sir Thomas Hetherington.
(*Above right*) Home Secretary Merlyn Rees.
(*Right*) The Old Bailey.

The Men at the Yard – the Administrators: (*Right*) Commissioner Sir David McNee. (*Below*) DAC David Powis. (*Below right*) DAC Ron Steventon.

**The Men at the Yard –
the Flying Squad:**
(*Top left*) Commander
John O'Connor.
(*Top right*) Commander
Don Neesham.
(*Above*) D/Supt. Tony
Lundy.
(*Right*) Ch. Supt. Bob
Robinson.

Operation Countryman – Headquarters:
(*Above*) Camberwell police station.
(*Below*) The top of the car park at Godalming police station.

Operation Countryman – Head Men:
(*Left*) Sir Peter Matthews. (*Right*) Arthur Hambleton.

Operation Countryman – the Investigators:
(*Left*) ACC Leonard Burt. (*Right*) DCS Steve Whitby.

The Accusers:
(*Above*) Two heroic blaggers going about their daily chores…
(*Below*) and Billy Tobin taking a rest from his.

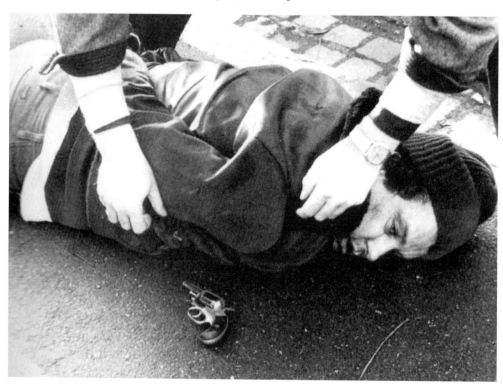

led nowhere, a cunning ruse to question an officer about a firearm which he knew nothing about, then Ackerman's failed prosecution, followed a bare three months later by a similar charge against Cuthbert – which, as we shall see, possessed the same humiliating lack of evidence.

*

With Cuthbert having been suspended for twelve months, Countryman decided to arrest and charge him; 'High time, too', many might say. After all, they had convincing evidence of serious criminality, thanks to the covert tape recording, and during the intervening period they had also obtained persuasive corroborative evidence to bring about a conviction. However, it was not only the charge which was contentious; so was the way in which the arrest had been achieved and the court proceedings which followed.

Phil Cuthbert had been charged with dishonestly handling a hi-fi music centre, an infra-red light, an ultra-violet light, a portable TV, a clock radio, an electric blanket, eleven containers of toothpaste, razor blades and nine packets of toilet paper, valued approximately at £500. These items had apparently been stolen from a Boots the Chemists' depot in Hertfordshire two years previously, and it was alleged that Cuthbert had assisted in their retention and disposal by or for the benefit of one Terry Wackett in the Edgware Road over that two-year period. Cuthbert had then appeared at Hatfield Magistrates' Court, where the prosecution was conducted not by the DPP's representative, who just a few days previously had been attached to the Countryman enquiry, but by a local country solicitor from Dorset. Cuthbert had been remanded in police custody for three days and was spirited away to Dorset.

It was the type of arrest and charge which, if a junior Flying Squad detective constable had carried it out, would have caused his detective inspector to take him on one side and tersely demand to know if his subordinate would not feel happier working at Upminster, Potters Bar or one of the Met's other outlying police stations; preferably in uniform.

Following Cuthbert's stay in Dorset, he appeared again at Hatfield Magistrates' Court on 12 November 1979 and was remanded on £10,000 bail until 10 December.

Hambleton would later say in a television interview:

> We arrested Cuthbert on a holding charge. It was to do
> with stolen property which we suspected he had been
> keeping. We wanted him out of the way because we

thought he had been squaring witnesses and interfering with honest policemen who might be able to give evidence. My officers also wished to interrogate him about information we thought he had about senior officers who had been receiving bribes, not only in the City but in the Met as well.

Michael Chance, representing the DPP, went to Godalming and, as he told me, 'I called for a report on the case as a matter of extreme urgency. They said the report had not been prepared. The report reached me shortly afterwards. I was shocked to find there was no evidence whatever that could possibly support a charge of handling stolen goods.'

The DPP was livid – understandably – and not for the first time. On 15 February 1980 he wrote as follows to City of London Commissioner, Peter Marshall:

Dear Peter,

Having given careful consideration to all the evidence, I have no doubt at all that it is quite insufficient to justify this, or any other charge. Quite apart from the fact that there is no corroboration from Wackett's claim that DCI Cuthbert knew that his informant was in possession of stolen property which is alleged to have occurred between the two, it could not in law amount to an offence under the 1968 act.

I feel bound to express my concern at the arrest and subsequent remand in police custody of DCI Cuthbert, particularly since Wackett, on whose allegation it was principally if not solely placed, was not even available as a witness.

It is indeed a matter of regret that the investigating officers proceeded without prior consultation with my department to which all such cases are properly referable but instead sought the assistance of the principal prosecuting solicitor of Dorset.

Whether DCI Cuthbert will seek further compensation by means of civil proceedings, remains to be seen . . .

Although DCS Steve Whitby 'pleaded' (in Hambleton's words) 'with the DPP's representative not to drop the charges', that was exactly what happened. On 25 February 1980 – just three days after Superintendent McLaren's astonishing bail application for Shaw – Chance told the Magistrates at Hatfield that 'The Director of Public Prosecutions has formed the view that the available evidence is quite insufficient to support this charge', and the case was dismissed.

'The first to be told was Cuthbert's solicitor', stated Hambleton indignantly, and that is what happens when one follows correct procedures.

That was Irving Shine, who outside the court stated, 'We shall write to the City Police Commissioner confirming the situation and requesting that Mr Cuthbert be reinstated.'

Well, there was a fat chance of that happening, because the City Police issued a statement saying, 'Detective Chief Inspector Cuthbert was suspended from duty on November 7 1978 and notwithstanding his appearance at Hatfield Magistrates' Court, he remains suspended from duty as the matters for which he was originally suspended are still under active investigation.'

Hambleton would later sorrowfully state, 'My chaps had worked very, very hard at cultivating informants, and at a stroke that confidence in us was lost. They thought, what's the good of us giving this evidence if the DPP wasn't going to prosecute?'

But it utterly beggared belief that a Police Force could act in such a way; it was clear that Countryman was completely out of control, that they were making up their own rules as they went along. Supporting a bail application for a serial armed robber after the officers in the case opposed it? Getting their own tame solicitor to represent them when they had the representative of the second highest law officer in the land in their office? Remanding a prisoner on a piddling charge in police custody for three days? On what grounds – that he was likely to step on the cracks in the pavement?

'I certainly think it was nevertheless unwise to consult the Dorset Police in-house lawyer when they were already in touch with one of my colleagues (now deceased) about other aspects of the enquiry', Chance told me. 'What I said at Hatfield Court was intended to reflect the reality of the situation. It was reported that evening in, I think, the *Evening Standard*. The decision to abandon the charge was received with fury, despite the fact that the essential ingredients of the offence were clearly absent.'

Met officers hugged themselves with delicious anticipation; what on earth would 'The Swedey' do next? Well, nothing really, said the sensible ones – Countryman really had shot their bolt. Nothing could trump *that*, they reasoned.

They were wrong. In a jaw-dropping act of impertinence, Burt now ordered the DPP's representative to leave the Countryman headquarters; he refused, and Burt and the rest of his staff sent him to Coventry.

Well, that's enough of that for the time being. Let's leave Burt, puce in the face, probably feeling like a one-legged man in an arse-kicking competition and wondering if his Dorset solicitor should apply for an eviction order in respect of the recalcitrant lawyer. Because now we turn to something that happened one week after the Cuthbert debacle. In fact, it was nothing to do with Countryman and everything to do with the City of London Police, who came within a gnat's whisker of being disbanded.

CHAPTER 17

Despite the hilarity of the Met officers at Countryman's latest gaffe, morale in the City of London was at a very low ebb; shoulders were being cautiously looked over, rumours and counter-rumours were rife and it was anybody's guess who, if anybody, would be suspended next. John Simmonds made efforts to keep organizational matters going and moved several officers around, some because they'd got into ruts, others to give them greater scope for their capabilities. One who fitted this scenario was a detective constable named Leslie Nugent. He was attached to Wood Street and was described as 'a quiet chap who did his job'; but Simmonds considered that Nugent had been at the station for too long, so he moved him to Bishopsgate, which was considered the busiest of the three stations.

Simmonds was also concerned at the number of night-time burglaries which had recently occurred on Bishopgate's ground and he decided to visit the station at night. There he met the night-duty CID team, Nugent and another detective constable named David Chapman. Simmonds takes up the tale:

> Chapman was an active detective and very up-front. By the way he expressed himself in my presence it was obvious that detective chief superintendents had not made too many night supervisory visits in the City. I gave him licence for his attitude and spoke of the state of recent crime reports. I had the chance to speak to Leslie Nugent on his own and asked him how the move was going. Leslie looked at me and said that I did not know what I had done to him. I tried to draw him out, but he would not expand further.

On Sunday, 2 March 1980, Simmonds was taking it easy at home on a day off when he received a telephone call from Detective Chief Inspector Tim Hillier from Wood Street. Hillier was one of the officers whom Moore had 'sidelined', but Simmonds knew him to be very sound and trustworthy, so when Hillier told him that he needed to see him very urgently and with no questions asked, at Archway tube station at the top of Holloway Road, there was no doubt in Simmonds' mind that this was a real emergency – and he was right.

As Simmonds pulled up at Archway, so Hillier got into his car, together with a Temporary Detective Constable named Graham Cruttenden. Simmonds recounts what happened next:

Graham told me he had just finished Night-Duty CID. During the night, there had been a call to Austin Reed outfitters, where a beat PC had found the premises inse-cure. The Night-Duty CID, the duty officer, dog handler and some others had attended, and in fact, although the premises were insecure, there had been no break-in. What happened next beggared belief: six officers then set about helping themselves to items from the shop. Graham had told them they must be mad, but they ignored him. One officer pressed a leather wallet into his hand and told him to have it; he threw it on the floor and told them he wanted nothing to do with it. Once they had their fill they then left the premises and recorded the situation as a burglary.

With the Force under the sword of Countryman, I just for the life of me could not understand what was in the minds of those officers. This could have been the end of the City Police.

I took Tim Hillier and Graham to my office in Old Jewry and took a full statement from Graham. I put in a call to Assistant Commissioner Ernie Bright as he was responsible for Force Discipline. Ernie felt that this was a serious matter and we should call in an outside Force to investigate it. I pleaded with him to give me the chance to show that the City Police were not as bad as the media were making us out. I said I would show them that we could do our own dirty washing. If we called in an outside Force they would take a day or two to get their act together and we might lose the goods. I was equally not confident that if we called in a similar team to Countryman that they would be any better than Countryman were.

Ernie accepted my argument and let me continue. I rang all the DCIs and DIs . . . and told them I wanted them in the office immediately; no one demurred. While I waited for them all to arrive, we obtained search warrants for the officers' addresses. When I had everyone in I told them that the future of the City Police rested in their hands; I was going to send them out in pairs to the addresses and any one of them could blow it by telephoning the officers concerned. As I was aware some of the officers knew the individuals well, I offered them the choice of which premises they preferred to do.

The teams went out and all recovered stolen property from the premises or from locations personal to the officers concerned. David Chapman and Leslie Nugent were two of those arrested. I spoke to Leslie later because I just knew this was not in his nature, but all he would say was that he tried to warn me. I have always felt sorry for him. He was working with a strong personality and did not have the strength to say 'no'. He was never a villain.

That last statement was somewhat obliquely backed up by a former City officer who, referring to the Austin Reed burglary, told me, 'That wasn't villainy; that was opportunism.'

When you compare it to what else had happened in the City Police – incitement to murder, accepting bribes on a massive scale, diluting evidence so that robbers and murderers could walk free, plus, of course, trying to fit-up John Simmonds' wife with a stolen watch – perhaps stealing goods worth £2,700 might be considered pretty small beer. I suppose it depends on your point of view.

'I'd just come on duty when I saw Les Nugent getting out of a police car in handcuffs', another City officer told me. 'It affected all of us.'

It especially affected Graham Cruttenden, who, at 6' 8" and weighing in at 20 stone, had led a pretty peripatetic life. Born in 1946, he had served in the Household Cavalry and as a fireman in Hertfordshire before becoming a member of Australia's Northern Territory police for three years. He joined Sussex police in 1975, before transferring to the City in 1977. Having seen his colleagues helping themselves to clothes, suitcases, squash rackets and golf balls, he did what he saw as his duty and reported them; it was a very brave thing to do.

So that was the Sunday. On the following Tuesday Inspector Brian Deacon ('a lovely bloke'), Sergeant Stanley Isley, Acting Sergeant and dog handler Fred Jolley BEM, Police Constable Richard Burgess, plus Chapman and Nugent, all appeared at the Mansion House Justice Rooms. All had been suspended from duty; now they were remanded until they were committed for trial at the Old Bailey.

When they appeared at that court on 1 September 1980, five of the officers pleaded guilty. Deacon – described as 'an outstanding officer' – was sentenced to eighteen months' imprisonment. Isley received fifteen months, Nugent, twelve months, and Jolley, aged forty-seven and with twenty-seven years' service, nine months. Sentence was deferred on Burgess.

Only Chapman denied the charge. PC Cruttenden told the court that when he entered the shop he saw four officers helping themselves to clothing and that Chapman had pushed two wallets into Cruttenden's anorak, saying, 'Go on, take them, they're tasty wallets.' Disregarding the stolen property which had been found at his home, Chapman's defence was that Cruttenden's evidence could not be relied upon because he was mentally unstable. To authenticate this, he called Hugh Moore; not as a character witness but as a defence witness.

Moore – who had been furious when Simmonds had neglected to inform him of the intended raids on the officers' premises – now attended the Old Bailey to state that because Cruttenden had had a period of sickness due to stress, he doubted his sanity. Moore had been credited with a high IQ – another officer told me that, having seen him previously at court, 'He was very good in the witness box; he was cunning and shrewd – he parried counsel with ease' – but he was not as clever as all that.

Appearing for the prosecution was the late Miss Ann Curnow QC (later Her Honour Judge Curnow), a barrister who was much admired and to my own personal knowledge was as sharp as a tack (during cross-examination in a rape trial, the defendant asked for a glass of water. 'Of course you must have some water', replied Miss Curnow soothingly. 'With all those dreadful lies you're telling, your mouth must be getting awfully dry!').

Miss Curnow produced a sheet from Cruttenden's file. It revealed that within days of Cruttenden returning from sick leave, Moore had personally sanctioned his attendance at a firearms course. It was not the sort of recommendation a senior officer would reasonably make if he believed the man concerned was suffering from mental instability. This was impossible for Moore to wriggle out of. It made him look a fool and quite probably contributed to the jury finding Chapman guilty.

The court was told that in the past ten years of Chapman's service he had been commended for bravery and efficiency on eleven occasions; nevertheless, he was sentenced to eighteen months' imprisonment.

Although Judge Buzzard told Cruttenden, 'You deserve the highest praise for resisting the great temptation to join in but more particularly the temptation to keep your mouth shut', it was too late to save his career in the City Police.

As John Simmonds told me:

Graham Cruttenden's life was made a misery. We moved him to Snow Hill police station but officers refused to work with him and there was graffiti in the toilets about him. His family became involved and they received hate phone calls and letters at home. In the end, he was unable to endure the pressure any longer and we arranged his transfer to another Force.

By the time the case had come to trial, Cruttenden had moved to Hampshire Constabulary. He said that it had been the hardest decision of his life to report his colleagues. He had considered forgetting the episode and resigning from the Force, but after a talk with his wife he decided to tell a senior officer what had happened.

But that was not the end of the controversies which surrounded Cruttenden. During his posting on the Isle of Wight, he became both a dog handler and a schools liaison officer, and in 1995 allegations were made that Cruttenden had committed indecent assaults on a boy a number of years previously; Cruttenden denied the allegations, and the person concerned decided not to pursue the matter. When the accusation was repeated a year later, the police started an investigation and Cruttenden was suspended from duty. Charged with offences of sexual abuse, Cruttenden hanged himself in his garage.

His partner complained that his oppressive treatment by Hampshire Police had resulted in Cruttenden taking his own life, and the controversy rumbles on, surrounding the life and death of a man who, whatever else might have been said about him, possessed considerable moral courage in the City of London.

*

Time to leave the badly bruised and battered City of London and return to see what Countryman and their intrepid crimebusters are up to. Actually, much the same as always . . .

CHAPTER 18

His real name was Stanley Houghton – he was known as Sacheverell Stanley Walton Houghton – and he was a consummate conman who also used the name De Houghton-Crewe. Born in 1940, he first hit the headlines in 1964 when he was sentenced to twelve months' hard labour in Cork for stealing silver and jewellery from a Dublin antique dealer – but he was not, alas, a former Irish Guards officer, nor had he been educated at Eton or been a member of the Foreign Office, as he claimed. He had, however, been one of a number of people concerned in the theft of £2 million in different currencies from Heathrow Airport in June 1976. Following the theft, a large amount of the money was taken to Dublin, and early in July the Garda recovered about £1 million. Other money had also been recovered, but there appeared to be a shortfall of £500,000. The insurance company offered a reward of £125,000 for information leading to the recovery of this money plus the arrest and conviction of those responsible. Having returned from Dublin, Houghton went straight to the police, saying he had information regarding those responsible for the theft, in order to claim the reward. It soon became clear to the officers that Houghton, despite his previous denials, was deeply involved in the theft himself, and he was charged, as were other members of the gang. At his trial, Houghton claimed that the police had led him to believe that he was being treated as an informant who would be immune from prosecution, but this was rejected by judge and jury, and Houghton, the possessor of five previous convictions for dishonesty (plus two substantial prison sentences) was sentenced to five years' imprisonment.

Max Vernon was a Detective Superintendent with CIB2; he was instructed by the Commissioner to investigate allegations of corruption made by Houghton from his Oxford prison cell. Houghton had stated that the detective superintendent whom he had first approached regarding the reward for the theft from Heathrow had accepted a bribe of £100,000.

'Previously, Houghton had been seen by Countryman officers', Vernon told me, 'a detective chief superintendent who until the enquiry had been a chief superintendent in traffic. His DI had been elevated to that rank, having previously been a sergeant, also in traffic. They had been touting for business in different prisons, promising criminals Royal pardons if they incriminated officers.'

Now Vernon went to Godalming to pick up the papers pertinent to the Houghton investigation, whereupon an officer refused him entry. Looking down at the recalcitrant officer from his imposing height of six feet four inches, Vernon told him that unless he was given access to the papers he would return with a warrant and arrest anyone who tried to stop him. That worked; but when he was permitted access to the papers he found:

> They were complete rubbish. They had taken no statements from the criminals. Instead, they had made statements themselves, saying what the villains had told them. I took a long and very detailed statement from Houghton. I proved that everything he said was a lie. He explained exactly where in a hotel he had met the superintendent. I went to the hotel and if I had followed his directions, it would have led me into the middle of the swimming pool. The missing foreign currency was accounted for because the value was wrongly based on the currency exchange rates at the time; a solicitor involved in the investigation came to the same conclusion. I don't believe the bribe ever existed.

*

That was just a further instance in which a cunning conman had bamboozled Countryman, but there were plenty more. Charley Scott told me:

> DCI Dave Bassett and I received information about a hold-up in the planning at the NatWest Bank, Elephant and Castle, which included Patrick Fraser and Henry Richard Wright, aka Harry the Rat. This was about 1980, as I recall – we caught them, got the guns and the money back, all charged – a good job.
>
> This was the time when the prison officers were on strike and no prisoners were appearing on remand. I pitched up at Tower Bridge Magistrates' Court – lo and behold, there were five of them for the hearing.
>
> Conversations took place and Harry said to me (supported by Patrick Fraser) that Countryman had been to see them in Brixton and had offered them a deal – essentially,

that they make allegations against C8 and they would walk
free. I shot back to the office and a senior officer told me
to do a 728 [internal report], and by midday this was on
the Commissioner's desk. Powis told us personally, 'Do
not cooperate with Countryman in any way.'

I asked Harry the Rat if he was going to put his hands
up, he replying that he would wait and see – kept his
options open, so to speak. There were some guilty pleas
– Patrick Fraser, as I remember got a twelve[1] – Harry
denied everything and got ten years. A short time later, a
number of prisoners were being transferred to a new nick
when the van was held up and a number of prisoners were
freed. Harry was on the van and although he was nothing
to do with the escape, he seized his opportunity and had
it away – it took a while to catch him!

★

One of the anomalies of the justice system was the way in which
results at court were recorded. If a defendant was not going to
be proceeded against any longer, he was either acquitted on the
judge's instructions or by the jury; or, if the prosecution offered no
further evidence on a charge, it would be recorded as 'to remain
on the file; not to be proceeded with without leave of the Court
or the Court of Appeal (Criminal Division)'. It came to the same
difference; it meant that the prisoner walked free from court, and
I never, ever heard of a case which had been resurrected from the
Court of Appeal. Ezra Pritchard, then a Detective Inspector with
the Flying Squad, in filling in the result portion of the form to be
sent to the Criminal Records Office, had, due to his enormous
workload, erroneously put in the wrong result – either 'acquitted'
or 'to remain on the file', or vice-versa. He had been interviewed
by Countryman 'loads of times' as he told me, but 'always as a
witness'. Whilst being interviewed by a detective chief inspector
from Countryman and providing him with a witness statement,
this discrepancy suddenly came to light.

'Suddenly, halfway through the statement, I was cautioned',
Prichard told me. 'The matter was soon cleared up, whereupon I
was told, "Right – now you're off caution!"'

His opinion of Countryman and their professionalism? 'Out of
their depth'.

★

Peter Burgess was an Area Car driver and in the late 1970s he was driving 'Lima Three' with PC Jon Shatford as the RT operator. He told me:

> We got an RT call from C8 who wanted assistance to stop a car. We stopped it in Patmos Road, SW9, where the street had been lined with corrugated iron, prior to building the Loughborough Estate there. When the Squad arrived, we took the two occupants of the car into Brixton police station and their car was brought in. That was our involvement and I forgot all about it.
>
> Sometime later Jon and I were interviewed by a super-intendent and a DS from Countryman. I was told, 'Some very serious allegations have been made about you – it's alleged that you forced their car off the road into the cor-rugated iron, pushed them over the bonnet and held guns to their heads.' I was astonished.

I spoke to Jon Shatford (who, some 20 years later, as Detective Chief Superintendent Shatford of the Flying Squad, masterminded the arrest of five men for the robbery at the Millennium Dome), who recalled the incident.

'I remember, the superintendent started with a curious phrase', he told me. 'He said, "You made sure they weren't going to get away with this one". I hadn't a clue what he was talking about.'

The *entente* became a little less than *cordiale* when Shatford, who had just come to the Metropolitan Police from his country roots, answered the questions in his West Country accent; this was thoroughly misinterpreted as disrespectful mimicry.

'You think we're all a bunch of swedes, don't you?' furiously demanded the note-taking sergeant.

'I thought', reminisced Shatford to me, 'that they were border-ing on incompetence.'

Incompetence? Like many post-war children, brought up on rationed food, I'm saving the best bit to last.

★

According to various sources, it was Leroy Terence Davies, an East End serial armed robber since the 1960s, who was responsible for launching the allegations of police corruption to Countryman; but this was not the case.

Davies had been arrested for a chainsaw attack on a secu-rity vehicle at Leverstock Green, Hertfordshire in 1977, when cash amounting to £231,000 was stolen. In the custody of the Hertfordshire Regional Crime Squad, Davies turned supergrass, and when he appeared at St Albans Crown Court on 24 July 1978 he pleaded guilty to seven counts of armed robbery, one charge of conspiracy to rob and asked for thirty-three offences – these included fifteen robberies and twelve conspiracies to rob – to be taken into consideration. During 'Operation Gold Dust' he had also named over thirty fellow criminals to his handlers; his barrister, Roger Frisby QC, told the court, 'The information he has given is about men who the police believe to be among the most violent and dangerous criminals in the country.'

The trial judge, Mr Justice Stoker, had obviously not heard about the usual five-year tariff which was routinely dished out to supergrasses; he sentenced Davies to ten years' imprisonment.

Davies appealed; his sentence was reduced to seven years, six months, but he served just over two years before being released in 1980.

Detective Superintendent Neil Dickens was in charge at Hertfordshire and he told me, 'Throughout all of my personal dealings with Leroy he never made any accusations to me about corrupt action of any police officers. I do recall he was at one time interviewed by police officers concerned with police internal investigations but I have no knowledge what transpired from that and do not remember whether they were CIB or provincial police officers.'

Precisely what Davies said – or may have said – to those officers is debatable. Did he point the finger of accusation at officers with allegations about which he had first-hand experience? Or was this second- or third-hand information, gleaned from others, because two other supergrasses were being used by Hertfordshire in a joint operation? Difficult to say. What is known is that Davies confessed all – or at any rate all he wanted the *Daily Express* to know about – in that newspaper's 15 July 1980 edition:

> After an attempted robbery in the Mile End Road in 1974, an inspector who knew I had done it demanded £500 for keeping quiet. I paid him after I had pulled another job to finance it.

This brings us to the next set of allegations investigated by Countryman.

CHAPTER 19

Superintendent Bob Robinson was attending Havering Magistrates' Court in respect of a complaint against police which he had investigated, when he was told by the gaoler, 'There's two gents to see you.'

They were Countryman officers, one of them a chief superintendent, who told him, 'We're taking you to the Yard.'

Robinson was not told he was under arrest but was in no doubt that he would have to accompany them. Upon arrival at the Yard, and because they had failed to book an interview room, they were obliged to sit in the canteen until one became available. During this time there was no intimation as to why he had been brought there.

But when the interview did get underway, it became clear that an allegation had been made that Robinson had received money in respect of a robbery some eight years previously, for which Leroy Davies had been arrested and which Robinson had investigated as a detective inspector at Leman Street police station.

However, what was not clear was who had made this imputation. Was it Davies – or somebody else?

'It seemed to me that they were on a fishing expedition', Robinson told me.

It became apparent to Robinson that because Davies had been acquitted after two trials, the Countryman officers believed this was due to assistance given to him. However, they were unable to tell Robinson what he had done in order to receive the money.

In fact, Robinson had behaved with propriety; when he received information that a juror had an association with Davies, he and the prosecuting counsel had brought this to the attention of the trial judge, who permitted the case to continue. At its conclusion, Robinson filed a comprehensive report regarding Davies' activities to C11, the Criminal Intelligence Unit at the Yard.

Knowing that he had nothing to fear, Robinson invited the Countryman officers to inspect his bank and building society accounts and signed an agreement permitting them to inspect the accounts from two years either side of the date of the robbery.

It is important to emphasize this, because the question of scrutinizing Robinson's accounts was not something which had been raised by the Countryman officers. It was a clear indication of innocence, because if Robinson had refused a requested to see details of his accounts, there was no way that they would have been legitimately allowed to do so. At that time, in order to inspect an account, a warrant had to be obtained under the provisions of the Bankers' Books Evidence Act 1879, and then only when a person had been charged with an offence.

Because of his transparent openness, the head of A10 Department, Deputy Assistant Commissioner Colin Vernon Hewett QPM ('a very decent man'), refused to suspend Robinson.

Several months passed before Robinson was recalled to the Yard to be interviewed, once more by the same Countryman officer, who had a prepared questionnaire.

His first question was, 'Where did you live in 1972?' and Robinson told him. The next question was, 'Who did you have the mortgage with?', and when Robinson replied that he didn't have a mortgage, it completely threw the interviewer and he had to abandon his questionnaire.

Before and after 1972, whilst most of the household bills had been paid by direct debit, Robinson had been in the habit of taking £80 per month out of his account for any extraneous expenses – and it was clear that Countryman believed that this sum was used to pay the mortgage. In fact, as Robinson explained, his mortgage had been paid off by increasing the monthly payments and with a lump sum from the bank, all of which was verifiable.

Every entry in the eight-year-old account was scrutinized and satisfactorily accounted for – until they came to two amounts of over £500 credited to the account which Robinson was unable to immediately explain. It was only on the train journey home that he realized these were cheques from the Metropolitan Police Friendly Society in respect of policies which had matured and which, of course, could be authenticated. This was later communicated to Countryman.

But Countryman were now becoming desperate; and in an effort to justify their actions they wanted to extend their search of Robinson's accounts – back to 1961, which was when he had been appointed to the CID. Robinson now took the view – with some justification – that they regarded him as 'a bent CID officer'. He told them so and refused either to allow them to extend their search into his accounts or to answer any further questions. The interview concluded with the ominous warning to Robinson that 'He might have to be seen again.'

A year went by. Robinson had held the rank of superintendent for eight years, had attended three boards for selection to chief superintendent (two during this waiting period) and had failed all of them. But after he was told that the enquiry had finished, he learned to his dismay that there had been a conversation between the overall head of Countryman and the interviewing officer on one side, and the Met's Deputy Commissioner and other senior officers on the other; and the question put to all of the latter had been: 'Do you have a mortgage? Yes? Well, Superintendent Robinson hasn't.'

They were wrong.

He did indeed have an £18,000 mortgage, having since purchased a new house. But during his questioning, at no time had Robinson been asked about his current position; they had not asked if he had moved from his original house, or if he had taken out a mortgage – and had they done so, he would have told them.

However, within a few days the Countryman officer came to Dagenham police station to return some items which Robinson had voluntarily handed over to prove his innocence at an early stage of the enquiry. When he came to sign the receipt for them, Robinson recalled a comment which his wife had made: that the Countryman officers could not have been very good at their job because they had not visited their house to observe their lifestyle. Consequently, when Robinson signed the receipt for the return of his property, he also wrote on it, 'You are formally invited to visit my home in respect of which I have an £18,000 mortgage, and no item in the house requires individual insurance.' When the interviewing officer asked why Robinson had written those words, he was told precisely why.

The upshot of this slipshod enquiry was that Robinson's offer was not taken up; and this man who had not been suspended, charged or subjected to any disciplinary proceedings whatsoever attended the next board and was promptly promoted to the rank of chief superintendent.

But if Davies' assertions published in the *Daily Express* were accepted by Countryman, there were some worrying features. First, in the article it was not an attempted robbery which Robinson had arrested him for; it was a successful one, which had netted several thousand pounds. And far from pulling off another job in order to pay the venal inspector, Davies was not on this occasion in a physical position to do so.

At the time of his arrest, Davies jumped 44ft from the window of his mother's flat to evade capture. As Robinson told me, 'We took a ruler and found that Leroy's arse had gone eight inches into the ground when he landed.' He was taken into St Leonard's Hospital for much needed treatment and was remanded in custody thereafter.

But in addition, Robinson had left the East End in May 1972. He had been posted to the Regional Crime Squad and there he stayed for seven months, before promotion to detective chief inspector took him to the Flying Squad, where he remained until 1974, when he was promoted to detective superintendent.

Therefore, if Davies had indeed paid an inspector £500 for his freedom, it could not have been when Bob Robinson arrested him, nor could it have been Bob Robinson who received the money in 1974, because by then he was an inspector no longer, he had left the East End and been posted to the Flying Squad as a superintendent.

It took me five minutes to check that out and verify it. So why couldn't Countryman have done so, instead of keeping him waiting for over a year? Were they so convinced of Robinson's guilt that they became blinkered to anything which would point to his innocence?

CHAPTER 20

The DPP's representative who had been ostracized following the Cuthbert prosecution debacle stayed at Godalming; it was Hambleton who left on 29 February 1980. Sir Peter Matthews, the Chief Constable of Sussex, now took charge of Countryman, leaving Burt as head of the investigation.

Hambleton retired as Chief Constable on 5 March – his successor, Peter Owen CBE, QPM (a former Met detective chief superintendent), had already been appointed – and on the same day Hambleton gave an interview to BBC Radio's *World at One* programme. He stated that the lower and middle ranks of the CID 'had not been very helpful' (although two weeks previously, in a rather heated debate in the Commons on the same matter, the Attorney General had stated, 'Whether junior officers may be exercising their rights not to answer questions, I do not know, but that is a right they are entitled to.').

Additionally, Hambleton stated that some criminals had feared reprisals if they came forward to give evidence, but as he staunchly announced, 'Anyone who speaks to Countryman and gives information will not be got at or fitted up.'

This was an incredibly reckless statement; it suggested, on the basis of no evidence whatsoever, that there was a real possibility that anybody offering information *would* be fitted up.

And if that were not bad enough, of some eighty officers, up to and including the rank of commander, against whom allegations of corruption had been made, Hambleton expected that twenty to twenty-five would eventually be charged. It was astonishing that such an announcement should be made in respect of an enquiry which was far from complete; not only that, but Hambleton was actually prophesying its outcome. Both the Met and City Police Commissioners sent out a joint statement in which, with barely controlled fury, they stated that they 'regretted Mr Hambleton's comments', which, they added, 'were dangerously premature'.

These were sentiments echoed the following day by Merlyn Rees, but paradoxically he added that although he was 'staggered' at the number of allegedly corrupt officers, he doubted that that number would face prosecution. It appeared that Hambleton was not the only one capable of prejudging the issue. Although he was now Shadow Home Secretary, Rees saw no harm at all in distancing himself from the very divisive political mess which Countryman had degenerated into, especially since the enquiry had been started at his instigation. Speaking on BBC Radio, Rees said it had been right to appoint an outside force to investigate corruption but rowed for the shore when he added, 'I have always had slight doubts about it, because it is extremely difficult for provincial officers to come into the Metropolitan, with 22,000 men, and find their way about.'

All well and good, but then Rees became horribly muddled when he said, 'I would have had no doubt that the Metropolitan could have done the job themselves.'

Then, when he was asked if he thought that informants would still have come forward if the Met had carried out the enquiry, Rees, who by now was going round in circles, limply replied, 'That was one of the reasons it had to be from the outside.'

Jonathan Aitken, the Conservative MP for Thanet East, suggested, 'I have gathered there are internal weaknesses in the Countryman investigating force itself which are also the cause of the disappointing progress so far' – and it could well be that he was right.

On 7 March the DPP announced that he had rejected four of the Countryman reports which recommended prosecution of six more Met detectives; this included John O'Connor, who was reinstated. Indeed, the DPP was highly critical of the way O'Connor's investigation had been handled.

The next day, the Home Secretary, the Right Honourable William Whitelaw KT, CH, MC, PC, DL (later Viscount Whitelaw), who had replaced Merlyn Rees on 4 May 1979, appeared on television to deny there had ever been any cover-up of police corruption.

On 9 March the BBC re-ran their controversial *Law and Order* series, a four-part detective programme which showed the CID – especially the Flying Squad's fictional Detective Inspector Fred Pyle – in a very bad light. Frank Williamson, the former Head of HM Inspectorate of Constabularies, had seen the original showing of the programme; piously, he refused to watch the re-run but did not lose the opportunity to tell the press, 'I have seen a number of detective inspectors in the Met who looked just like the leading character.'

★

On 24 March 1980 a truck on its way to Tilbury Docks containing silver ingots weighing three tons and valued at £3.4 million was stopped on the A12 trunk road by a robber dressed in a police officer's uniform. The crew were overpowered by the rest of the armed five-man gang, and the silver, which represented (at that time) Britain's biggest ever bullion robbery, was spirited away.

Tony Lundy and his team got to work, arrested the gang and found the whereabouts of the silver. Of the 321 ingots stolen, twelve – valued at approximately £120,000 – were missing. It was later alleged that there had been police involvement in the raid and that, together with the matter of the missing ingots, this was the subject of an internal investigation.

'It was DCS MacDonald from CIB2 who dealt with it', Bill Peters told me, adding, 'A decent man'.

Tony Lundy was uncertain: 'I'm not sure whether it was the [Chief Superintendent Alan] Stagg enquiry or later by South Yorkshire', he told me.

In fact, it was the Stagg enquiry. But did the investigation have an involvement by Countryman? No, surely not. After all, hadn't they been given strict terms of reference, to adhere to their original enquiry and not to undertake fresh enquiries without implicit permission? Of course they had. Which makes the following account as incomprehensible as it is hilarious.

Police Constable Tony Cook was, without doubt, the finest collator (an officer who keeps and analyzes criminal records) I ever met. He had transferred from Essex to the Met following the amalgamation of parts of Essex during the boundary changes in 1965 and brought with him a rich store of information on criminals of the area. He had initially been the collator at Collier Row; by the time this story unfolds in 1980, he was the collator at Romford police station. He now takes up the story:

> Suddenly, three men burst into my office. One of them introduced himself as a DI from Countryman. They were all very rude. The DI demanded whatever documentation I possessed about the hi-jacking of the bullion van.
>
> I told them I had no such documentation – I was told that if I was trying to obstruct them, I'd really be in trouble. I knew what they were talking about; I told them it had taken place at Mountnessing.
>
> 'So?' they said. 'Mountnessing's near Romford, isn't it?'
>
> I told them that Mountnessing was in the Essex constabulary, not the Met. I directed them to Brentwood police station so that they could receive instructions on how to proceed to Essex Police Headquarters at Chelmsford.

     I knew and had met some very fine CID officers in my
time, but I never met any as rude as these.

In thanking Tony Cook for his information I refrained from telling
him that it was quite likely that the inspector's rank was a made-up
one and that it was a further, strong possibility that none of the
charmless trio were CID officers at all.

★

Nor were the Countryman officers in search of Mountnessing the
only ones to be confused; readers of the 26 March 1980 edition
of the *Los Angeles Times* received a fair share of misinformation as
well:

> One criminal told a radio audience that he refused to give
> information to Countryman because corruption was too
> organized and its perpetrators too powerful. 'People just
> don't believe it', he said. 'There's no way I'm putting my
> life in my hands to go against them.'
>   'What did he fear?'
>   'Anything – killed, "fitted-up" (jailed on false evi-
> dence). You might end up doing 20 or 30 years . . .'
>   A woman is reported to have told Countryman that a
> senior detective helped plan an armored [*sic*] van robbery
> for which her lover went to jail. She is now being hidden
> away and there is a $17,000 'notice' or killing contract on
> her head, according to rumors.

A rather more measured report was published by *Police Review:*
'Countryman: A Failed Harvest?' in their 18 April 1980 edition
was a skilfully penned article by Met Detective Ian Will in which
he was critical of those whom he dubbed 'The Dorset Crusaders'.
He finished the piece with these words:
   The greatest problem confronting the authorities now is how to
bring Countryman to a dignified end. Whatever the operation ultimately produces in terms of convictions and regardless of whatever
official verdict is cobbled together in an attempt to salvage something, some results are clear already:

- criminals and other opponents of the police have been
  given enough ammunition to last them for years
- public confidence in the Met has been placed in real
  jeopardy

- the morale and public image of the force has been attacked with a virulence and complete disregard for the absence of proven fact which could almost be equated with subversion
- the objectivity and traditional independence of the DPP's office has been attacked
- and the professional competence and impartiality of the Countryman team has been called into question.

For Government, the public and the police, the message from Countryman is clear: it must never be allowed to happen again.

A clear-cut message, but what neither Ian Will nor anybody else knew was that the enquiry would trundle on for two more years.

★

On 12 April six men and two women civilians were held at Godalming police station on unspecified charges (later, seven of them were released without charge); the following weekend, more arrests of civilians were carried out.

And then the enquiry revealed a rather clandestine aspect. An unnamed man had apparently appeared in court. Several people were in the process of being interviewed by Countryman, but when the Yard was asked about the anonymous prisoner they replied (and this almost certainly came from the Yard's civilianized Press Bureau) that their information was that the man was still assisting with enquiries.

This was not quite true, because on Monday, 21 April 1980, Montague Fitzmaurice had appeared at Newham (West) Magistrates' Court and had been remanded into police custody for three days; when he appeared again at the same court on 24 April he was flanked by two Countryman officers. Michael Chance for the DPP told the bench that the charges involved inciting others to commit robberies against Securicor vehicles 'and other targets', over a period of months between September 1978 and February 1979, and 'that others were either serving substantial sentences or awaiting trial'. There was no application for bail, Fitzmaurice was not legally represented and once more he was remanded in police custody for another three days. This suggested that the prisoner was a supergrass in the making, but it was denied by a Countryman spokesperson, and in any event, was not true.

Fitzmaurice was later joined in the dock by Frederick Skipp, and the following January, for 'incitement to rob', each was sentenced to four years' imprisonment. It was Countryman's first conviction, albeit they were civilians rather than crooked police officers, and later three more civilians were charged with incitement to rob by Countryman.

However, it had put Press Bureau in an embarrassing position; they were later obliged to issue a statement saying that they had been told to withhold the news from the press. It appeared that for reasons of 'operational necessity', and for a period of over three days, senior Yard officers had not been told of the circumstances of the man's remand into police custody. It was a smack in the eye for them, suggesting untrustworthiness on their part, and also for Press Bureau. It would have been far better to have referred the newspapers to the Countryman office, or to have said, 'No comment', rather than obfuscate the truth; it made a nasty dent in Press Bureau's reputation for impartiality in supplying information to the press.

'Have you ever heard of the final straw?' suavely asks Robert Newton, as he holds his adulterous wife's boyfriend at gunpoint in Edward Dmytryk's 1949 thriller, *Obsession*. 'Well, you're it!'

Much the same thought must have been going through the minds of the two London Commissioners; they were furious at not being informed about the prisoners being processed through the courts, and they put out a combined statement expressing their concern, saying, 'Changes would be made' in view of the time the enquiry had taken and urging that matters should be expedited to allay public anxiety and to prevent police morale being adversely affected.

In spite of the spring weather, a chill wind of change was blowing across the Surrey countryside, particularly in the region of Godalming.

★

By May 1980 Burt was – as newspaper reports delicately put it – 'temporarily withdrawn' from the Countryman enquiry. It happened two months after the reinstatement of John O'Connor from the botched investigation which had rightly attracted so much criticism, and it was a withdrawal which became permanent. Burt returned to Dorset, where, it was said, he would be filling in for an officer sent on secondment to Hong Kong. Burt said that he would return to the enquiry. Indeed, this was a view held by other Countryman officers, but they were wrong, and so was Burt; he would never again be part of the investigation.

A CIB2 officer walked into his office to be told that from now on this would be known as 'The Ryman Enquiry'. When he asked why, he was told, 'The cunt's been taken out of Countryman.'

Now Chief Constable Matthews sought to confine the enquiry to its original terms of reference, and with regard to all the extraneous complaints which had been made he brought in DAC Ron Steventon from the Met's Complaints Investigation Bureau.

In their defence, Countryman stated that they had taken almost 2,000 statements, used 12 supergrasses, considered almost 200 (more accurately, 187) allegations and submitted 41 reports to the DPP. Of those allegations, 80 had been 'checked' – whatever that meant – and the remaining 107 were 'unchecked', or in more prosaic terms, rumours. But as we know, according to those officers who were either the subject of these investigations or reviewed them later, many of the statements were made by the Countryman officers themselves; they contained hearsay evidence and were of no evidential value whatsoever; the majority of the supergrasses failed to come up to proof (or had no intention of doing so in the first place); a great many of the 187 allegations were spurious; and many of the reports submitted to the DPP contained gibberish.

It did not stop questions being raised in the House of Commons. The Labour MP for Lewisham (West), Christopher Price, asked the Attorney General, Sir Michael Havers, how long it would be before the DPP reached his conclusions in respect of any further prosecutions and about the conflicting reports by Hambleton and Kavanagh that there had/had not been obstruction of the enquiry by police officers. This was the reply:

> The DPP has under consideration allegations against eleven officers as a result of the investigations. It is impossible to estimate when he will reach a decision in respect of any . . . I naturally sought to clear up the matter when it was reported in the press. Anybody, police officers or not, is entitled to refuse to answer possibly incriminating questions put by police officers in an investigation. When, like any other citizen, it is that right they are exercising, it is protected by law and cannot be treated as obstruction, so there is nothing inconsistent in what Mr Kavanagh said and my reply. I had a long interview with Mr Hambleton, and the DPP has seen him and he has never given details of obstruction of the sort reported in the newspapers.

However, before long, Hambleton would be doing just that.

CHAPTER 21

Now, many of the allegations of police misconduct were taken over by DAC Ron Steventon, with Detective Chief Superintendent Chris Draycott as his deputy. Draycott worked at Godalming for between nine and eighteen months, commuting each day from his home in Teddington, a round trip of 55 miles. He told me:

> I went to a meeting at Surrey Police headquarters. Peter Matthews was there, and Ron Steventon (with whom I got on very well. He was very straight and he liked me because I was trustworthy), plus the Countryman officers.
>
> I didn't have any problems with Countryman. After the meeting, Stevenson suggested I take the senior Countryman officers out to lunch. I was regarded with some suspicion at first but once they realized I wasn't a spy, we got on fairly well. In fact, one of the officers reminded me that I had once investigated a complaint against him and I had treated him very well.
>
> My job was liaison, checking the statements. They were not up to our standards; not as you or I would have liked.

That was a rather more tactful way of referring to Countryman's correspondence. Another CIB2 officer, taking a directly opposite view, told me:

> Their files were a shambles. They (Countryman) were paranoid about the Met being corrupt. Some of the skippers (sergeants) weren't too bad but most of the senior officers were bastards – really unpleasant, as well as being absolutely useless. One of them was referred to as 'Billy Liar'.

Detective Chief Superintendent Alan Longhurst liaised with Countryman officers from an office at the Yard, where he was answerable to the Commander of CIB2. This was Tony Lampard, of whom Longhurst said, 'He was not one of the hierarchy who let Countryman have their head, he was one of the steadying influences.'

Referring to Countryman, he told me, 'Most of their workload was taken from them and taken back to the Met. I was given the task with a squad of twenty-two officers to clear up their outstanding cases, i.e. to try to clear up the mess!'

However, Longhurst disagreed with other senior officers on one major point. 'Countryman did not exceed their brief', he told me. 'In fact, they were allowed to do so by the hierarchy at the Yard, who did not exercise sufficient control. When it all got too much, they were then restricted to their original brief and all these other cases ended up with my squad. I believe the powers that be initially did not want to be seen to be, or be accused of, obstructing Countryman.'

It's a fair point; in his memoirs, McNee said as much when he used the phrase, 'Spare the rod and spare the child', which, he added, 'was an adage we might have remembered with advantage.'

It was a task that kept Longhurst and his team fully occupied, but, as he told me, 'In the following two and a half years I did not find one case where there was a sufficiency of evidence to bring either criminal or disciplinary proceedings.'

The transference of allegations from Countryman to the Met did not meet with wholehearted approval from many of the complainers; these included a certain Miss Vivienne Rosaline Wilde, and her case prompted Jack Straw, at that time Labour MP for Blackburn, to demand to know from the Home Secretary if the DPP's day-to-day involvement with the investigations into police corruption compromised his position as an independent prosecuting authority. His complaint was that Miss Wilde's allegations against a senior police officer who, she said, had accepted bribes totalling £9,500 to help prisoners escape and had suppressed evidence, allegations which had initially been made to Countryman, had now been bounced back to the Met – all of which merits closer examination.

In November 1976 Leonard Thomas Wilde, who with some justification had been regarded as the mastermind behind the £12 million Bank of America robbery, was sentenced to twenty-three years' imprisonment (later reduced to twenty years by the Court of Appeal) and had a bankruptcy order of £500,000 imposed. Other members of the gang were jailed for between three and twenty-one years.

Leonard Wilde's alibi for the robbery had been that at the material time, he, his wife and daughter and a visitor named Mrs Susan Hilliard had been watching television. However, Mrs Hilliard had informed the police that she feared for her safety.

Miss Wilde, who had been charged with two counts of receiving money stolen from the bank, was one of few people in the trial to be acquitted. But in taking a highly unusual, almost unknown course of action, Judge King-Hamilton QC had Miss Wilde brought back into court, where he had this to say to her:

> Before you leave the court, there is something I would like to say to you. I just want to say this to you and please regard it as a solemn warning. If anything happens to Mrs Hilliard as a result of what you do or what you cause others to do as a result of the evidence she has given in this court, then you can expect no mercy at all.

What was apparently not made clear to Mr Straw was that a prison warder had been bribed, and was later convicted of conspiring to aid Wilde's escape; and that if the 'senior officer' in question had been discredited, it could have led to his suspension and Wilde walking free from prison.

Another unhappy complainer was Brian Davies, a convicted fraudster who had informed Countryman of his links with ten dubious London police officers, whom he had 'lavishly entertained' in return for favours of an unspecified nature. The entertainment included flying a detective constable to Paris to arrange his honeymoon, taking two more detective constables to see the hit show *Evita* in a hired Rolls-Royce, arranging concert tickets and wining and dining the officers. To authenticate his beneficence, Davies had ticket receipts, photographs and cheque book stubs; but in a statement to Countryman he stipulated:

> I do not wish to repeat my complaints to any member of the Metropolitan Police or any other police force . . . I do not wish the information I have given to be given to any other person.

Now why was this? Because Davies believed the whole of the Met to be bent? Or because he feared that those investigating the allegations in the Met were not as muddle-headed as their Dorset contemporaries, who had slavishly swallowed his assertions hook, line and sinker? His hopes were dashed, ten weeks later, when all the documentation was handed to CIB2, at the insistence of the DPP, who told Davies' solicitor that the complaint was beyond Countryman's brief. Two and a half years later, no one had been charged with any offence arising out of Davies' complaint.

There we can leave the furious Miss Wilde, the frustrated Mr Davies, DCS Draycott statement-checking and DCS Longhurst endeavouring to separate the wheat (if indeed there was any) from the chaff. We can also bid adieu to the four Countryman officers who allegedly resigned in the face of the despotic decision to permit investigation of these allegations by a competent unit.

Instead, we move on to a series of arrests which could have turned the tide in the investigation; but thanks to unparalleled stupidity and incompetence, didn't.

CHAPTER 22

A series of raids were carried out by detectives in the Home Counties and the West Country, and as a result, fourteen men and one woman appeared in the dock at Reading Magistrates' Court on the morning of 9 June 1980. Various of them were charged with different offences, which included a robbery at the Midland Bank in Sloane Street, Knightsbridge in the run-up to Christmas 1976. Only £405 was snatched from one of the tills; the gang had unsuccessfully tried to blast their way into a locked box containing £236,000, whilst they kept the public away at gunpoint. To divert any police officers who might be in the vicinity, one of the gang members had placed a fake bomb in Kensington, this being during the height of a murderous IRA bombing campaign in London.

There had also been a £90,000 robbery at Highbury in 1976, and other offences involved a conspiracy to rob Securicor between July 1975 and March 1976 and dishonestly handling jewellery valued at £78,000.

One of the prisoners was George Copley; remember, he had walked free from the Williams & Glyn's robbery two years previously, as had Frank Fraser Jr, who had also been freshly arrested. Fred Cutts was one of the Regional Crime Squad officers involved in Fraser's arrest. There was some prevarication by Fraser about opening his front door at 5 o'clock in the morning, until Cutts called through the letterbox that he had a telegraph pole strapped to a Land Rover and unless Fraser opened the door by the count of ten . . . The front door was quickly opened without further ado, although apparently Fraser was somewhat bemused upon leaving, since there was no sign of a Land Rover, with or without a telegraph pole appended to it.

Codenamed 'Operation Carter' and led by Detective Chief Superintendent Joseph Coffey from No. 5 Regional Crime Squad at Hertfordshire, it appeared that this was a rich haul indeed; and due to the elapse of time between the offences being committed and the arrests carried out, it appeared that someone had been supergrassing – and someone had.

One of the other prisoners was serial blagger Fred Sinfield. He had participated in the Williams & Glyn's robbery; now he, too, was turned and he named his accomplices.

By 18 September 1980 the number of people arrested had increased to eighteen men and two women; the amount of stolen jewellery seized had now swollen to a value of £200,000, and several hand guns had been recovered. The prisoners were now being quizzed about robberies which had occurred in London, Manchester, Liverpool, Bristol, Swansea, Bedford, the Thames Valley, Surrey, Essex, Hampshire and Cornwall. In particular, some were questioned about the robbery at Williams & Glyn's in the City of London.

By early March 1981 thirty-four people had been charged with offences countrywide involving property worth £3.2 million; and then disaster struck.

Sergeant Rodney Pook requested to speak to George Copley in prison; the DPP's representative, Kenneth Dowling, refused. But in March 1981 Pook went right ahead anyway and offered a deal: if Copley would admit his part in the Williams & Glyn's robbery and give evidence against certain London detectives, he would receive a sentence of just five years. It was a ludicrous offer because there was no way in which Pook or anybody else could guarantee such a sentence. Not that it really mattered, because the cunning Copley obviously knew of Pook's imminent arrival plus the fact that a deal was on the table and had taken the precaution of covertly taping their conversation.

Three months later, Copley, Fraser et al came up for trial on other robbery charges at Oxford Crown Court, where the defence produced the tape recording. The prosecution crumbled, the charges were dropped and when the trial for the Williams & Glyn's robbery started in July, that too similarly collapsed. Stephen Wooler for the DPP declared that the prosecution in respect of eight men had been 'hopelessly compromised'. Pook and another officer were suspended from duty, statements attributed to Fraser and Copley were found to be backdated and since, by imputation, senior officers must have had knowledge of the deception, Wooler told the court, 'The prosecution has got to think long and hard.'

Not for too long, though. The Williams & Glyn's charges were dropped, and although Frank Fraser Jr. was convicted of receiving some of the jewellery from the 1975 Bank of America robbery and received a five-year sentence, it meant that a very good chance of obtaining compelling evidence to convict those alleged to have been involved in a major robbery, plus corrupt officers who had obtained bribes in respect of the City of London robberies, had gone right out of the window.

★

George Copley wasn't the only one to utilize a covert tape recorder. The late Detective Superintendent Harry Mooney was a resourceful fellow; he featured prominently in the Kray enquiry and it was he who eventually coaxed the terrified barmaid in The Blind Beggar who had witnessed George Cornell's dispatch to testify that Ronnie Kray was responsible. A dozen or so years later, Mooney grew very irate with Countryman, who had interviewed him on several occasions; when they next demanded his presence for a grilling, he took with him a tape recorder concealed in a briefcase. Halfway through the interview he realized the tape was going to run out, so he excused himself with a visit to the lavatory, where he changed the tape over and returned to complete his questioning. When Countryman's account of the interview revealed sizeable discrepancies with what he had recorded, Mooney had a transcript made and took that, plus the original recording, to the Home Office. It resulted in a rather embarrassing confrontation with officers who began to wish that the moniker 'detective' had not been inserted in front of their inflated rank and who were returned to their native pastures to concentrate upon the inhabitants of those parts who had breached sections of the 1960 Road Traffic Act.

Mooney's evaluation of Countryman was, 'They couldn't catch a currant in a rice pudding.'

It's time to return to some of those who had provided evidence against detectives, and we'll start with those who featured in the trial of the Ross brothers, Rextrew and others. By the end of their trial, one of their accusers, Carpenter, had subsequently been convicted of burglary. Twomey was in custody charged with offences of armed robbery in 1981. The main prosecution witness was a supergrass, Edward 'Toggi' Ludlow, who had implicated Twomey in two raids during which a security guard was shot and wounded. In March 1983 Twomey was acquitted on two of the charges, but the jury failed to agree on the remainder; on 16 July, after a three-day retirement, a second jury failed to reach a verdict and Twomey was discharged. He had spent long periods in the cells during the trials 'because I had no interest in hearing lying accounts', but as he tearfully told reporters, 'I have been trying to lead an honest life for a long time; then along comes this diabolical so-called supergrass.'

Twomey had successfully sued the police in respect of the Paddington robbery charge and received £25,000. The currency he received from the police was rather more genuine than the notes he was peddling a few years later, when he went down for twelve months' imprisonment on a counterfeiting charge. And then he was arrested for being part of a four-man gang during a £1.75 million armed robbery at the Menzies warehouse at Heathrow in 2004 where a member of staff was shot at.

At his first trial in 2005 the jury failed to reach a decision. Two years later, two of the jurors claimed they had been threatened. The remaining ten told the judge they had reached a majority decision on the four defendants before being sent home for a Bank Holiday weekend. One of them stated he had been threatened over the weekend, thereby making it impossible for the others to achieve a majority.

The judge halted the proceedings halfway during the third trial after allegations of jury nobbling.

The prosecution took the highly unusual step of applying for a juryless trial and at their fourth and final trial the four men were convicted on 31 March 2010; Twomey was sentenced to twenty years and six months. A sixty-one-year-old self-confessed alcoholic, who states he has suffered three heart attacks, Twomey told the press that he believes he will die in prison.

★

In September 1981 I was walking along the 4th floor corridor of the Victoria Block at the Yard, when I was surprised to be confronted with the sight of a dignified Flying Squad detective superintendent named David Little skipping along the corridor and whooping with delight. The reason for his jocularity was that serial armed robber Billy Tobin, who thanks to some disputed evidence during the trial of Detective Inspector James Jolly, had walked free from court in respect of the murder and robbery at the *Daily Mirror* building, had finally been convicted of yet another robbery.

In December 1980, Tobin, part of a six-man gang, had been at the controls of a mobile crane which had smashed into the rear doors of a security van in an attempt to steal the contents, which amounted to £811,000. The Flying Squad had been waiting and videoed the raid, but it was a matter which required split-second timing. First, because it was known that the gang was armed. Next, because of the danger involved to the occupants of the security van. Last – and by no means least – because of the very close proximity of Kingsdale Comprehensive School in Alleyn Park, Dulwich. Even so, Flying Squad officers were hidden in the school's playground, and when Tobin and another gang member ran into the playground in an effort to escape, a Squad officer fired three shots, one of which passed through Tobin's jacket; he fell to the ground and in his pocket was found a loaded revolver. A masked member of the gang escaped, despite being clumped with a truncheon. Dave Little told me:

> I do remember one of the defendants tried to run down one of the officers, who fired shots in defence. One of the bullets went into the radiator of a parked car – a lady's car later overheated several miles away and the garage recovered one of our bullets. I had great difficulty explaining this to Mr Powis, as you can imagine!

In court, Tobin gave a statement from the dock – it meant he could not be cross-examined – stating that he was a victim of a frame-up arranged between a police informant (who was referred to in court only as 'Mr X') and certain police officers. He had gone to the scene with 'Mr X' in a van, not to carry out a robbery, good heavens no, but to photograph a corrupt police officer taking a bribe. When he saw the police running towards him, he fled the van, not wanting to get involved, but he had been, so there you are. The gun? Planted by police, naturally. It wasn't, he told the jury (who had been provided with police protection) the first time he'd been framed. He'd been arrested on five previous occasions, each time he'd been framed and each time he'd been acquitted. Certain police officers had been out to get him because once he'd refused to pay a bribe. Oh, and he'd had nothing to do with making threatening telephone calls to two women on the jury.

It wasn't good enough, not this time. He was convicted – on what Mr Justice Leonard described as 'the clearest evidence' – of attempted robbery and possessing a loaded revolver with intent to endanger life. Women screamed in the public gallery and there was also the sound of a scuffle when he was sentenced to sixteen years' imprisonment.

And that was not the end of it. In March 2001 Tobin was part of a four-man gang who attacked the crew of a security van who were to deliver cash to Lloyds TSB in Wye High Street, Ashford, Kent. Tobin punched one of the guards in the face, and although the intended prize was £400,000, the raiders escaped with just £6,000. Tobin was sentenced to life imprisonment in 2003, with a recommendation that he serve eleven years.

*

Leroy Davies, too, had a further brush with the law. In August 1981 – three months after Bob Robinson's promotion to chief superintendent – Davies was arrested following a robbery at the French Revolution public house at Putney, where he had allegedly fired a shotgun at police in order to facilitate his escape. His older brother, Glanville, was also arrested after a struggle and promptly implicated his sibling. On 7 April 1982 it took the jury at the Old Bailey just ninety minutes to acquit thirty-five-year-old Leroy after he told the court that he 'Would not have taken part with my brother in an inefficient robbery', which he described as 'a comedy farce'. Another contributory factor in Leroy's acquittal may have been that the jury were unaware of his sibling's detailed statement under caution in which he implicated his brother – it had been withheld from them in the interests of 'fairness'. Jailing Glanville for five years, Judge Lawson told the jury that they had come to a conclusion which he could not criticise 'but which did not accord with the facts' and added, 'I have no doubt as to the true identity of that gunman.' Leroy left both the court and his old identity of

'Leslie Newton' behind, having been provided with a new alias courtesy of Hertfordshire police.

It was clear that Judge Lawson thought Leroy Davies' testimony was unreliable; what a pity that Countryman couldn't have probed rather deeper into his veracity.

★

When the raid on Brink's-Mat warehouse near Heathrow Airport was carried out on 26 November 1983 and the robbers were somewhat surprised to discover that instead of large amounts of cash they had to make do with gold bullion valued at £26 million, it wasn't too long before the Flying Squad identified the 'inside man', namely Tony Black. When he rolled over (and that didn't take long, either) he identified a number of the robbers. One of those implicated was Tony White, who had made guest appearances at the line-up of arrests at the Williams & Glyn's and *Daily Mirror* robberies and had walked away from both. Now, once more, he was arrested, and although detectives said that during his interviews White admitted the offence and suggested 'doing a deal', this was later strongly denied by him.

White was charged with the robbery, together with 'Mad' Micky McAvoy (who with William Joseph Chadwick had been acquitted of the *Daily Express* robbery) and Brian 'The Colonel' Robinson. At the Old Bailey on 2 December 1984 the jury delivered their verdicts by a majority of ten to two – McAvoy and Robinson were found guilty and the following day were each sentenced to twenty-five years' imprisonment. White was found not guilty.

Prior to his arrest, White had lived in a second-floor flat in Redlaw Way, Bermondsey on the run-down Bonamy council estate and was drawing unemployment benefit. Following his acquittal, he opened a shoe shop, brought three properties for £33,000, £40,000 and £146,000 and spent £200,000 on renovations, before selling up and moving to Spain's Costa del Sol.

The Spanish police raided his villa in 1989 – the reason is unclear – but there they found £115,000 in cash and jewellery worth £100,000.

However, in August 1995 he was successfully sued in the High Court – where guilt is decided on 'the balance of probabilities' as opposed to the stricter parameters imposed in a criminal court – by the Brink's-Mat insurers, and Mr Justice Rimmer ordered him to pay £26,369,778, plus compensation of £2,188,600, to the insurers; White's wife was also ordered to pay over £1 million.

But two years previously, 'Operation Stealer' had got underway, a covert operation run by Customs and Excise. It led to the seizure of cocaine valued at £57 million, plus cannabis worth more than £8 million – and also to the arrest of thirteen people, including Tony White, who admitted being the financier. In July 1997 at Bristol Crown Court White was sentenced to eleven years' imprisonment.

*

Stanley Houghton went on to better things. In October 1992 he was sentenced to twelve years' imprisonment at the Old Bailey for kidnapping a fine art dealer, and while he was in his prison cell he devised a plan to lure a millionaire businessman to an island, where he would be injected with LSD and heroin and tortured into ordering his staff to transfer huge sums into accounts controlled by Houghton. This was denied by Houghton, who told the jury at the Old Bailey that what had been revealed by the prosecution was nothing more than 'pure fantasy', to stave off boredom whilst he was in prison.

'You cannot imprison me for acting foolishly', he told them, adding that 'The only things that kept me going were my love of classical music, my Catholic faith and the visits of my Aunt Muriel.'

Although he and another man were acquitted of conspiracy to murder, after three days' deliberation the jury of six men and six women found Houghton guilty of inciting his co-defendant to kidnap. Judge Gerald Gordon told him:

> I have to consider not only punishment but the protection of the public. You are at present a person who is highly likely to go back to dangerous crime on release, if not before. It does seem to me I have no option but to pass a life sentence.

*

Houghton's partner in crime, Stephen Raymond, also prospered; for a time, anyway. As cunning as ever, when he attended bankruptcy proceedings in respect of the Heathrow theft, he barefacedly told the panel that he had given £25,000 of the proceeds to his friend Tom Driberg. It was providential that Driberg, who by the time of the alleged transference of funds had been elevated to the peerage as Baron Bradwell of Bradwell Juxta Mare in the county of Essex, had sadly passed away, just three months after the theft.

Free from his prison sentence, Raymond defrauded Granada Television of electrical goods worth £500,000, and for that and other excesses he was jailed for eight years. In 1989 he escaped from HM Prison, Oxford, but in 1994 he was charged with the escape, plus conspiracy to supply and manufacture ecstasy. It was suggested he had earned £20 million out of it and, what was more, had put £600,000 aside for jury nobbling, should he be caught. Although the officer in the case requested that the trial judge authorize jury protection, Raymond screamed across the courtroom that he had bribed him; he later admitted to journalists that he had done nothing of the kind – this was after he was acquitted, of course.

By 2000 Raymond appeared to have semi-retired to respectability at a château in France, from where he set up a cordon bleu cookery college; but not a bit of it.

He had a couple of dry runs before attempting to smuggle 693kg of cocaine, worth £35 million, into the country via Rotterdam; but the Dutch police, acting on a tip-off from HM Customs and Excise, seized the consignment and, ultimately, Raymond. In vain he tried to convince the jury at Snaresbrook Crown Court that he was only importing cannabis. In July 2005 His Honour Judge Martyn Zeidman QC told him:

> This was a major, sophisticated attempt to bring a huge quantity of cocaine into our country. Those who try to profit out of this evil cannot justifiably complain when they receive severe punishment. It is a means of deterring others and reflecting society's horror at such activities.

He then sentenced Raymond to concurrent terms of twenty-eight and eleven years' imprisonment.

And that was Stephen Patrick Raymond, who had studied law, often represented himself in court, operated under a multiplicity of aliases, involved himself in a variety of serious crimes, accused police officers of corruption and was a master conman and manipulator. When he was arrested he would often turn his back on his interrogators and face the wall, telling them to come back later. I don't believe that it's pitching matters too high to say that when he met the Countryman officers he must have regarded them in the same way that a particularly hungry lion at the Colosseum in ancient Rome would have observed a reasonably plump Christian.

★

I want now to go back to one David Lawson Ewin. It's true that he never treated Countryman as his playthings, but he deserves a mention, because you will recall that due to John O'Connor's suspension at the behest of Countryman he walked free from court on charges of robbery and murder.

Born in 1957, Ewin had a chequered criminal background and, coupled with this, a fanatical hatred of the police. In May 1979 he was jailed for eighteen months for malicious wounding, but before he could be released, on 22 February 1980 he pleaded guilty to receiving stolen jewellery valued at £160,000 belonging to Lady Chelsea, taking a car without consent and a £6,800 house burglary, and was sentenced to three years' imprisonment. This was followed with an eight-year sentence for armed robbery, and whilst he was incarcerated in HMP Parkhurst on the Isle of Wight, Detective Superintendent Bill Hatfull of the Flying Squad was surprised to receive a telephone call from the chief security officer there to say that Ewin 'wanted to clear the slate' and confess to all of the crimes he'd committed. Amongst these offences were the apparent murders of taxi drivers in France and Belgium. Hatfull made the necessary enquiries via Interpol and could find no evidence of any such murders being reported, but nevertheless, together with a detective constable, set off to Parkhurst. He now takes up the tale:

> I saw the chief security officer, who told us that he had set a room aside for our interview but he didn't believe Ewin's motives to be genuine. He was concerned and told us that he was going to strip-search Ewin beforehand. We later discovered that Ewin had been attending art classes in the prison and had got hold of some drawing pencils which he had sharpened to a point, then bound together with tape and stuffed down the back of his trousers. The chief security officer was convinced that this was because Ewin intended to attack us. He was put back in his cell and the following day, he refused to talk to us or even see us.

That was not the end of the story. In July 1992 Ewin was sentenced to five years' imprisonment, again for armed robbery. On 28 February 1995, whilst on licence for this offence, he was spotted in a stolen Toyota in Barnes, South-West London, by a police armed response unit. Ewin's hatred of police was now shown in its full glory. One of the officers, in full uniform, tried to stop Ewin, who was one and a half times over the drink-drive limit and had traces of cannabis, cocaine and heroin in his bloodstream. He drove off dragging the officer with him and crashing into other vehicles; eye-witnesses described him as 'driving like a maniac'. The wheels of the Toyota spun with such force that the road's tarmac melted. The officer then had to leap out of the way of the stolen car which Ewin drove straight at him. Believing that he was in mortal danger, the officer drew his firearm and fired two fatal shots.

This officer – Police Constable Patrick Hodgson – became the first Metropolitan Police officer to be charged in these circumstances with murder and manslaughter. He stood trial three times; on the first occasion, just as the trial was ending, someone from the public gallery howled abuse at the jury (they often do, don't they?) and a mistrial was declared. On the second, the jury was unable to agree, and on the third, he was acquitted.

Ewin's mother, outraged at the verdict, indignantly stated, 'People steal cars all the time – there was no need to shoot'.

Perhaps security guard John Potter was looking down from heaven; he had had the business end of a sawn-off shotgun pressed against his stomach on 12 October 1978 at Northfields Underground Station before it was discharged, practically cutting him in two and cutting short his fifty-one-year-old life. From his celestial position, and since he would have been only too aware of the culprit's identity, Mr Potter might have begged to differ.

*

There were others who had made false allegations against police to Countryman; now the complaint papers had passed to the Met and were being dealt with by CIB2. What follows is a hilarious account of what happened, told to me by an anonymous detective chief inspector from that department:

> I got two–three to investigate; I went down to the Isle of Wight to interview one of the prisoners and was accompanied by my woman detective sergeant, who was wearing a tight dress. At that time, the prisoner had to personally tell us he did not want to be interviewed.
>
> However, he got no further than 'I don't . . . ' and saw my sergeant, whereupon he said something like, 'Well, I can give you a moment to tell me what you want.' He not only stayed but admitted (though not in writing) that his complaint was bogus and was made because there was a rumour going round that Dorset officers either interviewed the prisoners over lunch at a local pub or took them out somewhere for the day.

The second and third time I went down, my sergeant was dressed in what we called 'prison garb', and this consisted of a slightly see-through blouse, a skirt and black stockings. We got to interview the prisoners every time, and on the second visit the prisoner went for lunch and came back with his mate, 'who'll back me up, if required'! Don't recall the complaints, but there was talk of 'prison gossip'. There may have been a third complaint, but none of them were taken any further than the prison interview. I recall the attitude as 'Well, it was worth a try – forget it.'

There can be no doubt that all of these complaints were of a spurious nature; if they'd been true, the sex-starved cons would have wished to amplify, not deny their accusations, whilst spending extra time ogling the luscious CIB2 cutie!

CHAPTER 24

And now it's time to return to the City of London, where this all began.

The City Commissioner had promised John Simmonds the next Senior Command Course allocated to that force, but when it arrived, Simmonds felt, given the prevailing circumstances, it would be wrong for him to leave the City and better to stay and fight it out. It was a pity, on two counts: firstly, successfully completing that course, given his reputation for practical experience and honesty, could have elevated him to the highest ranks in any of the United Kingdom's police forces; secondly, it was never offered again. But perhaps it was for the best; Simmonds was getting very disillusioned with the police and the Establishment.

Although the leak about the impending investigation had obviously come from Hugh Moore in the first place, there was only Cuthbert's word for it, and without any supporting evidence, Moore would never be prosecuted. Peter Marshall, the Commissioner, had told Simmonds that when Moore had reached twenty-five years' service he was going to get him to leave; but when that time arrived, a row developed between the two men and Moore refused to go, saying that he had done nothing wrong and unless the Commissioner could prove anything to the contrary, he was staying.

Simmonds told me:

> Personally, I would have got him to go by isolating him from all contact; I had seen that happen in the Met with a superintendent and it worked. It was dawning on me that it was not going to be 'in the public interest' for a man as senior as Hugh to be put before the courts for these allegations. I based this on my attendance at a cocktail party at the DPP's office, where my invitation had been with other Met officers and not from the City. I was on the periphery of a group of police and DPP staff when the question of Countryman came up. If I wanted to be convinced that Dorset Constabulary had been chosen because the Establishment did not expect them to make much of a job of it, what I heard that day would have made my mind

up for me. I told Peter Marshall that if Hugh Moore was still with the Force when I had my twenty-five years in, I would be the one to leave . . . but I don't think he was taking me too seriously. He made no effort to dissuade me and just accepted it.

In late December 1981 Simmonds was invited to a luncheon with the outgoing chief security officer and the personnel officer of British Petroleum. It led to the offer of the departing officer's job being made to Simmonds, and with the proviso that he could not leave the City until 2 June 1982, when he would have completed twenty-five years' service, he accepted.

He gave notice that he was leaving the City and, as he told me:

No one said much about it. It was my perception that they were pleased to see me go and if the conversation I had heard some time before in the DPP's office was anything to go by, so was the Establishment.

A while after I gave notice of my intention to leave, Hugh got a bit aggressive to me at one stage when I was in his office, so I decided that I would 'tell him his fortune'. I felt it was about time I told him what I thought of him and the way he had run things. I said I was aware that he had got some of his 'bent cronies' in the Force to check into my background and asked him how far he thought that had got him. He seemed surprised that I knew this but said he would get something on me.

He told me that he had an ace up his sleeve; he was going to prove I was a liar and that Phil Cuthbert could not have said the things he did to me and I had made them up. (He was conveniently forgetting what Cuthbert had said on tape!) I said that if he was a real policeman and knew that I was a liar, he should go immediately to the DPP with his evidence and get the trial stopped. He had no answer to that, and I left him fuming.

Just before the trial, I attended a function at the Freemasons' Hall, and as I entered I saw a detective chief inspector who had served with me and was a friend of Phil Cuthbert's. He was with some other police officers, he shook his head at me and openly made a Masonic sign, indicating that I had betrayed Freemasonry. I was disappointed with his behaviour, I had not let the Craft down, it was the crooks who had done that. I was abiding by the oath that I took as a police officer and obviously, to him, that was not acceptable if it involved the Craft. It was

this incident that was the final straw for me. I had witnessed obnoxious behaviour by senior and junior police
officers, graffiti in police stations, personal threats, intim-
idation of my wife and friends and ostracism from many
colleagues. Now I had Freemasons in Freemasons' Hall
publicly denouncing me. I resigned from the Freemasons
and now firmly hold the belief that the Police Service and
Freemasonry should not be allowed to mix.

Five days after Simmonds' resignation from the City Police, on 7
June 1982, the trial of Cuthbert and Golbourn commenced at the
Old Bailey.

★

'I was the Assistant Director heading a DPP Division called "Police
A" at the time of Cuthbert's trial', Michael Chance told me. 'I and
my team dealt with all allegations of criminal offences involving
officers from the Met and many other forces. The DPP had a small
team of law clerks at the Old Bailey who assisted counsel . . . I
remember going to talk to Michael Hill at the court on one occasion. I'm not sure if I or one of my colleagues prepared the case
for trial but I expect I obtained the Attorney General's consent [to
proceed with a charge of corruption]. Police A was an exceedingly
busy division.'

Both men pleaded not guilty to two charges each of conspiring
to obtain gifts of money by seeking to secure bail for accused men
and presenting evidence which was only such as would lead to dis-
charge or acquittal. The prosecution was led by forty-seven-year-
old Michael Hill QC, a barrister so committed to his work that he
frequently stayed up all night evaluating evidence for the following
day's trial. He became a Recorder in 1977 and was Senior Treasury
Counsel between 1977 and 1979; he was said – with considerable
justification – to be particularly devastating in cross-examination.

Hill told the jury of the circumstances of the robberies which had
been committed in the City and their investigations, the granting of
bail and the dropping of the charges: 'The Crown say that what went
on in these two investigations was not just curious . . . these two men
entered into corrupt dealings with an agent for the arrested persons,
the object of which was for these persons to buy their freedom.'

Golbourn's job was to 'watch Cuthbert's back' and to share in
the proceeds. It was also said that Cuthbert and an informer had
tried to trick an insurance company into paying them an unde-
served reward of £3,000.

Cuthbert had been approached by forty-two-year-old Alfred William Sheppard ('a professional criminal') on behalf of two of the robbers. Cuthbert wanted £10,000 for bail for each individual, said Hill; he added that the man in charge of the police investigations was Detective Superintendent Ernest Bransgrove, who appeared for the police in bail proceedings.

'It was not clear', said Hill, 'if Mr Bransgrove was a party to the corruption or was Mr Cuthbert's "creature"' – a curious and rather outdated term which my *Concise Oxford Dictionary* (New Edition) describes as being 'One who owes his fortune to, and remains subservient to, another'. It was an expression which would be repeated during the six-week trial.

Sheppard, said Hill, handed over the money to the officers at a restaurant opposite Bishopsgate police station. This was followed by negotiations for 'help or outers' in respect of the charges which the men faced.

Let's take a closer look at Sheppard.

★

Alfie Sheppard claimed that he had had nine other corrupt dealings with eighteen police officers, going back to 1963, and knew of eight other officers who took bribes. In 1968 he had been acquitted at the Old Bailey of being concerned in a £49,000 wages snatch. However, on 24 April 1979 he and a John Frampton were each sentenced to five years' imprisonment for conspiracy to rob a Croydon dairy, an offence of which he and his solicitor James Saunders stated, once again, that he was totally innocent. Countryman had expressed an interest in the case because Sheppard had told them that he had been a go-between in obtaining bail for robbers from police in the City of London, in return for £80,000. Moreover, since May 1979 Sheppard had apparently made a number of detailed statements to Countryman, had produced what he claimed were wrappings from some of the bundles of stolen notes which he had handed to the police and had also provided handwritten instructions from a crooked police officer telling the robbers what response to make to questions in court in order to get bail.

All very interesting, and Countryman officers tried to get Sheppard released by laying evidence of a wrongful conviction before a Judge in Chambers at the Court of Appeal. In fact, Countryman were so buoyant at the thought of Sheppard's release, which they thought to be imminent, that they arranged a safe house for him and his wife. But apparently James Saunders decided not to proceed with the application after it appeared that Sheppard had been seen in prison by Metropolitan Police officers, who informed him that charges in respect of more than a dozen burglaries and robberies, going back over a period of more than ten years, were being considered against him.

Countryman officers believed this was an attempt to discourage Sheppard, who apparently knew a thing or two about police malpractice, from talking; when he was still being held in custody, his story appeared in the 21 December 1979 edition of the *Daily Mirror*, in which he stated that he and Frampton had paid £500 each for bail through an intermediary to 'a City of London detective'. The intermediary was a John Hannam, who two weeks later told his own story to the *Daily Mirror*: having handed over the £1,000 a few weeks later, the City of London officer said that 'word had got around' and handed Hannam £700 and three post-dated cheques; Frampton's wife Doreen told the press, 'One of them kept bouncing.' It was after her husband and Sheppard were jailed that she complained to the Yard. Hannam made a statement to CIB2, after which he was arrested and charged with burglary – his press release was given from Brixton prison after he was refused bail. The matter was investigated by CIB2 – then Countryman stepped in and decided that this investigation was 'slipshod'.

On 29 April 1980 Detective Chief Inspector Marsden and Detective Superintendent Martin from CIB2 were put on uniform duties, allegedly for not properly investigating a Countryman-generated complaint. AC(C) Kelland looked at the offending report and was unable to detect any evidence of gross neglect or dishonesty on behalf of the investigating officers; he called for an independent review to be carried out by Deputy Assistant Commissioner John Radley, who concluded that the enquiry they had conducted had been carried out efficiently and honestly. They were reinstated to CIB2. Martin retired in due course on pension; Marsden retired with the rank of detective chief superintendent.

Regarding that matter, I spoke to James Martin (*not* the Superintendent Martin referred to above), who coincidentally had served in A10/CIB2 as a detective chief inspector, a detective superintendent and a detective chief superintendent ('the closest thing to being a leper!'), and what he had to tell me brought a great deal of clarity to the situation: 'I'd be most surprised to find a case hadn't been fully investigated, because reports went all the way to the top and the DPP insisted on meticulous reports.'

Back now to Alfie Sheppard, who also claimed that he had been asked to falsely testify against George Henry Ince, accused of hi-jacking an articulated lorry containing silver bullion worth £393,758, an offence which occurred on 2 May 1972. At the conclusion of his trial at the Old Bailey on 29 November 1973, Ince was sentenced to fifteen years' imprisonment. Unfortunately, it took three and a half years for Sheppard to come forward with this information to Ince's solicitor, who coincidentally was James Saunders and who, on 22 April 1977, confessed that he was 'in a quandary'. He told the press, 'I am so convinced Ince is innocent that I do not want to delay his release from prison by giving the Home Office further evidence which could take several months to be checked by the police.'

Frankie Sims, who like Ince had claimed he was elsewhere at the time, had also been convicted for the same robbery and similarly stated that Ince was innocent, and questions about the conviction were raised in the House. Moereover, when I had dealings with Ince ten years after that, *he* told me he was innocent. However, the sentence was not remitted.

So that was the background to Alfie Sheppard, who had been involved in criminality since the 1950s: a go-between, facilitating bail and watered-down charges for other criminals as well as fattening the wallets of corrupt police officers, getting another 'Mr Fixit' to arrange bail for himself – for a crime he hadn't committed – as well as offering to act as a witness for another criminal in respect of a crime which *he* hadn't committed. Not an appetizing proposition – in fact, quite an unpalatable one – but as 'Nipper' Read told the lawyers when he was tasked with going after the Kray twins, if he could have got a set of bishops and businessmen to testify against them, he would have done so. Since he could not, he would have to 'go down the sewers' after witnesses. In these types of case, police have to use the best ammunition available.

Because if what Sheppard was saying about the corrupt practices in the City of London was true, it was absolute dynamite.

Chapter 25

Sheppard – to whom someone had mischievously sent a pair of crutches – told the jury that Cuthbert was 'a criminal who chose to be a policeman'; he was reported to have sent a greetings telegram to a criminal who had asked him to get him bail and dilute the evidence in his case which read, 'From one good firm to another'. Cuthbert, Sheppard told the court, had told him that if everything fell into place, he and other corrupt officers 'would have the keys to the City'; and if what Sheppard said was correct, when he admitted being the go-between in a deal where more than £80,000 changed hands, he certainly had a point. Sheppard said that Cuthbert had also asked him to carry out robberies, using his police knowledge, and that since 'there was a fortune to be made in the City', one target was the Post Office headquarters, where he 'knew the form'.[1] Cuthbert had told him, said Sheppard, that 'he wanted to be rich and very quickly, so he could retire and live off the proceeds.'

Perhaps the worst – and probably the most damaging – of the allegations made by Sheppard was that following the *Daily Mirror* robbery Cuthbert had been unperturbed by the security guard's murder, calling him 'a busybody' for getting in the way.

All very damaging; and yet, as in all cases when one person makes allegations face-to-face against another, it was often a case of 'Yes-you-did, No-I-didn't' during cross-examination in the witness box. This extended to the junior officer who admitted taking £150 in crooked money from Cuthbert. It was, however, a little bit different when it came to John Simmonds and the covert tape-recording.

As he told me, 'I didn't have a bad time in the box; the tape really said it all.'

As indeed it did; but whatever the tape divulged, it could not be the subject of a further recording in court – this was strictly forbidden by the Criminal Justice Act, 1925, which also forbade the taking of photographs in court. It didn't fail to stop an application being made to the trial judge by a BBC reporter named Graeme McLagan for at least part of the trial to be recorded. This met with an unequivocal refusal by the Recorder of London, who said:

To permit it would be to produce the thin end of a wedge
of mammoth and uncomfortable proportions, so that
before long it would be difficult to stop the taping of the
entirety of a criminal trial by a number of interested third
parties and it is in my view neither desirable or necessary.

It was hardly surprising. Sir James Miskin QC had been the
Recorder of London since 1975 and he was a person of rather
strongly held views; at a Mansion House dinner, for example, he
referred to a black man as 'a nig-nog' which sent much of the audience into a state of swoon. I was present in court during one of
his last trials prior to the onset of the Alzheimer's disease which
afflicted him. His once mellifluous voice had become quite hoarse
– he was now known as 'Whispering Jim' – but his meaning was
clear enough when he addressed a member of an armed robbery
team (coincidentally, also black) who, due to irrefutable evidence
which had been produced at the eleventh hour, had admitted the
offence.

'I'm going to give you credit for pleading guilty', croaked Sir
James, and after a short pause added, 'but it won't be much'!

Cuthbert obviously believed that Moore was going to let him
carry the can and told Simmonds, 'When I saw him, I thought I'm
going to be the patsy . . . which is why I got a bit upset . . . which is
why I'm protecting myself now.'

This was the ideal moment for Simmonds to respond, 'Yeah,
well I want to know . . . we are in a stage now where I want to know
the full story.'

In a condensed version of the recording, this was what Cuthbert
had to say:

> Hughie did the *Daily Express* job, Guv'nor and I know
> what Hughie copped on the *Daily Express* job . . . twenty
> grand . . . One of the sergeants got £300 . . . that was
> his share out of the twenty grand and he got the fucking
> hump with it, thought it was a liberty . . . a lot of money
> changed hands, Guv'nor, it's happened in the Met, it's
> happened in the City, it's happened in all the counties,
> it has happened for years and years. The job is different
> now. I don't do fucking things like that. I'm not saying
> that somebody doesn't get a bit of bail and a drink goes
> in, fuck it, that will always happen, you will never stop it,
> but we don't let fucking robbers go for money, I've never
> let robbers go for money in my life. I never would. And if
> anybody has, it's not down to me. Hughie's run fucking

Bishopsgate and half the City Police for years and years
and years; he's been the greatest villain unhung ever since.

Referring to Bransgrove, Cuthbert told Simmonds, 'He did all the
remands, Guv'nor, he did all the bits and pieces. I didn't do fuck-
all. All I did was to go and meet a couple of guys and took an
envelope.'

When the subject of the bribes was brought up, with Simmonds
saying, 'The stories I've heard, between sixty to ninety grand',
Cuthbert replied, 'If somebody had it, if somebody fucking had it,
I don't know about it.'

'Well, what did you have, then?' asked Simmonds, and was told,
'Ninepence, nothing'.

'Yeah, yeah', scoffed Simmonds, and Cuthbert replied,
'Guv'nor, leave me alone, you never expect me to say that, do you?'

'No, no', agreed Simmonds, 'but when people turn round to me
and say it's . . . I've had various stories, sixty grand.'

'Everybody on that incident room . . . had a drink, everybody', said Cuthbert, 'We're talking about fifties, we're talking
about fifties, honestly, I'm talking about fifties. A soppy drink
for nothing, 'cos they grafted and knocked themselves out . . .
all the fucking evidence we gave was bent, I wouldn't mind, not
supposed to let them go. Never again, I tell you . . . they got
fucking ridiculous.'

By 1 July Cuthbert was in the witness box fighting for an acquittal. There was, of course, no denying that he had made those comments to Simmonds, but he stated that at the time he was drunk,
adding, 'I can tell I was well under the weather.' He told the jury
he had drunk four pints of lager before meeting Simmonds and
had continued to drink whilst they had their meeting. He had been
'talking rubbish' and he stressed that there was no foundation to
the allegations that Hugh Moore, any of the other officers in the
City police or the Metropolitan Police officers he had named were
corrupt.

It did not stop Michael Hill taking him through each incriminating comment he had made on the tape recording, but to a series
of pointed questions Cuthbert's replies were much of a muchness:
'I'm talking a load of rubbish . . . It's all made up. I've absolutely
no idea why I said it . . . I'm still making it up . . . Completely made
up, Sir.'

It was not a particularly convincing set of denials, and Cuthbert's
credibility took a dent when Hill quoted from the tape: 'Hughie did
the *Daily Express* job, Guv'nor, and I know what Hughie copped on
the *Daily Express* job, off Chadwick.'

Hill then asked, 'Can you offer us no explanation of how you came to say that?'

Cuthbert replied, 'I think I was saying what Mr Simmonds wanted me to say. I don't recall saying it and I can only speculate.'

'Why Chadwick?' asked Hill

Cuthbert replied, 'Don't know, sir.'

'He was one of the defendants who was tried for the *Daily Express* job and acquitted', stated Hill.

Cuthbert replied, 'I'll take your word for it, Sir.'

But Cuthbert did not need to take Hill's word – or anybody else's – for it, because he knew. There was no way he could *not* have known, because two years after the robbery three men stood trial at the Old Bailey for that offence and were acquitted, one of whom was 'Mad Micky' McAvoy and another was William Joseph Chadwick. Michael Hill certainly recalled it, because he was prosecuting, and the trial of the three men was taking place within a week of the murder and robbery at the *Daily Mirror* building – the offence which Cuthbert was investigating, just as he had the robbery at the *Daily Express*.

Five days later, Hugh Moore stepped into the witness box. In the same way that he had spoken up for DC David Chapman during the Austin Reed burglary case almost two years previously, Moore now appeared as a defence witness for Cuthbert. Then, Moore had been made to look a fool over his testimony for Chapman; now, his even dodgier evidence for Cuthbert would be disastrous.

Matters got off to a bad start: when Moore entered the witness box, took the oath and announced himself, the trial judge, the Recorder of London, immediately cautioned him, telling him that he did not have to say anything unless he wished to do so, but that whatever he said would be taken down and might be used in evidence against him. It was the kind of warning that might cause the staunchest police officer's Adam's apple to bob up and down, but Hugh Moore carried on, telling the court that he had not disclosed details of the internal investigation into robberies at Williams & Glyn's bank or the *Daily Express* to Cuthbert during their meeting in September 1977. Not only that, he said, but it would have been impossible for him to have done so, since he himself was unaware of the investigation.

And now Michael Hill produced the documents which almost four years previously John Simmonds had retrieved from the safe at the City Police Headquarters. It was the safe in the office where Moore had once been the detective superintendent, the safe whose combination had never changed until it had been changed by Simmonds, the same safe which that very evening someone had tried to force open. These were the documents which detailed the allegations of corruption in respect of the three City robberies which had been discussed at the meeting between Peter Marshall, the City Commissioner, Wilford Henry Gibson CBE, QPM, the Assistant Commissioner 'A' Department from the Yard – and Moore.

Shown the documents, Moore stated that he could not remember seeing them. But Hill had not shown him all the documents. Now he passed over Moore's own list of the contents of the complaints file. Like the other papers, they were dated six weeks prior to Moore's meeting with Cuthbert. This list included the internal reports and letters; and once more he was asked if he had known of the allegations before his meeting with Cuthbert, especially since there were comments in his own handwriting.

'Looking at this, I must have done', replied Moore. 'I'm sorry if I misled anyone. I have no recollection of seeing this before. I apologize.'

Hill asked about the allegations heard in court that Moore had a history of corruption. 'It's not only without foundation', replied Moore, 'but it is impossible to have been achieved, even if I had wished to.'

'You are not on trial today', said Michael Hill, witheringly. 'I do not intend to cross-examine you any further.'

'If I were permitted to say so, I would take exception to that remark', replied Moore and went on to say that he had been subjected to a great deal of adverse publicity during the trial and was quite willing to answer any questions.

However, the judge told him not to worry, adding, 'So long as it is understood that it is not on my behalf that counsel refrains from asking questions.'

It was not Moore's finest hour.

*

On 20 July 1982 the jury was out for a bare two hours before returning unanimous guilty verdicts against both Cuthbert and Goldbourn which the judge described as an 'inevitable and sensible series of verdicts'.

Bemoaning the fact that the maximum sentence for conspiracy to corrupt was two years' imprisonment, despite the fact that in 1976 a Royal Commission had recommended it be raised to seven – it was compared unfavourably with the maximum sentence for theft, which was ten years' imprisonment – the judge told the defendants:

Justice in England has been for countless years the admiration of the whole world. Corruption by police officers strikes at its very roots. I have watched juries understandably refusing to convict on uncorroborated evidence of decent policemen and I don't blame them with their knowledge of how men like you behave. Each of you has tried unsuccessfully to pull the wool over these sensible jurors' eyes. You failed.

He then jailed Cuthbert ('the intellectual superior and undoubted leader') to two consecutive terms of eighteen months' imprisonment and Golbourn (whom he described as Cuthbert's 'cheerful assistant') to twelve months' imprisonment on each offence, again to run consecutively.

The Times accurately reported 'The Destruction of a High Flyer', and as Cuthbert, with twenty-three years' service, and Golbourn were led away to commence their respective three- and two-year sentences, the judge praised the Countryman officers:

They must have been faced with a nearly impossible problem, with which, in my judgement, they dealt fairly and admirably, including the nursing of witnesses who, but for that nursing, might have got cold feet and denied justice.

But neither the judge, the DPP nor any senior police officer uttered any comment on Simmonds' input to the investigation; several people expressed surprise that Simmonds had not received a letter of commendation from the City's Commissioner. Whilst Countryman officers preened themselves outside the Old Bailey – at least two of them incongruously wearing Flying Squad ties – there was speculation: would Cuthbert live up to the threat he made – 'If I go down, I'm not prepared to be the patsy' – and become the first police supergrass?

The *Daily Telegraph* thought this might be a possibility, and its headline read, 'Bail Racket Police Chief May Turn Supergrass for Countryman', but it was probably more out of hope than expectation.

'If Cuthbert informs on others, the probe could widen dramatically,' America's *Christian Science Monitor* told its readers. 'If he stays silent, probe officials have told British newsmen they may have to yield to pressure and go home.'

'He has the potential to provide the icing on the cake', said one Countryman officer. 'I couldn't possibly put a figure on how many arrests we could expect, because if he decides to help us, there could be a domino reaction, with others agreeing to talk as well.'

But Cuthbert didn't talk. Neither did anybody else. Despite the fulsome praise meted out to Countryman by the judge, they had left the stable door open – wide open – for far too long. And despite the judge's condemnation of Cuthbert as 'the undoubted leader' (and in the dock, he certainly was), this was not a view shared by John Simmonds.

Over thirty-five years later he told me, 'He was, in my opinion a victim of a corrupt hierarchy; a follower, rather than a doer.'

Given everything that had happened, including the wrecking of Simmonds' career, these were remarkably generous words.

Nevertheless, Hugh Moore moved in quick with a statement of rebuttal, which read as follows:

> Mr Cuthbert has since admitted in evidence that the allegations were completely without foundation.
>
> Between 1976 and 1978 I was seconded to the Home Office and played no part whatsoever into the Williams & Glyn's robbery. I did commence the investigation into the *Daily Express* robbery but moved to the Home Office many months before any arrests were made and I never had any contact at all with those arrested.
>
> I have never accepted a bribe nor been involved in any way with any criminal activities. No evidence was even given at the trial to suggest otherwise – contrary to what might have been supposed by readers of some of the media coverage.
>
> It was also suggested during the tape that I may have tipped off one of the accused, Mr Cuthbert, of Operation Countryman's interest in him. Again, that is totally unfounded and there is no truth whatsoever in that allegation. On the day that Mr Cuthbert alleged that I had tipped him off, I was not even aware of the investigation by an outside force, other than by the Metropolitan Police.
>
> Reference was made on the tape to an enquiry some years before and the inference was made by Mr Cuthbert that the complaints against myself and other officers were true, although 'not proved'. In fact the complaints have since admitted that the complaints were false and in an attempt to 'frame' the investigating officers.
>
> Mr Cuthbert has since withdrawn his allegation, also.

Well, it sounded almost believable – except for 'not being aware of the investigation by an outside Force', when quite clearly

he was. As for his assertion that he was seconded to the Home
Office (in fact, the Regional Crime Squad, which was run by the
Home Office) at the time of the Williams & Glyn's robbery, this
was quite true. And the jury – plus anybody else present at the
trial – would have recalled that when Cuthbert told Simmonds,
on the tape, 'Hughie's fronting me, trying to fucking frighten
me, because Hughie had a drink out of that fucking *Daily
Express* job . . . er, er, out of the Williams and Glyn's job . . .'
Simmonds contradicted him, saying, 'He was on the Regional
Crime Squad.'

'I know he was, Guv'nor', replied Cuthbert, 'but he had a drink
out of it.'

Not unreasonably, Simmonds asked, 'Well, how can he have a
drink out of it when he's on the Regional?'

There was a little more conversation, Simmonds querying,
Cuthbert insisting, before Simmonds asked, 'Well, for what reason?'

'Because he was coming back to the City, and because he was
Hughie Moore and because he worked with all of us and he, you
know, he was in a position of power, up there on the Regional
Crime Squad and covered things, same as all the blokes on the
Robbery Squad had a drink out of it, going right up to the fucking
top of the tree . . . They're putting me in as the bad man because I
did the fucking business, that's why, 'cause I had to go and do – see
the people. I never met any of the villains, nobody like that, I was
fucking asked to do it.'

In detailing where the corruption went, 'right to the top of the
tree', Cuthbert also said, 'It's a funny world, this City, because
everybody knows after a couple of years what everybody does
because you have to know in the City and the rules used to be if
you were a DI or a chief inspector in Division, you went through
the fucking sliding scale, that was it, the same as it used to be at the
Yard, Guv'nor, don't pretend. I used to bung Roy Yorke and Jim
Marshall, and it used to go up the fucking top of the tree, used to
go up to the ACs [Assistant Commissioners].'

All right, let's take a look at these luminaries.

Roy Yorke had been the wearer of two hats – Commander of
C9 Department (the Met's Provincial Crime Branch, which acted
as a liaison and arrest facility for constabulary forces) and also
Commander of C12, the Regional Crime Squad. He had held
that position from 1 January 1970 until 26 April 1972, when he
took control of the Metropolitan Police's No. 2 District. There he
remained until he retired on New Year's Eve 1973, having served
34 years and 304 days; he had also collected nine Commissioner's
commendations. How much contact Cuthbert would have had

with him is debatable; but let's leave Yorke for now and go on to the next accused officer.

Jim Marshall, who had served continuously on the Flying Squad and the Regional Crime Squad since 1965 and retired as a detective chief superintendent, was certainly about at the time when Cuthbert was on the Regional Crime Squad, but he was also rather busy. He was being commended by the Commissioner (as well as a number of judges) for 'ability and tenacity in a case of robbery with violence', 'determination and detective ability in arresting a persistent and experienced criminal for officebreaking and possessing explosives' and 'detective ability and initiative leading to the arrest of a gang of active criminals for armed robbery'. Additionally, he was highly commended for 'outstanding courage, determination and devotion to duty in overpowering and detaining a violent gang of criminals armed with loaded firearms', which led to a £20 award from the Bow Street Magistrates' Reward Fund, plus Her Majesty The Queen conferring on him the British Empire Medal for Gallantry – oh, and between the high commendation and the decoration, he was also further commended for 'persistence and ability leading to the arrest and convictions of a gang of criminals for conspiracy to rob'. He had collected eleven commendations – coincidentally, the same number as had been awarded to both Cuthbert and Moore – and when he retired, it was prior to the revelations being made which would result in the creation of Operation Countryman. He retired on 22 May 1977, having served 29 years and 236 days which, together with 129 days war service, neatly brought his total up to exactly 30 years service, classified, like Roy Yorke's, as 'exemplary'.

Who does that leave? Although Cuthbert spoke of bunging ACs in the plural, really there was only one that fitted the bill and that was the Assistant Commissioner (Crime).

Peter Ewan Brodie OBE, QPM, educated at Harrow, a product of Lord Trenchard's 'officer class', seconded to the Ceylon Police during the Second World War before becoming Chief Constable of Stirling and Clackmannan, Chief Constable of Warwickshire and HM Inspector of Constabulary for England and Wales, before being appointed Assistant Commissioner 'C' Department, Metropolitan Police? The man who at one stage prior to his retirement in 1972 was tipped to become the next Commissioner? Can you seriously see Cuthbert – or anybody else – sliding up to his office on the 5th floor at the Yard and, with a furtive wink, slipping him a grubby brown envelope?

As Cuthbert was prone to say, 'Don't be rude, Guv'nor!' – but let's face it, all things are possible. Those three officers all had impeccable records, but then again, so did Commander Ken Drury and Detective Chief Superintendent Bill Moody and they came a tumble, to the tune of five and twelve years' porridge respectively (see Introduction), so why shouldn't Messrs Yorke, Marshall and Brodie be similarly as straight as corkscrews?

No reason at all, except for two matters. When illicit payments are obtained and disseminated by detectives, money only goes to those who are in the know – and it was common practice for those receiving the money to say to the distributor, 'Well, the Guv'nor's got to have his corner, y'know' – when 'the Guv'nor', whoever he might be, was blissfully unaware of what was going on and the extra money was simply going into the corrupt officer's pocket.

That was a classic example of the words from an old Flying Squad stanza:

> . . . and to his eternal shame,
> copped his dough in another man's name.

That's one matter, and the second is this: despite naming those (and other officers) to Simmonds, Cuthbert swore, on oath at the Old Bailey, that none of those assertions of corruption were true. Because if he were to later say that they were true, it would mean that he had lied on oath, thereby committing the offence of perjury. As an experienced detective, having attended courses at the Detective Training School, Cuthbert would have been fully aware that the courts take a very dim view of perjury, for which the penalty is seven years' imprisonment. But as we know, Cuthbert never did change his story – so those accusations must have been false, mustn't they?

Still, I expect the Countryman officers had a fine time interviewing the likes of Messrs Brodie, Yorke and Marshall in their retirement, and who possibly emerged from the discussions with their feelings well and truly hurt.

★

The tabloids, of course, had a field day. First came revelations from vivacious Tina Duncan, whom Golbourn had met in 1976 when she was a trainee manageress at The City Stores pub. During their two-year relationship, during which she described herself as being 'his bit on the side', Ms Duncan told how Golbourn would give her envelopes containing £500 or £1,000 'to keep safe'. Telling the newspaper, 'I had mountains of gold', she described in detail the gifts which Golbourn bestowed on her: £100 for a dress, a ring at

Christmas and £200 to buy presents and a £700 gold watch for her birthday. At one stage the money flow seemed to have dried up; that changed at approximately the same time as the robbery and murder at the *Daily Mirror*.

In 1978 Golbourn met up with single mother of four, Valerie Groves, who vowed to marry him at the end of his sentence. She denied completely any suggestion that like Ms Duncan she had been 'showered with gold', saying that he had been unable to support her and the children; but since by that time Golbourn had resigned from the police and was working as a wood-machinist in an East End factory, perhaps that was hardly surprising.

★

Not that the fallout from the trial really mattered now, because it had pretty well been settled in the House of Lords on 30 July. When Lord Jenkins of Putney asked the Lord Chancellor, 'Whether the tape-recording played at the Old Bailey during the trial of Detective Chief Inspector Philip Cuthbert has been considered by the Director of Public Prosecutions with a view to further proceedings?' he received the rather unequivocal reply, 'The matter has been considered by the Director of Public Prosecutions. On the evidence presently available, no further proceedings are contemplated.'

It was all over bar the shouting; and in the week, and then the months, that followed, there was enough of that.

PART IV

Leaving

And therefore, if I cannot prove a lover
To entertain these fair, well-spoken days,
I am determinéd to prove a villain.

Shakespeare, Richard III

CHAPTER 26

Stephen Sherlock Ross (later Baron Ross of Newport) was the Liberal MP for the Isle of Wight, where a number of his constituents were serving prisoners, many of them with grievances to declare. Ross ('call me Steve') started Phase Two in the battle of the innuendoes. This was as the result of working with journalists from the *Guardian* and Granada Television over a period of months and included allegations that police had not only accepted bribes but had also taken part in bank raids.

Within two days of both City police officers' convictions, David Steel MP, the Leader of the Liberal Party (later Lord Steel of Aikwood KT, KBE, PC), clashed in the Commons with the Prime Minister, Margaret Thatcher (later Baroness Thatcher LG, OM, PC, FRS, FRIC), when he stated that the lack of prosecutions arising from Operation Countryman threatened to bring the police force into disrepute.

When the Prime Minister replied that the police were the first to want to root out corruption in their ranks, adding that most police officers did their jobs magnificently, Steel exploded.

'We do not need lectures about the dedication of the police service', he riposted. 'What I am concerned about is the failure to tackle the alleged network of corruption and dishonesty in one unit. Operation Countryman has cost the taxpayer £4 million and appears to have been frustrated. The Government must take action.'

He added that he would be seeking a meeting with William Whitelaw, the Home Secretary. Mrs Thatcher's comments, he later suggested, were 'inadequate, evasive and irrelevant'.

The morning following Steel's remarks, Assistant Commissioner Gilbert Kelland must have choked on his breakfast boiled egg when he heard the following announcement on the Independent Radio News:

A new scandal is threatening the Metropolitan Police. Stephen Ross, the Liberal MP for the Isle of Wight, is claiming that twenty police officers up to the rank of assistant commissioner should be investigated on corruption charges. He has called for a Royal Commission to investigate police corruption in London after following up information given to him by prisoners on the Isle of Wight, and Mr Ross says he is hoping to meet the Home Secretary to discuss the allegations next week.

Nobody wants to criticise the police unreasonably at a time when they are under pressure, particularly after the recent bombings. But I don't think anybody, any citizen of the country, can be happy at some of the accusations that have been made, and they have come from so many different sources that I think that this is a time now to clean the whole thing up. If we are going to reorganize the Metropolitan Police, well, for God's sake let's do it properly this time.

Well, this was something which Kelland definitely did *not* wish to hear, in particular the reference to Assistant Commissioners, because the imputation of dodgy dealings was not directed at the Assistant Commissioners in charge of administration, traffic or training; it was a reference to the Assistant Commissioner in charge of crime – and that was him!

The morning toast was undoubtedly left cold in the rack when Kelland hot-footed it to the Yard; there was a hurried discussion with the Commissioner and the Met's solicitor which resulted in the following communiqué being sent to the head of IRN:

Referring to the news item(s) involving Stephen Ross MP of 23.7.82, your attention is drawn to the apology printed in *The Times* newspaper of 17 February 1982 following a similar defamatory allegation made in *The Times* diary. Would you please ensure that a retraction is made at once whilst the legal position of the assistant commissioners is considered?

The Commissioner hit out in a statement the same day, attacking 'unfair allegations of unsubstantiated allegations . . . which undermine police morale', and the retraction was duly made and no legal proceedings on behalf of the police were instituted; a pity, maybe, since the broadcast was decidedly defamatory, but perhaps the higher echelons at the Yard hoped these allegations would die a death. No chance.

Later the same day, it was announced that there would be a meeting between the two Liberal MPs and the Home Secretary the following Thursday.

'Our concern', said Steel, 'is to find out what the Government intends to do about the apparent obstacles placed in the way of Operation Countryman.'

Right on cue, a spokesman for the Home Office replied, 'We are anxious to hear what Mr Steel and Mr Ross have to say.'

They didn't have to wait until the following Thursday, because on the same day as the announcement Ross told the listeners of BBC Radio's *World at One* that his informants had been police officers, convicted prisoners and journalists, and although he declined to say who had provided the list of twenty names he told the audience, 'Operation Countryman has been thwarted both by the Home Office and by Scotland Yard. The provincial policemen involved in the investigation have made many recommendations to the DPP and nothing has come of them.'

On 25 July the *Observer* published an article mentioning that '75 names remain on lists of unfinished business compiled by Operation Countryman' and that a secret team of 'specially selected detectives' were conducting enquiries into the theft of silver bullion, valued at £3 million, carried out in March 1980 outside London. The Yard stated that having put out a statement to repudiate these matters forty-eight hours previously, they were 'not prepared to discuss or comment on any subsequent stories which are printed in newspapers'.

The Attorney General for England and Wales, Sir Michael Havers (later Baron Havers PC, QC) *was* prepared to comment – the credibility of the DPP's office had been impugned – and he did so, the same day, in the *Sunday Times*. Suggestions that the DPP's office had obstructed the corruption enquiries 'were completely and absolutely untrue', he declared and he added that the lack of 'real independent evidence' had prevented more corruption trials of police officers as a result of Operation Countryman. He said:

> I think the police are having a very rough time at the moment. They are, as a force, superb, first class. To raise this thing, naming ranks and leaving it hanging in the air, is, I think, most unfair to the police, generally. There is no reason why Mr Ross, if he has the evidence, should not have sent it to me and the Director of Public Prosecutions, officially. It is terribly easy to make allegations and villains have every reason to do so. It is very straightforward. If it is simply a villain against a police officer, or anyone else, I wouldn't prosecute. Most of the Countryman cases were entirely based on villains' allegations. I have agreed with the DPP's decision in every case.

And if that were not enough, Sir Michael reinforced this on the BBC Radio Programme, *The World this Weekend*, later the same day. He stated that both he and Sir Thomas Hetherington, the Director of Public Prosecutions, had 'felt very frustrated' over the past three years because there was often no evidence to put before the courts to back up allegations of corruption. However, he criticized the way in which the two Liberal MPs had publicized the corruption allegations, saying:

> If you have got evidence of criminal offences which involve a number of the whole group, the proper way to deal with that is to send those details, either to me or the Director of Public Prosecutions. You can certainly say afterwards you have done it. But not to start naming ranks of people, particularly when you get to ranks when there are very few of them and of course, cast a slur upon the whole force of 25,000 people.

Following the meeting with the Home Secretary on 29 July, Mr Steel told reporters that Mr Whitelaw had said he would consult with the Lord Chancellor, the Attorney General, the Commissioner of the Metropolitan Police and the Chief Constable of Surrey, now the actual head of Operation Countryman. He envisaged that the proposed enquiry would be heard in secret by a senior Queen's Counsel, and witnesses would be given immunity from prosecution. The resultant report would be published, naming names, and the offenders would be put before the courts as well as facing police disciplinary procedures. Ross added that unless action was taken in the next few months, he would raise the matter in the Commons, where Parliamentary privilege would protect any member who named names. But the Commons would not be sitting again until October; however there was another weapon in the pro-Countryman armoury. It was called *World in Action*.

*

The programme was broadcast on the evening of 2 August 1982. Some aspects of it have been mentioned previously, but the content was a real tour de force of trashing the police. Heading the cast was Arthur Hambleton, who declared that the statement which said Countryman had never been obstructed was not true and that it had been signed 'to save Countryman'. His men, said Hambleton, felt that the DPP's office was not supporting them, morale was affected and informants began to wonder if it was worthwhile their

giving Countryman information. He said that he was angered by the
way in which Deputy Commissioner Kavanagh had claimed allegations eventually passed to the Yard were often frivolous, although
paradoxically, Hambleton also stated that some of the allegations
made to Countryman were false and that within the first year of
the enquiry sixteen officers were cleared of misconduct. However,
he added the corollary that he did believe many other accusations
were true. In addition, he stated that Kavanagh had told him not
to accept any further enquiries, which, he said would be dealt with
by the Yard. Hambleton disputed claims that he had exceeded his
brief to deal purely with the allegations regarding the three City of
London robberies. After he had retired, he said, the Yard had put
its own men on to investigating the allegations, 'So basically, you
may say that we were stopped from clearing up the Yard.'

Next came John Cottingham Alderson CBE, QPM, who had just
retired as Chief Constable of Devon and Cornwall Constabulary. A
police officer since 1946, he had served in the Dorset Constabulary
as its Deputy Chief Constable and also in the Met from 1966 to
1973, when he had been Assistant Commissioner 'D' – in charge
of training. He had been called to the bar and was a member of
the Liberal Party, as well as being on the committee of the Royal
Humane Society and a consultant on human rights. A champion
of community policing, he was generally regarded as being 'soft'.
Now he told the programme that he believed that Countryman's
work on the Metropolitan Police was wound down because it was
'politically embarrassing' and that he believed that for some CID
officers, corruption was a way of life and 'institutionalized'.

Precisely what Alderson had to back up these claims is debatable; he had never had any input into the Countryman investigation, nor as the Assistant Commissioner in charge of training at the
Yard, four years prior to the commencement of the enquiry, would
he have had any up-to-date knowledge of the state of affairs in the
CID.

And to back up the others, the rather tainted Alfie Sheppard
appeared, fresh from his run at the Old Bailey, to say that with his
main source of income gone, crime was becoming unprofitable: 'It
was like working for the police.'

The Yard hit back, the same night, with a statement claiming
that the programme 'was misleading and factually wrong in many
places' and stating:

> It is extraordinary that a former chief constable should
> say that he issued a statement from Dorset Headquarters
> which he knew to be untrue and that in itself hardly adds

to his credibility. Firstly, it is quite wrong to say that the enquiry into Metropolitan Police officers ended when Mr Hambleton resigned. The independence of the enquiry was preserved by Sir Peter Matthews, Chief Constable of Surrey, agreeing to take command. Sir Peter took over 18 months after the start of the enquiry which had not then produced any results. Because of the general concern with the lack of progress, Sir Peter delegated enquiries which had no connection with the Countryman terms of reference to the Complaints Investigation Bureau. Corruption cannot be condoned but gossip from criminals is not evidence, as every policeman knows. Fair play applies as much to policemen as it does to the rest of the public and to condemn a class on uncorroborated allegations is less than natural justice.

This was followed by a leader in the 5 August 1982 edition of *The Times*, in which two basic questions were asked: first, was there a substantial measure of corruption in the Metropolitan Police, and second, had there been a cover-up by the police, as Hambleton had suggested? The solution, suggested the leader, was this:

A special investigating unit is needed, whose sole function would be to investigate allegations of corruption against policemen. It should be independent of any police force and staffed by a combination of police officers working long-term for the unit and others on temporary secondment. The essential point is that the unit should have its separate identity and objectives and be accountable, not to a police force but to the Police Complaints Board, the Inspectorate of Police or the Home Secretary.

And then one week after the *World in Action* programme, *The Times* published a ludicrous article under the heading 'Countryman Causes 300 to Leave Force', in which they claimed that during the Countryman investigation 313 London officers had left the force, of whom 44 had been convicted of criminal offences, and a further 194 had resigned whilst under criminal or disciplinary action. When these wild inaccuracies were pointed out, *The Times* withdrew the comments the following day.

All very well; but since 'The Thunderer' had a reputation for accuracy, it meant that public confidence in the police took yet another knock.

★

So what of Messrs Ross and Steel's demand for an investigation *right now*? And if the Home Secretary did agree to an enquiry into the enquiry, who would be called and what would they say?

Merlyn Rees, for a start; as the then Home Secretary, he had agreed to Countryman running the investigation, but had recently said that, in retrospect, it had been wrong to let a small rural force like Dorset investigate the City and the Met, because they were unable to comprehend the complex issues faced by big city forces and posed by big city criminals. So why pick them in the first place?

What action did the Home Office take when Hambleton complained? The enquiry might make Whitelaw trawl back to find out what, if anything, was said or done. And with regard to Hambleton, if the situation had been as desperate as he had stated, why wait two years before publicly voicing his concerns? What – the enquiry would certainly want to know – was the exact nature of the evidence on which he based his assertions of corruption? How accurate were the criminals' assertions? Were the police officers who were accused too clever for the investigators?

Did the enquiry spiral out of control? Did it go too far? Was it as unproductive as the Yard had suggested? The DPP and his staff had been accused of, at best, being less than helpful, at worst of being obstructive. Was Countryman overzealous – or the DPP too timid?

All these questions and many more would only be answered as and when the Home Secretary's enquiry group was formed.

But it wasn't. On 21 October Whitelaw wrote to Steel refusing his request for an enquiry and telling him that he had concluded that 'There was no evidence of an obstruction of a kind which would have prevented those responsible from doing their job.'

Meanwhile, the Countryman personnel had been considerably depleted at Godalming, where just three officers – one a detective chief superintendent – were left. This was in respect of the investigation into the City Police Detective Superintendent Ernie Bransgrove, who had, almost as an afterthought, been suspended from duty since 7 October 1981 – over three years from the commencement of the enquiry, over three years since Cuthbert had named him on the tape as being involved in corrupt practices.

Still the matter rumbled on. At a Commons sitting on 25 October 1982, Alf Dubs, MP for Battersea South (later Baron Dubs of Battersea), discovered from the Attorney General that no further matters from Countryman were before the DPP for a decision; he then went on to comment on the public disquiet about the failure of Countryman and asked the Attorney General whether he did not feel that he and the DPP had a responsibility to carry out an investigation into the whole sorry affair? In response to this, and to a question put by Arthur Davidson QC, Labour MP for Accrington, who asked how closely the DPP kept in touch with and advised those carrying out the investigations, the Attorney General had this to say:

> The problem was that the original Countryman investigation was carried away on a wave of optimism. Figures as high as 80 potential cases were given at one time, but when the evidence in respect of those cases was looked at with care, many times it was found to be hearsay upon hearsay. Often, the evidence was from people with serious convictions who may have had a score to settle against particular police officers or against the police force in general.
>
> When the complaints of obstruction came to light, as the Hon. Gentleman will recall, the then Chief Constable in charge of the investigation issued a statement, denying that there had been any obstruction. Shortly after that, I had a long meeting with him and Sir Peter Matthews, who was to take over from him. We went through everything that was there and in the end, the sort of obstruction that I could identify in the complaints was, for example, that the Director had not agreed to a general immunity against anybody that we wanted to call as a witness, even though that might be in a serious armed robbery case, such as the Williams and Glyn's bank case. For years, the Director has refused to give such blanket immunities. I am sure that all Right Honourable and Honourable Members will agree that is proper.
>
> There were one or two complaints about the Director's representative working in Surrey with the Countryman force. When one looked into them, they were found not to be cases of obstruction of any kind. The meeting ended with a resolve on all sides that the enquiry should go forward with renewed vigour.
>
> The Director of Public Prosecutions did everything he could to keep closely in touch, but unfortunately, from time to time, Countryman officers did things that could not be justified. Without telling the Director that they had done so, they arrested a senior officer on a charge that had nothing to do with Countryman. He did not learn about it for some weeks. There was found to be no evidence when the facts were analysed and the officer had to be discharged.

In another case, the Countryman officers sought to support a bail application in a Surrey case involving a villain in Surrey when the Surrey police were opposing bail. Mr Hambleton admitted to me at the meeting that both of those actions were wrong. Those were the sorts of problems that were occurring. Tight control can be exercised by the Director, only if somebody reacts to that tight control when it is sought to be imposed.

The matter ground to a halt during Question Time in the Commons on 18 November 1982, when there were denials of 'police-baiting' by Labour MPs and accusations of 'generalized smears on a fine body of men' from across the floor. Eventually, the Home Secretary stated:

> I believe the right person to pursue this corruption is the new Commissioner, the Deputy Commissioner and the Assistant Commissioner (Crime). If I set up another enquiry, it would look as if I did not have confidence in them. I have confidence in them and that is why I am determined to back them ... The view of the House is clear that we have to root out corruption in the Metropolitan Police and we have to decide on the right way of doing that. I have told the House how I think it is right to pursue that and I hope the House will back me in going forward in that way. The new Commissioner and the new situation should look to the future and not constantly hark back on the past. I intend to look forward to the future and I believe I shall be fully backed by the House.

The 'old Commissioner', Sir David McNee, had gone. It had been an eventful tenure. True, he had increased the numbers of police from 22,500 to 26,500 and got 1,500 extra officers on the beat by banning Panda cars in the middle of London. But there had been civil disturbances at Grunwick, Lewisham, Southall and, by far the worst episode, Brixton. On the terrorist front, there had been the Balcombe Street siege and the storming of the Iranian Embassy. There had also been the death of Blair Peach; but a particularly low spot came when Michael Fagan gained access to the Queen's bedchamber at Buckingham Palace, then a swift resignation was demanded (and just as promptly offered and accepted) after the Queen's Police Officer of ten years standing, Commander Michael Trestrail RVO, admitted a relationship with a male prostitute. Political correctness had not then taken hold of humanity by the scruff of its neck, and consequently the wordplay on 'Queens' provided the press with a field day.

Before legging it hot-foot back to his native Glasgow, Sir David made a farewell speech in which he took particular care to lambast his nemesis, saying, 'It must be very discouraging to my officers, who have done so much hard work against corruption, to have this drip, drip, drip called Countryman and the allegations that corruption is institutionalized in the Metropolitan Police – that is rubbish.'

The 'new Commissioner' referred to by the Home Secretary was Sir Kenneth Leslie Newman GBE, QPM, KSTJ, LL.B, CIMGT. Asked about Operation Countryman and the recent controversy over police corruption, Sir Kenneth drily replied, 'I have seen some evidence that the press are treating these Countryman cases with less care than perhaps they should.'

Now that he was free of the toils of office, Sir David McNee obviously felt that Hambleton had not been sufficiently punished for his allegations of obstruction and so went to work with a will; when the *Sunday Mirror* published his views, he came out with all guns blazing:

> There are bound to be problems in an enquiry involving a force as large as London. However, it is a man of questionable judgement who decides the sole cause of his problems is wilful obstruction. In a police officer, such a quality borders on the naïve; after all, suspected villains whoever they might be are not inclined to confess all at the first question. A suspect has rights and a police officer under suspicion has the same rights, too. If a copper is good at his job, he will not roll over, screaming, 'Obstruction! Obstruction!' every time someone declines to answer a question. He will get on with the job and find a way to get at the truth.

Arthur Hambleton declined to comment on those remarks; he contented himself with saying that 'he was considering his position'.

★

Countryman had pretty well been laid to rest but not, it seems, forgotten, especially by the City of London Police.

Les Knight was an inspector with the Suffolk Constabulary. One of his senior officers had previously served in the City Police and he had arranged for a three-monthly exchange between officers in the two forces. In 1984 Knight was seconded to Snow Hill police station and during the week he ate in the officers' mess. At weekends it was closed, and as the duty inspector was the only rank above that of sergeant who was on duty, he ate in the 'other ranks' mess. He told me:

> My first weekend visit was an eye-opener. I entered the mess to see half the shift crowded on to one table and the other table totally empty. I got my food and sat at the empty table. Within seconds, my senior sergeant approached and said, 'We don't use that table – it was the Countryman's.'
>
> I tell you this as an example of their deep resentment and general distrust of county forces.

Although the Countryman officers had departed from the City some two years earlier, this does tend to show that they were neither forgiven nor forgotten.

CHAPTER 27

So – what happened next?

After eighteen years as Chief Constable of Dorset, in retirement Arthur Hambleton devoted a great deal of time to the Dorset St John Ambulance Service and the Red Cross; he spent his remaining years between Dorset and Skipton in Yorkshire. He died, aged ninety-six, in Dorset County Hospital, following a short illness in 2012.

Len Burt retired from Dorset Police in 1984. He became chairman of the Bournemouth Fine Wine Society, joined the Society of Dorset Men and led the Ragamuffins, a luncheon club which became known for its fund-raising. Clearly deeply affected by the failure of Countryman, he died in 2010 at the age of seventy-eight.

It was John Simmonds' proud boast that he was unemployed for nine hours after he left the police and slept through seven of them. He went on to have a hugely successful second career with British Petroleum, but at what cost to the general public? I have no doubt that, but for this hiatus in the City of London, Simmonds could eventually have been appointed Commissioner of the Metropolitan Police. And what a Commissioner he would have made! He would have brought to the appointment a variety of gifts: honesty, integrity, huge experience and a commitment to reform. With two exceptions – the peers Imbert and Stevens – Commissioners with all of those attributes have been thin on the ground in recent years. As Simmonds said:

> A number of officers came up to me after the trial and told me they had always known certain people who were part of the enquiry were bent. Some also apologised to me for not giving me more support while I was in the Job. Others even admitted that they had believed the 'propaganda' that had been put about that I had fitted up Phil Cuthbert and only when they heard the evidence did they believe the truth.
>
> To me, this was all too little, too late.

Ernie Bransgrove retired from the City of London Police and was living in Billericay, Essex, when on 15 December 2009 he was killed instantly in a head-on car crash. Assistant Commissioner Ernest Bright retired and died, aged seventy-eight, on 25 January 2007. The Commissioner, Peter Marshall, retired in 1985 and died of cancer, aged seventy-six, on 20 February 2007.

And Hugh Moore? As we know, he successfully resisted the Commissioner's efforts to oust him in 1980 when he had completed twenty-five years' service; he stayed on and prospered, implementing the City's anti-terrorist policies and conducting investigations into the Bank of Credit and Commerce International and the Maxwell empire. Although he never advanced beyond the rank of commander, a position he held for over fifteen years, he was awarded the Queen's Police Medal for distinguished service in 1992.

He died of a heart attack, whilst still serving, on 4 December 1993. Eleven days previously, at Great Ormond Street Hospital, he had tackled a bogus charity collector who was also a violent thief, and from the cuts he sustained on his arms, legs and face, the coroner ruled that he had been unlawfully killed. In the history of the City Police, it was only the second time that this had happened; the first had been over eighty years earlier, when Sergeants Bentley and Tucker and PC Choate were shot dead by Russian anarchists, killings which led to the famous 'Siege of Sidney Street'.

So was Moore a hero or – as he had been termed by Phil Cuthbert – 'the greatest villain unhung'? Well, perhaps a bit of both. Moore has to be commended, no doubt about that, for attempting, at the age of sixty-four and having not been in the best of health for some time (I was told by a colleague, 'Countryman had unhinged him'), to arrest a considerably younger violent criminal.

Then there is the matter of evidence, and there was little enough of that. A jury can be instructed that they can convict on circumstantial evidence, as they did in the case of Florence Ransom in 1940. She murdered three people with blasts from a shotgun. Nobody heard or saw her do it; she didn't confess to it, saying she was miles away from the scene at the time of the murder; nor were any incriminating fingerprints found. But in his very first murder investigation, the head of the Flying Squad, Detective Chief Inspector Peter Henderson Beveridge MBE, proved that every single thing she said was a lie, and this led to her conviction.

However, there was nowhere near anything like a sufficiency of circumstantial evidence to warrant Moore's arrest, let alone convict him. He had warned Cuthbert of the impending enquiry, there's little doubt about that; he denied this in court, on oath, saying that he was not even aware of the enquiry being launched, then had to retract his answer when papers were produced showing he had known of the investigation. But he stood firm on one matter – that he had not forewarned Cuthbert – and there was no independent evidence to show that he did; suspicion, certainly, but suspicion is not, and never has been, evidence.

Did he receive money from Cuthbert? Cuthbert had said he did, but again there were no independent witnesses or independent evidence to confirm it, and in the witness box both Cuthbert and Moore denied it on oath. Was there any evidence of sudden affluence in the Moore household and/or bank accounts at the time of the arrests of the robberies in the City? Did Countryman look for evidence of this? If they did, they couldn't have found any.

Was it Moore who attempted to extract the documentary details of the internal enquiry from the safe in the superintendent's office and then try to force the cabinet open? This is a possibility. He had previously used that office, knew the safe's combination and had no reason to believe it had been changed, given that many of the City CID's practices had lapsed into a moribund state.

Was he party to the attempt to fit up Simmonds and his wife? Probably not. Moore would have had legitimate access to all of the CID officers' details under his command, and the fact that whoever was responsible got the Simmonds' address right but the postcode wrong suggests that Moore was not responsible for supplying those details. It was not a case of leaving a false trail, either – for the fit-up to be fully effective (given the amount of planning which had gone into it), it was imperative that the post code be correct.

Moore championed the cause of officers who were thought to be crooked, denigrated those who were straight, was singularly unpleasant to John Simmonds and on two occasions appeared in court as a defence witness for crooked police officers; on both occasions he was found to be less than truthful.

Hero? Yes. Good man or bad man? You decide.

PART V

Conclusions & Comparisons

The only thing necessary for the triumph of evil
is that good men do nothing.

Edmund Burke

CHAPTER 28

A nd that was that.

Austin Mitchell, the Labour MP for Grimsby, tabled separate questions to the Attorney General and the Home Secretary in January 1984, asking if they would prohibit membership of Masonic lodges to police officers, and in 1985 the Commissioner published a book – a copy of which was handed to every member of the Met – entitled *The Principles of Policing and Guidance for Professional Behaviour*. It was regarded as a pretty sycophantic treatise, along the lines of 'be nice to everybody and be prepared to be firm (but not overbearing) when absolutely necessary'. Inevitably, Freemasonry collected a couple of pages to itself, full of 'dos and don'ts', none of which would really have mattered to anybody who was on the Square. But to somebody contemplating the Craft, these were the most perceptive words:

> The police officer's special dilemma is the conflict between his service declaration of impartiality, and the sworn obligation to keep the secrets of Freemasonry. His declaration has its statutory obligation to avoid any activity likely to interfere with impartiality or to give the impression that it may do so; a Freemason's oath holds inevitably the implication that loyalty to fellow Freemasons may supersede any other loyalty.

It really didn't make any difference. In fact, Masonic Lodge No. 9179 opened in January 1986. It was known as the Manor of St James, for the exclusive use of Met officers who'd worked in the West End. Among the founder members was Gilbert Kelland, and the membership included two deputy assistant commissioners, twelve commanders, two dozen chief superintendents, a dozen superintendents and a score or more from the other ranks. All were willing to be blindfolded with a noose draped around their neck and a dagger placed against their heart, and to be warned that if they broke their vows of secrecy and loyalty they would have their throats cut and their tongues torn out by the root, before going into dinner. *Bon appétit!*

However, if corruption with Masonic overtones bubbled to the surface again, at least the Commissioner could say, 'Well, I did warn them!'

In his book, *The Brotherhood*, Stephen Knight is convinced that the corruption involved in the three big robberies in the City would never have occurred had the erstwhile Commissioner, James Page, not been corrupted by joining the Freemasons, which in turn led to him promoting otherwise unsuitable officers. It's a moot point, and I think it's unfair to totally blame Freemasonry for all the ills that befell the City – or the Met for that matter. When it comes down to it, there are some cops who are going to be wrong 'uns whether they're Freemasons or not – it's as simple as that.

Is there a place for Freemasonry in the police? Well, as we know, John Simmonds thought the two couldn't mix. I remember chatting to a detective superintendent whom I'd known for years and who was a very useful, hardworking copper, and I asked him, 'Didn't you ever fancy going on the Flying Squad?'

'I'd like to have done', he replied, 'but I'm not on the Square.'

'What's that got to do with anything?' I said. 'I was on the Squad but I'm not on the Square' – but he simply shrugged, and we went on to other matters. Obviously, he thought this was a prerequisite for becoming a member of the Sweeney, yet thinking about it, there were strong Masonic influences on the Flying Squad during my time there. One senior officer who was very high up in his Lodge only brought people on to the Squad who were fellow Masons, not because they were suited to Flying Squad work, because quite conspicuously many of them were not. Amongst them were some pretty dire characters, I can tell you. Not necessarily bent, but useless – not only at Squad work, I mean, but at any kind of police tasks. One of them was a lethargic Squad driver. Late one afternoon, I received a tip-off that a serial armed robber who was top of my 'wanted' list would be at a certain place at a certain time, within half an hour.

'Quick, get the car!' I said. 'We're going to South London; I've got one to nick!'

'I can't go!' he exclaimed indignantly. 'Tonight's my Lodge meeting!'

I'm afraid the driver didn't keep his appointment, although I kept mine – and the capture of the armed robber led to twenty-six more arrests.

That's on the negative side. I accept that Freemasons do an enormous amount of good with their charitable works and by helping each other in business; a notable exception is the one referred to above. But the two men who acted as my referees when I applied to join the Metropolitan Police were both Freemasons, and all of my friends and acquaintances are as well. They know that I'm not, and never have been, on the Square, but I've never received anything other than friendship, kindness and assistance from them.

Mind you, I was once asked if I'd like to become a Freemason, and this was when I was first appointed a detective constable. I thanked the officer concerned but courteously declined, for two reasons. The first was that I believed that entry into the Masons required the type of expenditure, for Masonic impedimenta, which represented funds I didn't possess; most of my cash was being spent on my four children, all of whom possessed the appetites of starving timber wolves. The second reason was that in those days it was commonplace for suspects to be interviewed in the CID office, at the interviewing officer's desk. The officer who had made me the offer of inclusion into the Craft had the habit, once the interviewee was seated, of producing a sign from the drawer of his desk, which read:

ONLY THE POOR NEED GO TO JAIL

This, I thought, might well be a bad omen.

Taking everything into account, I suppose becoming an honest, decent Freemason or a crooked one is the difference between appreciatively sipping a glass of Château Margaux and getting smashed out of your brains on cheap Nigerian brandy, able to take the enamel off a bucket – just a matter of keeping a sense of proportion, and knowing what's best, that's all.

*

From time to time over the years, Countryman's head would pop up above the parapet. In March 1998, Jim Fitzpatrick, Labour MP for Poplar and Canning Town, asked the Secretary of State for Home Affairs, Alun Michael MP, 'if he will release the conclusions of the report of the Operation Countryman investigation'.

To this he received the unequivocal reply, 'No. Disclosure is a matter for the Commissioner of Police of the Metropolis. Investigating officers' reports are, as a class, regarded by the courts as subject to public interest immunity.'

Countryman surfaced on another occasion, too, but this was not made public until thirty years after the event. In 1977, HRH Prince Charles became keen that the royal family should demonstrate more support for the police and expressed these thoughts to the Commissioner. Sir David was extremely enthusiastic, and since this was the royal jubilee year, he thought that the Met should be given a new prefix and thus become 'The Royal Metropolitan Police'.

He imparted his views to the Permanent Under-Secretary at the Home Office, Sir Robert Temple Armstrong (later Baron Armstrong of Ilminster GCB, CVO), who was less than excited with the idea. The matter was batted from department to department for a period of two years; it died a death after Sir Robert sent the Commissioner a rather scathing memo in which he made reference to Operation Countryman: 'No less than sixty-four officers of the Metropolitan Police . . . are under investigation on allegations of serious corruption. It would not be a very happy background to the acquisition of the title royal'. He added that 'charges are about to be brought', as indeed they were; although of course, every Metropolitan Police officer who was charged was acquitted.

★

Various requests have been put by researchers to the City of London and Dorset Police under the Freedom of Information Act for details of the Operation Countryman investigation; for the most part these were answered in the structured, wooden way in which today's police civilian staff are instructed to deal with people seeking assistance. Those researchers could have saved themselves a great deal of time by applying to the National Archives, where they would have discovered that the files were ordered closed for eighty-four years; access to them may be granted on New Year's Day 2067.

CHAPTER 29

Before we finish, I want to deal with a couple of comparisons to the Countryman enquiry. Let's take a look again at the Austin Reed burglary. Within three days of hearing of the offence, John Simmonds with a limited number of detectives had arrested those responsible and recovered the stolen property, and the perpetrators had made their first appearance in court. In the space of six months from the date of the offence to sentencing, the matter had been dealt with. Well, the purists might say, so what? It was a relatively straightforward matter, even though it involved six dishonest police officers, five of whom pleaded guilty. Right, a fair point; so let's reflect on another internal police investigation.

In 1989 the Deputy Chief Constable of Cambridgeshire, John Stevens (later Baron Stevens of Kirkwhelpington KStJ, QPM, DL, FRSA), was asked to undertake an enquiry in strife-torn Northern Ireland in respect of allegations of collusion between the security forces (which included the Royal Ulster Constabulary) and terrorist groups. He took with him a maximum staff of twenty (although in the next two years it was often far fewer). Due to the terrorist threat, the team changed their hotels every three days. Nights out to pubs and restaurants were completely out of the question. Four months into the enquiry, their office was deliberately burnt to the ground. Their accommodation and workplace melded into one, Antrim Road RUC station in the north of Belfast. When driving out of the heavily fortified RUC station, officers were forbidden to turn right; the traffic lights at the junction with Cavehill Road were a favourite haunt of 'dickers' (terrorist spotters) and snipers. At that time, according to Interpol, Northern Ireland was the most dangerous place in the world to be a police officer; the risk factor was twice as high as in El Salvador, deemed the second most dangerous country.

But Stevens' team – none of them armed, all of them subject to a high threat level – got results. The first arrest was carried out three weeks after the team's arrival; and then the pace really accelerated. During the next two years, during which murders featured largely in their investigations and no end of obstructions were placed in the enquiry team's way, especially by the Special Branch and Army intelligence – ninety-four arrests were carried out, there were eleven trials and forty-four convictions (most of the defendants pleaded guilty) for more than a hundred and fifty terrorist-related offences. And that, it must be emphasized, was just in the first two years of the enquiry – in the years which followed, the conviction rate grew to ninety-seven.

And how did this success come about? Even though the team were working in a completely alien environment – none of them had ever been to Ulster before and one hadn't even previously been on board an aeroplane – they were competent detectives who received strong leadership from highly professional senior officers. John Stevens had been a working detective for most of his career, was commended on twenty-seven occasions for bravery and detective ability and became Commissioner of the Metropolitan Police. Moreover, the entire team worked closely and harmoniously with the Northern Ireland Director of Public Prosecutions.

Now compare that to Countryman. In the first two years of their enquiry, with a workforce of over ninety, investigating a police force in an area one-fortieth the size of Belfast, they had seen one detective inspector suspended and charged (who was later acquitted) and one detective chief inspector suspended, then charged with a minor offence containing a fart-full of evidence which was chucked out at the Magistrates' Court at the behest of the Director of Public Prosecutions, whose representative was then sent to Coventry.

By the autumn of 1980 no one, not even someone as famed for stretching credulity to its limits as Baron Münchausen, could possibly have described Countryman as a success story. And two years after that, when it was all over, it had tallied up a cost of over £4 million. With almost laughable understatement, the *Morning Star* solemnly reported, 'Countryman wasn't entirely successful'.

It begs the question – was it worth it? And was there a core of corruption in the City of London police?

Well, two police officers were convicted of serious venality and six more (who were nothing to do with the Countryman enquiry) were found guilty of theft; but it was felt that many more had slipped through the net. However, it has to be stressed that the first two officers had been brought to book largely through the hard work of John Simmonds (and the other six, wholly through his efforts). Had he not covertly recorded Cuthbert's admissions, it is highly debatable whether the men would have ever stood trial.

As for the Met, of the eight men who were charged, six were acquitted by their peers and the other two had no evidence offered against them. One would have thought that on the face of it there was certainly a core of corruption inside the Met given that allegations were made against 187 of its officers, but allegations of what? Many of the allegations were dismissed because of their sheer stupidity, but in the event, not one criminal or disciplinary prosecution emerged. Countryman had done their best, especially in the case of John O'Connor, where it appears that an attempt was made to well and truly frame him; although they fared less well with the bumbling enquiry into Bob Robinson, an affair which suggested those well-known phrases or sayings which include the words 'left-hand', 'right-hand', 'arse' and 'elbow'.

Before Countryman got underway, my pal Peter Connor had a put-down which he used to display contempt for inadequate officers in the police: 'He couldn't detect an elephant in a field of potato crisps.' It certainly seemed suitable for Countryman, but it also suggests one other matter.

Was the Dorset Constabulary deliberately selected because the Home Secretary, HM Inspector of Constabularies, the Director of Public Prosecutions and everybody else involved in the decision-making knew that they'd make such a complete bollocks of the investigation? John Simmonds was of that opinion and so were several other people that I spoke to – so was this the case?

Personally, I don't think so. Yes, it was a flawed decision by Merlyn Rees, but realization of Countryman's ineptitude only came later to him, as indeed it did to many other senior officials. I don't think anybody could have prophesied how completely out of control they would become, squirrelling away allegations which, even to the meanest aid to CID, would have been such obviously complete bunkum, and making the most nonsensical promises to criminals in return for assurances which, in the majority of cases, were not kept.

Did the Met obstruct Countryman? In fact, it was the Met's hierarchy who let them get away with too much, for too long. It was Don Neesham who tried to put a brake on Countryman's out-of-control activities, and he paid the price. Parallels can be drawn between Neesham and Julius Caesar: like Caesar, Neesham was immensely popular with 'the lower and middle classes', and like Caesar, Neesham was thought by the senior officials to be too powerful. The difference was that when Caesar's demise came, 2,035 years before Neesham's, he was stabbed twenty-three times – Neesham, only once.

In that case, did the Director of Public Prosecutions obstruct Countryman? The answer to that must be an unequivocal 'No'. The Director had to apply his usual 51 per cent chance of a conviction litmus test to each case; and in the vast majority of cases there was either insufficient evidence or no evidence at all to support a conviction. Had Countryman's investigators possessed sufficient knowledge and experience to realize that hearsay, rumours and bullshit do not equate to evidence, the matter might have been different; but they didn't, so it wasn't.

When allegations of police corruption are made, a rigorous investigation must ensue and every effort be made to clamp down on those responsible and, where it's possible, kick them right out of the police force and straight into a prison cell. But it is not a case for the faint-hearted or the soft-headed, either. Burt told Graeme McLagan – he who wished to re-record the tape played at the Old Bailey during Cuthbert and Golbourn's trial – 'People get what they deserve. If they're not prepared to put in the effort to sort something out, then they deserve what they get.'

That's not good enough. Burt had little idea of leadership and no comprehension whatsoever of how to run a major enquiry. He had few died-in-the-wool CID officers to aid him; he would constantly sing the praises of 'his detectives', but for the most part they were over-promoted, make-believe 'tecs who had so little experience, knowledge of the criminal law, common sense or credibility that they did not even resemble detectives in a children's story book.

It makes me angry – waste, unprofessionalism and ineptitude always makes me angry.

I've already mentioned the effect that these investigations had on some of the officers concerned and their families, something that could so easily have been circumvented by investigating officers who knew what they were doing. It is, I think, perfectly summed up by one officer whom I contacted to ask him exactly what had happened to him; this was his reply:

> The events that you refer to occurred some thirty-seven years ago and caused me, my family and colleagues . . . enormous distress, my health suffered and it was family and friends that helped me through a very difficult period. I . . . have moved on from that upsetting time and I have no wish to revisit what happened to me.

Similarly, I mentioned the three men who walked free from a murder and robbery charge because the prosecution refused to call John O'Connor whilst he was suspended, on charges which we know were utterly specious. Other charges were dropped in respect of defendants who were awaiting trial because the investigating officers were suspended, and we know details of some of them; but not all.

Consider this: at one stage there were a number of officers suspended from duty. All of them detectives with heavy caseloads,
with any number of prisoners – in police parlance – 'on the grid'
(awaiting trial). And whilst they were suspended, none of the officers – like John O'Connor – would be called to give evidence, and
so, again in police parlance, the prisoners 'walked'. I can't multiply
the number of suspended officers by the number of cases they had
awaiting trial, or the number of defendants involved in each case,
because I simply don't know. But if I suggest that it meant literally
scores of certainly guilty armed robbers walking free from court,
ready and able to go out and commit further armed robberies and
terrify, harm and perhaps murder the decent citizens of London,
would that really be an exaggeration? I don't think so.

Former Detective Superintendent Ezra Pritchard has a very
interesting view on the exploits of Countryman which is certainly
worth considering:

> I suspect/believe that when appointed they were misled
> by those appointing them that there was endemic cor-
> ruption. This was based on vivid accounts given by hard-
> ened old/big time villains. The few firms of solicitors who
> were constantly being briefed by these villains no doubt
> actively jumped on the bandwagon and encouraged them.
> Being able to discredit any officer in a case enhanced the
> chances of a not guilty verdict. This would then in turn
> enhance the solicitor's reputation with the consequence of
> further high paid (legally aided!) work coming their way.
>
> I suppose those of us working on the higher echelon
> villain had little problem, in fact probably a grudging
> understanding, why they were making the allegations
> against officers. They saw it as a legitimate tactic in their
> attempt to avoid conviction because conviction for high-
> level crime brought long incarceration.
>
> Solicitors, jumping on the bandwagon, began to
> feed the media, and a few of the less able people in the
> media began to run stories. The nature of the 'media
> beast' meant the others began to worry about being left
> behind, and also jumped on the bandwagon. This resulted
> in them feeding on each other. In these TRUMP days it
> would be called 'fake news'!
>
> When Countryman were appointed I am convinced
> that they assumed this was a simple job brought about
> by a 'mind set' forged in their day-to-day work in a rural
> non-metropolitan environment. They made that fatal

mistake, which I'm afraid has bedevilled inexperienced
investigators over the years, of unquestioning belief
in an allegation. This may have been brought about in
part because some of the allegations were put forward/
initiated by solicitors. Their provincial working environment would, I suspect, inhibit them from questioning a
solicitor's motive. In most rural areas a solicitor is usually
thought of as someone of some standing and integrity.

Those words do make sense; witness Countryman calling their
own Dorset solicitor to administer proceedings with regard to the
ill-fated attempt to prosecute Cuthbert on the dishonest handling
charge, plus what appeared to be their slavish adherence to what
was said to them by several defence solicitors regarding their own
clients. Unfortunately, their approbation of lawyers did not always
extend to the office of the Director of Public Prosecutions.

Senior police officers (and other politicians) have wonderful,
weasel words when something goes, horribly, catastrophically
wrong: they whimper, 'Lessons have been learnt.' Let's hope they
have; because when the next big corruption scandal suddenly
appears – and it will – never again must the Government, Chief
Constables, HM Inspector of Constabularies or Uncle Tom Cobley
and all, ever appoint something as ludicrously inept as 'The Dorset
Crusaders' to investigate it.

End Notes

Author's Note

1. For further details of this expedition, see *The Real Sweeney*, Robinson, 2005

Introduction

1. For further details of the foregoing cases, see *Whitechapel's Sherlock Holmes*, Pen & Sword True Crime, 2014
2. For further details of this case, see *Scotland Yard's Ghost Squad*, Wharncliffe Books, 2011
3. For further details of this case, see *The Scourge of Soho*, Pen & Sword True Crime, 2013
4. For details of this, and the foregoing cases, see *The Sweeney – The First Sixty Years of Scotland Yard's Crimebusting Flying Squad, 1919–1978*, Wharncliffe Books, 2011

Chapter 1

1. For details of this (and other Serious Crime Squad cases) see *You're Nicked!*, Robinson, 2007

Chapter 6

1. For full details of this case, see *The Brave Blue Line – 100 Years of Metropolitan Police Gallantry*, Wharncliffe Books, 2011
2. For full details of this highly embarrassing experience, see *Rough Justice – Memoirs of a Flying Squad Detective*, Merlin Unwin Books, 2001

Chapter 18

1. In fact, Patrick Fraser was sentenced to eleven years' imprisonment

Chapter 25

1. And so, it seemed, did somebody else. On 13 July 1979 an armed gang escaped with a £50,000 payroll from the Central Post Office, King Edward Street, EC1 after courageously firing three shots at a grandmother who tried to block their way.

Bibliography

Ball, John, Chester, Lewis and Perrott, Roy, *Cops and Robbers*, André Deutsch, 1978

Copperwaite, Paul, (ed.), *The Mammoth Book of Undercover Cops*, Robinson, 2011

Darbyshire, Neil and Hilliard, Brian, *The Flying Squad*, Headline, 1993

Davidson, Earl, *Joey Pyle: Notorious – The Changing of Organized Crime*, Virgin Books, 2003

Fido, Martin and Skinner, Keith, *The Official Encyclopedia of Scotland Yard*, Virgin Books, 1999

Fraser, David, Fraser, Patrick and Marsh, Beezy, *Mad Frank and Sons*, Sidgwick and Jackson, 2016

Gillard, Michael and Flynn, Laurie, *The Untouchables*, Cutting Edge, 2004

Hogg, Andrew, McDougall, Jim and Morgan, Robin, *Bullion Brink's-Mat: The Story of Britain's Biggest Gold Robbery*, Penguin Books, 1998

Jennings, Andrew, Lashmar, Paul and Simson, Vyv, *Scotland Yard's Cocaine Connection*, Arrow Books, 1991

Kelland, Gilbert, *Crime in London*, Harper Collins, 1993

Kirby, Dick, *Rough Justice – Memoirs of a Flying Squad Detective*, Merlin Unwin Books, 2001

— *The Real Sweeney*, Robinson, 2005

— *You're Nicked!*, Robinson, 2007

— *Villains*, Robinson, 2008

— *The Guv'nors – Ten of Scotland Yard's Greatest Detectives*, Wharncliffe, 2010

— *The Sweeney – The First Sixty Years of Scotland Yard's Crimebusting Flying Squad 1919–1978*, Wharncliffe, 2011

— *Scotland Yard's Ghost Squad – The Secret Weapon against Post-War Crime*, Wharncliffe, 2011

— *The Scourge of Soho*, Pen & Sword, 2013

— *Whitechapel's Sherlock Holmes*, Pen & Sword, 2014

Knight, Stephen, *The Brotherhood*, Granada Publishing, 1984

McLagan, Graeme, *Bent Coppers*, Weidenfeld & Nicolson, 2003

McNee, Sir David, *McNee's Law*, Collins, 1983

Millen, Ernest, *Specialist in Crime*, Harrap, 1972

Morton, James, *Bent Coppers*, Little, Brown, 1993

Morton, James, *Supergrasses and Informers*, Warner Books, 1995

— *Gangland*, Vols 1 & 2, Time Warner, 2003

Pearson, John, *The Profession of Violence*, Panther Books, 1973

Rowland, David, *Bent Cops*, Finsbury Publishing, 2007

Ryder, Chris, *The RUC – A Force Under Fire*, Methuen, 1989

Short, Martin, *Lundy – The Destruction of Scotland Yard's Finest Detective*, Grafton, 1991

Slipper, Jack, *Slipper of the Yard*, Sidgwick & Jackson, 1981

Stevens, John, *Not for the Faint-Hearted – My Life Fighting Crime*, Weidenfeld & Nicolson, 2005

Thomas, Donald, *Villains' Paradise*, John Murray, 2005

Waldren, Michael J., *Armed Police – The Police Use of Firearms Since 1945*, Sutton Publishing, 2007

Index